**THE GUINNESS
DICTIONARY OF**
QUOTATIONS
FOR ALL
OCCASIONS

THE GUINNESS
DICTIONARY OF
QUOTATIONS
FOR ALL
OCCASIONS

COMPILED BY

GARETH SHARPE

GUINNESS PUBLISHING

Design: John Rivers

Selection Copyright © Gareth Sharpe, 1994

Reprinted in 1995

The right of Gareth Sharpe to be identified as Author of this Work
has been asserted in accordance with the Copyright, Design &
Patents Act 1988.

This Publication Copyright © Guinness Publishing Ltd 1994
Published in Great Britain by Guinness Publishing Ltd,
33 London Road, Enfield, Middlesex

'GUINNESS' is a registered trademark of Guinness Publishing Ltd

Typeset in Palatino by
Ace Filmsetting Ltd, Frome, Somerset
Printed and bound in Great Britain by
Cox & Wyman Ltd

A catalogue record for this book is available from the British Library

ISBN 0–85112–753–3

ACKNOWLEDGEMENTS

Over the last three years I have received help from so many people and organizations in compiling this collection, that it would be impossible for me to thank them all individually here. I can only express my gratitude broadly to everyone who contributed in any way, whether or not I was able to take their advice or include their suggestions; it was on their willingness to get involved that this book relied most heavily.

Having said that, there are some very generous people whose help with this book really was invaluable, and to them I feel I must say a special 'thank you'.

First of all, thanks go to my wife Linda, who not only put up with me throughout the compilation of these pages, tiptoeing around the piles of books and scraps of paper without complaint, but who also helped with the research, and wore her fingers to the bone typing entries into the database from which this volume emerged.

Second, I would like to thank Ian Draper, who saved my computer from being hurled out of the house in a very un-user-friendly way on more than one occasion, and who advised me on every aspect of my computer, especially when I couldn't make it do what I wanted.

Finally, I would like to thank those who helped in specific areas of research, and whose contributions also definitely merit mention: my father, whose knowledge of poetry was indispensable; Liz, whose help and enthusiasm was inspirational; and my mother and father-in-law – Joyce and Philip Symes – for their assistance on biblical quotations. I would also like to thank the following for their substantial help in the task of researching this book: John & Helen Bogle, Mark Copage, Kent Garbutt, Howard & Jacqui Jobson, David Loader, Philip Loader, Fleur Pettie, Bernie Thompson, and of course the unsung heroes of many a reference work – the libraries.

ACKNOWLEDGEMENTS

CONTENTS

ACKNOWLEDGEMENTS   5

INTRODUCTION   11

FINDING THE RIGHT QUOTE   12

QUOTES ON QUOTES   13

1 – WORDS OF WISDOM   15
Guidelines – Worldly Observations – Wry
Comment – Happiness And How To Achieve It –
Hard Truths – Instructive Sayings – Support and
Sympathy – Ten Inspired Quotes

2 – BIRTHDAY   30
Humorous – Insulting – The Down Side – A
Special Day – Youth – Staying Young – Middle
Age – Age And The Signs Of Ageing – Growing
Older: The Benefits – Growing Older: The
Drawbacks – Old Age – Celebration And
Drinking

3 – CHRISTMAS AND OTHER HOLIDAYS   42
Christmas – Traditional Christmas – New Year –
Easter – Traditional Easter

4 – AFFAIRS OF THE HEART   47
Humorous – Sex And Lust – Courting – Advice
For Lovers – Flattery – Declarations of Love –
From The Heart (Expressions of Love) – The
Essence Of Love – Proposals – Love On The
Rocks

5 – MATRIMONY   62
Humorous – Engagement – Marriage: The
Positive View – Marriage: The Cynical View –
Second Marriage – The Bride – The Groom – To
The Happy Couple – Biblical – Advice To the
Newly Weds

6 – MOVING / NEW HOME   77
Of Houses And Home – House Buying –

First Home – Home Ownership: Pleasures And
Problems – Bless This House

7 – HOME AND AWAY   81
Travel – Foreign Travel – Foreigners And Foreign
Countries – Parting And Leaving – Farewell And
Bon Voyage – Planes, Trains And Automobiles –
Climate And Weather – Absence – Homesickness
(Missing Friends And Relatives) – Holidays And
Tourism – Town And Country – Home And
Homecoming – England And The English –
Scotland, Wales And Ireland – France – Italy –
Other European Countries – America – Canada –
India And The Far East – Australia And New
Zealand

8 – BABIES AND CHILDREN   99
Birth – Birth Rhymes – Babies – Parenthood –
Children: The Positive View – Children: The
Negative View

9 – MOTHER'S DAY / FATHER'S DAY   108
Mothers – Mothers And Young Children –
Fathers – Parents – Grandmothers And
Grandfathers

10 – TOGETHERNESS   113
Humorous – Anniversary – Enduring Love –
Happy Memories – Of Wives – Of Husbands

11 – RETIREMENT   119
Retirement: Early, Late Or Not At All – Well-
earned Rest – Quitting While You're Ahead –
Living With Leisure (Busily Doing Nothing) –
Life Beyond Retirement

12 – ILL HEALTH (GET WELL)   124
Medicine: Cures And Remedies – Sickness –
Accidents – Hospitals – Doctors And Physicians
– Convalescence

13 – DEATH AND BEREAVEMENT   128
Remembrance – Consolation – Of A Better Place
– Tributes To The Good And Great – Grief – Final
Rest – An End To Suffering – In The Line Of

Duty – The Bible – Of Death – The Inevitability
Of Death – Life And Death – Black Humour –
Epitaphs

14 – GOOD LUCK   141

Humorous – Advice – Opportunity – Faith And
Trust – Luck – Hope – Worry And Fear – Success
And How To Achieve It – Taking The Plunge –
Aiming High – New Job – Major Challenge –
Education And Study – Exams

15 – SUCCESS AND HAPPINESS   153

Humorous – Achievement (Acknowledgement
Of) – Good Fortune – Perseverance – The Good
Life – Congratulations (Begrudged)

16 – THANKS AND FOND REGARDS   157

Gratitude – Friendship – Hospitality –
Compliments – Generosity

17 – MISFORTUNE   162

Humorous – Philosophical Thoughts –
Encouragement – Advice – Sympathy –
Optimism – Set–back – Disappointments – Errors
and Mistakes – Failure – Honourable Defeat –
Mishaps – Cold Comfort – The Bible

18 – APOLOGY AND FORGIVENESS   176

Coming Clean – Denial – Justification, Excuses
And Reasons – Capitulation And Apology –
Regret – Burying The Hatchet – Forgiveness –
New Resolve – Love In Adversity – Making Light

19 – ABSENCE   189

Punctuality And Arriving On Time – Lateness –
Unwilling Absence – Strategic Absence – Excuses
– The Error Of Absence – Invitation Declined

20 – PUBLIC SPEAKING   193

Opening Lines – Meetings And Discussions –
Advice On Speeches And Speaking – Audiences –
Replies And Retorts – Drawing To A Close – Toasts

IF ALL ELSE FAILS   201

INDEX   203

INTRODUCTION

Everyone enjoys hearing a particularly witty turn of phrase or apt quotation during an after-dinner speech or public address; just coming across an appropriate quotation can illuminate our thoughts in a most telling way, and indeed for most of us the opportunity to speak or write a meaningful message occurs at this more personal level.

Finding the right words for a particular occasion can prove a chore, but the thousands of famous quips and quotations served up within these covers, from the frivolous and off-beat to the touchingly sentimental or profound, will serve as a rich resource to anybody seeking a means to improve or lighten a speech, write that special letter, or simply seeking inspiration.

A long time has been spent collecting and assessing entries, and although my personal preferences must be in evidence I hope a high content of wit or excellence is equally to the fore. I have also tried to assemble the 'bon mots' of our more notable commentators, and limited the use of material from less well-known works and persons (except when it was particularly relevant), as I have found that a quotation is often more successful in its impact if there is some recognition of the source. By this token many of those who have a particular interest in quotations will be familiar with much, although I suspect by no means all, of the contents herein.

So, for all those looking for help in a challenging situation, or those whose verbal interest is more particular, I hope this book will help you to enjoy and appreciate some of the wittiest and profoundest utterances from many of the greatest and humblest minds of our times – and beyond.

FINDING THE RIGHT QUOTE

The chapters and subheadings in this book are designed to help you locate the quotation required as quickly and as easily as possible. However, it is important to note that there is a certain amount of overlap between sections.

To get the most from this book it may be necessary to browse in more than one section to find the most suitable quotation.

For example, some chapters have a section of humorous items; these will be of a general nature pertinent to that particular chapter heading. However, more specific quotes relating to a designated sub-heading may be directly listed under that sub-heading whether humorous or not because the core of the subject is indivisible. Therefore, those wishing to find a light-hearted birthday quote for someone in middle age may look in 'The Signs of Ageing', 'Humorous' or either of the two 'Growing Older' sections as well as the specific sub-heading 'Middle Age'.

It should also be remembered that a quote is what you make it and does not always have to be used in its original context. With a little imagination a lot of fun can be had with some of the less obvious quotes even if this does result in some deviation from the true meaning.

QUOTES ON QUOTES

There is no less invention in aptly applying a thought
found in a book, than in being the first author of the
thought.
Pierre Bayle (1647–1706) French Protestant philosopher

The wisdom of the wise and the experience of ages may
be preserved by quotation.
Benjamin Disraeli (1804–81) British statesman and
novelist

By necessity, by proclivity, and by delight, we all quote.
Ralph Waldo Emerson (1803–82) American poet and
essayist

When a thing has been said and said well, have no
scruple. Take it and copy it.
Anatole France (1844–1924) French novelist and poet

I quote others only the better to express myself.
Michael Montaigne (1533–92) French essayist

It is gentlemanly to get one's quotations very slightly
wrong. In that way one unprigs oneself and allows the
company to correct one.
Lord Ribblesdale (1854–1925) British aristocrat

When someone has the wit to coin a useful phrase, it
ought to be acclaimed and broadcast or it will perish.
Wolfman Jack Smith American disc jockey

To select well among old things is almost equal to
inventing new ones.
Nicolas Charles Trublet (1697–1770) French clergyman
and essayist

CHAPTER ONE

WORDS OF WISDOM

❖ ❖ ❖ GUIDELINES ❖ ❖ ❖

It is always the season for the old to learn.
Aeschylus (525–456 BC) Greek playwright *Fragments*

A little preparation saves a lot of frustration.
Anon

If a man will begin with certainties, he shall end in doubts; but if he will be content to begin with doubts, he shall end in certainties.
Francis Bacon (1561–1626) English philosopher and statesman *Proficiency and Advancement of Learning*

Be so true to thyself, as thou be not false to others.
Francis Bacon *Of Wisdom for a Man's Self*

A business must have a conscience as well as a counting house.
Montague Burton (1885–1952) British tailor

The advice of friends must be received with a judicious reserve: we must not give ourselves up to it and follow it blindly, whether right or wrong.
Pierre Charron (1541–1603) French theologian and philosopher

Where large sums of money are concerned, it is advisable to trust nobody.
Agatha Christie (1890–1976) English author

When you have nothing to say, say nothing.
Charles Caleb Colton (1780–1832) English clergyman and writer

Nothing in life is to be feared. It is only to be understood.
Marie Curie (1867–1934) French physicist

It is a capital mistake to theorize before one has data.
Sir Arthur Conan Doyle (1859–1930) Scottish writer

Friendship consists in forgetting what one gives, and remembering what one receives.
Alexandre Dumas (1803–70) French novelist

What's money? A man is a success if he gets up in the morning and goes to bed at night and in between does what he wants to do.
Bob Dylan (1941–) American singer and songwriter

I am only one,
But still I am one.

I cannot do everything,
But still I can do something;
And because I cannot do everything
I will not refuse to do the something that I can do.
Edward Everett (1794–1865)
American statesman and scholar

The test of a first-rate intelligence is the ability to hold two opposed ideas in the mind at the same time, and still retain the ability to function.
F. Scott Fitzgerald (1896–1940)
American novelist *Esquire*
Feb. 1936

Money is like an arm or leg – use it or lose it.
Henry Ford (1863–1947)
American industrialist
Forbes Magazine

You cannot repent too soon, because you do not know how soon it may be too late.
Thomas Fuller (1608–61) English writer and clergyman

Do what is easy as if it were difficult, and what is difficult as if it were easy.
Baltasar Gracian (1601–58)
Spanish writer and Jesuit priest

The human mind is like an umbrella – it functions best when open.
Walter Gropius (1883–1969)
German architect *The Observer* 1956

Snatch at today and trust as little as you can in tomorrow.
Horace (65–8 BC) Roman poet and satirist *Odes*

If you can dream and not make dreams your master . . . you'll be a man, my son.
Rudyard Kipling (1865–1936)
English writer *If*

If you can keep your head when all about you
Are losing theirs and blaming it on you.
Rudyard Kipling *If*

If you can fill the unforgiving minute
With sixty seconds' worth of distance run,
Yours is the Earth and everything that's in it,
And – which is more – you'll be a man my son!
Rudyard Kipling *If*

Civility costs nothing and buys everything.
Baron de Montesquieu
(1689–1755) French philosopher and jurist

There is only one rule for being a good talker: learn to listen.
Christopher Morley (1890–1957)
American novelist and essayist

The real art of conversation is not only to say the right thing in the right place but to leave unsaid the

wrong thing at the tempting moment.
Dorothy, Lady Nevill (1913–)
English author

Do as you would be done by.
Proverb

We should not judge of a man's merits by his great qualities, but by the use he makes of them.
François, Duc de la Rochefoucauld (1613–80) French writer *Maxims*

The truly honest man is the man without pretensions.
François, Duc de la Rochefoucauld *Maxims*

Neither a borrower nor a lender be:
For loan oft loses both itself and friend,
And borrowing dulls the edge of husbandry.
This above all: to thine own self be true.
And it must follow, as the night the day,
Thou canst not then be false to any man.
William Shakespeare (1564–1616)
English playwright and poet
Hamlet

If you tell the truth, you don't have to remember anything.
Mark Twain (1835–1910)
American writer

Generosity gives assistance, rather than advice.
Marquis de Vauvenargues (1715–47) French moralist and soldier
Reflections and Maxims

It is a good rule in life never to apologize. The right sort of people don't want apologies, and the wrong sort take a mean advantage of them.
P. G. Wodehouse (1881–1975)
English novelist

WORLDLY
❋ ❋ OBSERVATIONS ❋ ❋

It is not a mistake to turn back if you are on the wrong road.
Anon

One man's folly is another man's fortune.
Francis Bacon (1561–1626)
English philosopher and statesman
Fortuna

Envy has no holidays.
Francis Bacon *Invidia*

Man prefers to believe what he prefers to be true.
Francis Bacon *Aphor*

Money is a good slave, but a cruel master.
Francis Bacon

Men talk of killing time, while time quietly kills them.
Dion Boucicault (c.1820–90) Dublin-born dramatist and actor

A man convinced against his will
Is of the same opinion still.
Samuel Butler (1612–80) English satirist

Life is like playing a violin solo in public and learning the instrument as one goes on.
Samuel Butler (1835–1902) English author, painter and musician

The optimist proclaims that we live in the best of all possible worlds; and the pessimist fears this is true.
James Branch Cabell (1879–1958) American novelist and critic

I am convinced that a light supper, a good night's sleep, and a fine morning, have sometimes made a hero of the same man, who by an indigestion, a restless night, and rainy morning, would have proved a coward.
Philip Stanhope, Earl of Chesterfield (1694–1773) English statesman, orator and wit

Compromise used to mean that half a loaf was better than no bread. Among modern statesmen it really seems to mean that half a loaf is better than a whole loaf.
G. K. Chesterton (1874–1936) English critic and novelist

War is sweet to those who do not fight.
Desiderius Erasmus (c.1467–1536) Dutch humanist *Adagia*

One of the funny things about the stock market is that every time one person buys, another sells, and both think they are astute.
William Feather: quoted in *Reader's Digest*

The past is a foreign country: they do things differently there.
Leslie P. Hartley (1895–1972) English writer *The Go-Between*

A moment's insight is sometimes worth a life's experience.
Oliver Wendell Holmes (1809–94) American physician and writer *The Professor at the Breakfast Table*

The news is always bad, even when it sounds good.
Aldous Huxley (1894–1963) English novelist and essayist

Advice is what we ask for when we already know the answer but wish we didn't.
Erica Jong (1942–) American poet and writer

Discretion is the polite word for hypocrisy.
Christine Keeler (1942–) English model and showgirl

The way of a fool seems right to him, but a wise man listens to advice.
Proverbs 12:16

It is not that which is beautiful that pleases us, but that which pleases us is called beautiful.
Leo Rosten's Treasury of Jewish Quotations

Nobody gives anything as freely as they give advice.
François, Duc de la Rochefoucauld (1613–80) French writer *Maxims*

One is never as happy or as unhappy as one imagines oneself to be.
François, Duc de la Rochefoucauld *Maxims*

One is never as ridiculous for the qualities one has, as for those that one pretends to have.
François, Duc de la Rochefoucauld *Maxims*

He who is slowest in making a promise is most faithful in its performance.
Jean-Jacques Rousseau (1712–78) French political philosopher and novelist

O beware, my lord, of jealousy;
It is the green-eyed monster which doth mock
The meat it feeds on.
William Shakespeare (1564–1616) English playwright and poet
Othello

Hegel was right when he said that we learn from history that men never learn anything from history.
George Bernard Shaw (1856–1950) Irish dramatist

Knowledge comes, but wisdom lingers.
Alfred, Lord Tennyson (1809–92) English poet

Education is an admirable thing, but it is well to remember from time to time that nothing that is worth knowing can be taught.
Oscar Wilde (1854–1900) Irish playwright, novelist and wit
The Critic as Artist

The only thing to do with good advice is to pass it on. It is never of any use to oneself.
Oscar Wilde

❀ ❀ WRY COMMENT ❀ ❀

To err is human, but to really foul things up requires a computer.
Anon

Life is rather like a tin of sardines. We are all looking for the key.
Alan Bennett (1934–) English dramatist and actor

Cynic, *n*: a blackguard whose faulty vision sees things as they are, not as they ought to be.
Ambrose Bierce (1842–1914) American journalist
The Devil's Dictionary

Bigot, *n*: one who is obstinately and zealously attached to an opinion that you do not entertain.
Ambrose Bierce *The Devil's Dictionary*

Let us all be happy and live within our means, even if we have to borrow the money to do it with.
Charles Farrer Browne (1834–67) American humorist *Natural History*

An atheist is a man who has no invisible means of support.
John Buchan (1875–1940) Scottish novelist and statesman

I have noticed that nothing I never said ever did me any harm.
Calvin Coolidge (1872–1933) 30th American President *Congressional Records*

There is only one difference between a madman and me. I am not mad.
Salvador Dali (1904–89) Spanish artist

Three may keep a secret, if two of them are dead.
Benjamin Franklin (1706–90) American statesman

As the horsepower in modern automobiles steadily rises, the congestion of traffic steadily lowers the possible speed of your car. This is known as Progress.
Sydney J. Harris (1903–76) American journalist

When in doubt, make a fool of yourself. There is a microscopically thin line between being brilliantly creative and acting like the most gigantic idiot on earth. So what the hell, leap.
Cynthia Heimel American writer

It's going to be fun to see how long the meek can keep the earth when they inherit it.
Kin Hubbard (1868–1930) American humorist

It is always the best policy to speak the truth, unless of course you are an exceptionally good liar.
Jerome K. Jerome (1859–1927) English humorous writer, novelist and playwright *The Idler*

If you can keep your head when all about you are losing theirs, it's just possible you haven't grasped the situation.
Jean Kerr (1923–) American playwright

Life is too short to do anything for oneself that one can pay others to do for one.
William Somerset Maugham (1874–1965) British writer

An idealist is one who, on noticing that a rose smells better than a cabbage, concludes that it will also make a better soup.
Henry L. Mencken (1880–1965) American journalist and linguist

He who kills a man's son, rapes his wife and buries his daughter alive in an ant hill, should not expect to sit at that man's table without the subject coming up.
Not The Nine O'Clock News (Not 1983)

He who teaches his son to swim at the top of the waterfall will not long be a father.
Not The Nine O'Clock News (Not 1983)

He who wears a bullet-proof jacket cannot complain if he gets shot in the b******s.
Not The Nine O'Clock News (Not 1983)

Practically anything you say will seem amusing if you're on all fours.
P. J. O'Rourke (1947–) American writer

There are two kinds of people in the world: those who believe there are two kinds of people in the world and those who don't.
Ross F. Papprill (1908–75) *Attributed*

All the troubles of men are caused by one single thing, which is their inability to stay quietly in a room.
Blaise Pascal (1623–62) French mathematician and man of letters

Never do today what you can put off till tomorrow.
Punch 1849

If you want to be considered smart, agree with everyone.
Leo Rosten's Treasury of Jewish Quotations

There is no cure for birth and death save to enjoy the interval.
George Santayana (1863–1952) Spanish philosopher, poet and novelist *Soliloquies in England and Later Soliloquies*

While it may be true that a watched pot never boils, the one you don't keep an eye on can make an awful mess of your cooker.
Edward Stevenson *Wall Street Journal* quoted in *Reader's Digest*

The fascination of shooting as a sport depends almost wholly on whether you are on the right or wrong end of a gun.
P. G. Wodehouse (1881–1975) English novelist

❀ ❀ HAPPINESS AND ❀ ❀ HOW TO ACHIEVE IT

Contentment consists not in great wealth but in few wants.
Anon

The grand essentials of happiness are: something to do, something to love, and something to hope for.
  Allan K. Chalmers

Be wiser than other people if you can, but do not tell them so.
  Philip Stanhope, Earl of Chesterfield (1694–1773) English statesman, orator and wit *Letter to his Son* 19th November 1745

Happiness is a mystery like religion, and should never be rationalized.
  G. K. Chesterton (1874–1936) English critic and novelist *Heretics*

I have tried too in my time to be a philosopher; but, I don't know how, cheerfulness was always breaking in.
Oliver Edwards (1711–91)

Whether happiness may come or not, one should try and prepare one's self to do without it.
  George Eliot (1819–80) English novelist

There is more credit and satisfaction in being a first-rate truck-driver than a tenth-rate executive.
  B. C. Forbes (1880–1954) American author *Epigrams*

Early to bed and early to rise, Makes a man healthy, wealthy and wise.
  Benjamin Franklin (1706–90) American statesman *Poor Richard's Almanac* 1758

All happiness depends on a leisurely breakfast.
  John Gunter (1938–) English designer

Mix a little foolishness with your serious plans: It's lovely to be silly at the right moment.
  Horace (65–8 BC) Roman poet and satirist

Believe that life is worth living and your belief will help create the fact.
  William James (1842–1910) American psychologist and philosopher *The Will to Believe*

Opportunities flit by while we sit regretting the chances we have lost, and the happiness that comes to us we heed not, because of the happiness that is gone.
  Jerome K. Jerome (1859–1927) Engish humorous writer, novelist and playwright

It is right to be contented with what we have, never with what we are.
  James Mackintosh (1765–1832) Scottish philosopher

God gives us the ingredients for our daily bread, but He expects us to do the baking.
  E. C. McKenzie American writer and compiler

Ask yourself whether you are happy, and you cease to be so.
  John Stuart Mill (1806–73) English philosopher and social reformer *Autobiography*

We are here to add what we can to, not get what we can from, life.
William Osler (1849–1919)
Canadian physician

A good name is more desirable than great riches; to be esteemed is better than silver and gold.
Proverbs 21:30

It's great to be great, but it's greater to be human.
Will Rogers (1879–1935)
American humorist–philosopher

Carry your own lantern and you need not fear the dark.
Leo Rosten's Treasury of Jewish Quotations

Happiness is not a state to arrive at, but a manner of traveling.
Margaret Lee Runbeck

Happiness is not having what you want, but wanting what you have.
Hyman Judah Schachtel
American clergyman *The Real Enjoyment of Living*

Ideals are like the stars: we never reach them, but like the mariners of the sea, we chart our course by them.
Carl Schurz (1829–1906)
American statesman and journalist

Do something for somebody every day for which you do not get paid.
Albert Schweitzer (1875–1965)
Alsatian medical missionary

There are two things to aim at in life: first, to get what you want; and, after that, enjoy it. Only the wisest of mankind achieve the second.
Logan Pearsall Smith (1865–1946)
British writer *Afterthoughts*

❄ ❄ HARD TRUTHS ❄ ❄

Plough or not plough, you must pay rent all the same.
Anon

If you're not part of the solution, you're part of the problem.
Anon

The march of the human mind is slow.
Edmund Burke (1729–97) Irish statesman and philosopher

Superstition is the religion of feeble minds.
Edmund Burke

The will is never free – it is always attached to an object, a purpose. It is simply the engine in the car – it can't steer.
Joyce Cary (1888–1957) English novelist

Annual income twenty pounds, annual expenditure nineteen pounds nineteen and six, result happiness. Annual income twenty pounds, annual expenditure

twenty pounds ought and six,
result misery.
   Charles Dickens (1812–70)
English novelist *David Copperfield*

A little learning is a dangerous
thing, but a lot of ignorance is just
as bad.
   Bob Edwards *From a quotation by
Alexander Pope*

It is well known, that among the
blind the one-eyed man is king.
   Desiderius Erasmus (c.1467–1536)
Dutch humanist *Adagia*

It is harder to conceal ignorance
than to acquire knowledge.
   Arnold H. Glasow

The paths of glory lead but to the
grave.
   Thomas Gray (1716–71) English
poet

The life so short, the craft so long
to learn.
   Hippocrates (Fifth century BC)
Greek physician

One of the mysteries of human
conduct is why adult men and
women all over England are ready
to sign documents which they do
not read, at the behest of canvassers
whom they do not know, binding
them to pay for articles which they
do not want, with money which
they have not got.
   Gerald Hurst (1877–1957) English
author and historian

There's only one corner of the
universe you can be certain of
improving, and that's your own
self.
   Aldous Huxley (1894–1963)
English novelist and essayist *Time
Must Have a Stop*

No man was ever endowed with a
right without being at the same
time saddled with a responsibility.
   Gerald W. Johnson (1890–)
American author and journalist

Life can only be understood
backwards; but it must be lived
forwards.
   Soren Kierkegaard (1813–55)
Danish philosopher *Life*

The claim to equality is made only
by those who feel themselves to be
in some way inferior.
   C. S. Lewis (1898–1963) Irish-born
academic and writer

He who thinks only of number one,
remember, it is next to nothing.
   Philip Loader (1966–)
Restaurateur

It is hard to believe that a man is
telling the truth when you know
that you would lie if you were in
his place.
   Henry L. Mencken (1880–1965)
American journalist and linguist

Man is quite insane. He wouldn't
know how to create a maggot,

and he creates Gods by the dozen.
Michel Montaigne (1533–92)
French essayist

We are all inclined to judge
ourselves by our ideals; others by
their acts.
Harold Nicolson (1886–1968)
British diplomat and author

Freedom is the right to tell people
what they do not want to hear.
George Orwell (1903–50) English
novelist

Words are like leaves; and where
they most abound, much fruit of
sense beneath is rarely found.
Alexander Pope (1688–1744)
English poet

Those who never change their
minds love themselves more than
the truth.
Franz Schubert (1797–1828)
Austrian composer

Oh how bitter a thing it is to look
into happiness through another
man's eyes.
William Shakespeare (1564–1616)
English playwright and poet *As
You Like It*

Like the waves make towards the
pebbled shore,
So do our minutes hasten to their
end.
William Shakespeare *Sonnets 60*

Experience is the name everyone
gives to their mistakes.
Oscar Wilde (1854–1900) Irish
playwright, novelist and wit *Vera,
or The Nihilists*

❋INSTRUCTIVE SAYINGS❋

Cut your own wood and it will
warm you twice.
Anon

You should never take advice from
any man, however well he
knows his subject, unless he also
knows you.
Balaam (Thomas Pitt; 1653–1726)
Grandfather of William Pitt the
Elder

Never forget what a man says to
you when he's angry.
Henry Ward Beecher (1813–87)
American congregationalist
clergyman and writer

Study the past, if you would divine
the future.
Confucius (551–479 BC) Chinese
philosopher *Analects*

Tsze-kung asked, saying, 'Is there
one word which will serve as a rule

of practice for all one's life?' The Master said, 'Is not Reciprocity such a word? What you do not want done to yourself, do not do to others.'
Confucius *Analects*

How often have I said to you that when you have eliminated the impossible, whatever remains, *however improbable*, must be the truth?
Sir Arthur Conan Doyle (1856–1930) Scottish writer *The Sign of Four*

Admitting Error clears the Score And proves you Wiser than before.
Arthur Guiterman (1871–1943) American author

The more haste, the lesse speede.
John Heywood (c.1497–c.1580) English playwright and musician *Proverbs*

Who has once the fame to be an early riser may sleep till noon.
William D. Howells (1837–1920) American novelist and poet

Caution is the eldest child of wisdom.
Victor Hugo (1802–85) French poet and author

Knowledge is of two kinds. We know a subject ourselves, or we know where we can find information upon it.
Dr Samuel Johnson (1709–84) English writer and critic *Letter to Lord Chesterfield* 1775

Always forgive your enemies – but never forget their names.
Robert F. Kennedy (1925–68) American politician

If it ain't broke, don't fix it.
Bert Lance (1931–) quoted in *National Business*

You can fool some of the people all the time and all the people some of the time; but you can't fool all the people all the time.
Abraham Lincoln (1809–65) 16th American President *Attributed*

The courage to speak must be matched by the wisdom to listen.
E. C. McKenzie American writer and compiler

A wise man, to accomplish his end, may even carry his foe on his shoulder.
Panchatantra (Fifth-century collection of Indian animal fables)

If you want people to think well of you, do not speak well of yourself.
Blaise Pascal (1623–62) French mathematician and man of letters

A mouse never trusts its life to a single hole.
Plautus (c.250–184 BC) Roman comic writer

Not to go back, is somewhat to advance,
And men must walk at least before they dance.
Alexander Pope (1688–1744) English poet *Satires and Epistles of Horace*

If you do not raise your eyes you will think you are the highest point.
  Antonio Porchia Argentine writer *Voces*

A man surprised is half beaten.
  Proverb

Blessed is the man who finds wisdom, the man who gains understanding, for he is more profitable than silver and yields better returns than gold.
  Proverbs 3:13–15

It's easy to run into debt, but hard to crawl out even at a slow walk.
  John D. Rockefeller (1839–1937) American oil magnate and philanthropist

Everybody is ignorant, only on different subjects.
  Will Rogers (1879–1935) American humorist-philosopher

The door to success has two signs: Push – and Pull.
  Leo Rosten's Treasury of Jewish Quotations

The sole advantage of power is that you can do more good.
  Lucius Annaeus Seneca (c.55 BC–c. AD 40) Roman rhetorician

Give every man thine ear, but few thy voice; take each man's censure, but reserve thy judgment.
  William Shakespeare (1564–1616) English playwright and poet

Liberty means responsibility. That is why most men dread it.
  George Bernard Shaw (1856–1950) Irish dramatist

Education is what survives when what has been learnt has been forgotten.
  Burrhus F. Skinner (1904–90) American psychologist quoted in *New Scientist*

Reading is to the mind what exercise is to the body.
  Richard Steele (1672–1729) Irish essayist, dramatist and politician

I have often regretted my speech, never my silence.
  Publilius Syrus (First century BC)

A man has made at least a start on discovering the meaning of human life when he plants shade trees under which he knows full well he will never sit.
  D. Elton Trueblood (1900–) American Quaker scholar

Procrastination is the thief of time.
  Edward Young (1683–1765) English poet *Night Thoughts*

❀ ❀ ❀ SUPPORT AND SYMPATHY ❀ ❀ ❀

The wisest of the wise may err.
  Aeschylus (525–c.456 BC) Greek playwright *Fragments*

Problems should be solved by those who see them.
Anon

We didn't all come over on the same ship, but we're all in the same boat.
Bernard Baruch (1870–1965) American financier and statesman

Miracles happen to those who believe in them. Otherwise why does not the Virgin Mary appear to Lamaists, Mohammedans, or Hindus who have never heard of her.
Bernard Berenson (1865–1959) American art critic *New York Times Book Review*

It is sometimes the man who opens the door who is the last one to enter the room.
Elizabeth Bibesco (1897–1945) English writer and poet *The Fur and the Palm*

A good scare is worth more to a man than good advice.
E. W. Howe (1853–1937) American author

Writing is not hard. Just get paper and pencil, sit down and write it as it occurs to you. The writing is easy – it's the occurring that's hard.
Stephen Leacock (1869–1944) Canadian humorist and economist

Knowledge advances by steps and not leaps.
Thomas B. Macaulay (1800–59) English author

A man should never be ashamed to own he has been in the wrong, which is but saying, in other words, that he is wiser today than he was yesterday.
Alexander Pope (1688–1744) English poet

No one can make you feel inferior unless you consent.
Eleanor Roosevelt (1884–1962) American humanitarian

Let me assert my firm belief that the only thing we have to fear is fear itself.
Franklin D. Roosevelt (1882–1945) 32nd American President

I had rather have a fool to make me merry, than experience to make me sad.
William Shakespeare (1564–1616) English playwright and poet *As You Like It*

They are able because they think they are able.
Virgil (70–19 BC) Roman poet

This world is a comedy to those that think, a tragedy to those that feel.
Horace Walpole (1717–97) English man of letters

❋ ❋ TEN INSPIRED ❋ ❋ QUOTES

I think, therefore I am.
René Descartes (1596–1650)
French philosopher and
mathematician *Le Discours de la methode*

Dost thou love life? Then do not
squander Time, for that's the stuff
Life is made of.
Benjamin Franklin (1706–90)
American statesman

Truth never damages a cause that
is just.
Mohandas K. Gandhi
(1869–1948) Indian leader
Non-Violence in Peace and War

Every individual has a place to fill
in the world, and is important, in
some respect, whether he chooses
to be so or not.
Nathaniel Hawthorne (1804–64)
American novelist

The price of wisdom is above
rubies.
Job 28:18

The chains of habit are too weak to
be felt until they are too strong to
be broken.
Dr Samuel Johnson (1709–84)
English writer and critic

There is no good in arguing with
the inevitable. The only argument
available with an east wind is to
put on your overcoat.
James Russell Lowell (1819–91)
American poet and essayist

The mind is its own place, and in
itself can make a Heav'n of Hell, a
Hell of Heav'n.
John Milton (1608–74) English
poet

Nine-tenths of wisdom is being
wise in time.
Theodore Roosevelt (1858–1919)
26th American President

There are as many opinions as
there are people: each has his own
correct way.
Virgil (70–19 BC) Roman poet

CHAPTER TWO

BIRTHDAY

❀ ❀ ❀ HUMOROUS ❀ ❀ ❀

You have a rare gift – A Birthday
Present from me!
Anon

Orang-utans teach us that looks are
not everything – but darned near it.
William Cuppy (1884–1949)
American critic and humorist

My Birthday! 'How many years
     ago?
Twenty or thirty?' Don't ask me!
'Forty or fifty?' How can I tell?
I do not remember my birth you
     see!
Julia C. Dorr (1825–1913)
American writer *My Birthday*

You know you're getting old when
your idea of hot, flaming desire is a
barbecued steak.
Victoria Fabiano quoted in
Reader's Digest

You know you're getting old when
you can make the wrinkles that
you see in the mirror disappear just
by taking off your glasses.
Farmers' Almanac quoted in
Reader's Digest

The same old charitable lie
Repeated as the years scoot by
Perpetually makes a hit
'You really haven't changed a bit!'
Margaret Fishback (1904–85)
American poet *The Lie of the Land*

A diplomat is a man who always
remembers a woman's birthday
but never remembers her age.
Robert Frost (1874–1963)
American lyric poet

I can tell a woman's age in half a
minute . . . and I do.
William S. Gilbert (1836–1911)
English comic opera and verse
writer

You know you're getting old when
the candles cost more than the
cake.
Bob Hope (1903–) American
comedian

A man is only as old as the woman
he feels.
Groucho Marx (1895–1977)
American comedian *Attributed*

You've heard of the three ages of
man – youth, age and 'you're
looking wonderful'.
Cardinal Francis Spellman (1889–
1967) American Catholic prelate

A woman may race to get a man a
gift but it always ends in a tie.
Earl Wilson (1907–87) American
columnist

❋ ❋ ❋ INSULTING ❋ ❋ ❋

All they will tell me is that you are of 'a certain age'. – I guess in your case that would be the stone age.
  Anon

Most women are not so young as they are painted.
  Max Beerbohm (1872–1956) English writer and caricaturist *A Defence of Cosmetics*

A man is as old as he's feeling,
A woman as old as she looks.
  William Collins (1721–59) English poet *The Unknown Quantity*

She may very well pass for forty-three
In the dusk with a light behind her.
  William S. Gilbert (1836–1911) English comic opera and verse writer *Trial by Jury*

When a man has a birthday he may take a day off. When a woman has a birthday she may take as much as five years off.
  E. C. McKenzie American writer and compiler

You are old;
Nature in you stands on the very verge
Of her confine.
  William Shakespeare (1564–1616) English playwright and poet *King Lear*

❋ ❋ THE DOWN SIDE ❋ ❋

Mine eyes, my brain, my heart are sad,
  sad is the very core of me;
All wearies, changes, passes, ends: alas! the
  Birthday's injury!
  Richard Burton (1821–90) English orientalist and explorer *Kasidah*

Time, the avenger!
  George Gordon, Lord Byron (1788–1824) English poet

Youth is a blunder; Manhood a struggle; Old Age a regret.
  Benjamin Disraeli (1804–81) British statesman and novelist

Time goes, you say? Ah no!
Alas, time stays, we go.
  Henry A. Dobson (1840–1921) English author and poet *The Paradox of Time*

Wrecked on the lee shore of age.
  Sarah Jewett (1849–1909) American writer

The tragedy of old age is not that one is old, but that one is young.
  Mark Twain (1835–1910) American writer

❋ ❋ A SPECIAL DAY ❋ ❋

Is it birthday weather for you, dear soul?

Is it fine your way,
With tall moon-daisies alight, and
    the mole
Busy, and elegant hares at play . . . ?
  Cecil Day Lewis (1904–72) Irish
poet and critic *Birthday Poem for
Thomas Hardy*

Believing hear, what you deserve
    to hear:
Your birthday as my own to me is
    dear . . .
But yours gives most; for mine did
    only hand
Me to the world; yours gave to me
    a friend.
  Martial (c.43–c. AD 104) Roman
poet *Epigrams*

How can you resist someone who
sends flowers to your mother on
your birthday, thanking her for
making him the happiest man in
the world.
  Nancy Reagan (1923–) American
actress

The main purpose of children's
parties is to remind you that there
are children more awful than your
own.
  Katharine Whitehorn (1926–)
British columnist *How To Survive
Children*

❀ ❀ ❀ **YOUTH** ❀ ❀ ❀

I notice that youth has become
something of a habit with you . . . I
wonder whether you will ever give
it up.
  Anon

Youth would be an ideal state if it
came a little later in life.
  H. H. Asquith (1852–1928) British
Liberal statesman

A Man that is young in years, may
be old in hours, if he have lost no
Time.
  Francis Bacon (1561–1626)
English philosopher and statesman
Of Youth and Age

Key to the door: 18, 21, or 5, if both
parents are working.
  Mike Barfield (1962–) *Dictionary
For Our Time – 'The Oldie'*

Youth is a disease that must be
borne with patiently! Time, indeed,
will cure it.
  R. H. Benson (1871–1914) British
novelist

Ah! happy years! once more who
would not be a boy!
  George Gordon, Lord Byron
(1788–1824) English poet *Childe
Harold*

It is better to waste one's youth
than to do nothing with it at all.
  Georges Courteline (1860–1929)
French humorist

Everyone has talent at twenty-five.
The difficulty is to have it at fifty.
  Edgar Degas (1834–1917) French
painter and sculptor

You will recognize, my boy, the first sign of old age: it is when you go out into the streets of London and realize for the first time how young the policemen look.

Edward Seymour Hicks (1871–1949) British actor and author

Towering in the confidence of twenty-one.

Dr Samuel Johnson (1709–84) English writer and critic

Should you be a teenager blessed with uncommon good looks, document this state of affairs by the taking of photographs. It is the only way anyone will ever believe you in years to come.

Fran Lebowitz (1951–) American journalist and photographer

Remember that as a teenager you are in the last stage of your life when you will be happy to hear that the phone is for you.

Fran Lebowitz

If youth be a defect, it is one that we outgrow only too soon.

James Russell Lowell (1819–91) American poet and essayist

How soon hath Time, the subtle thief of youth,
Stolen on his wing my three and twentieth year!

John Milton (1608–74) English poet *Sonnet for his Twenty-third Birthday*

One good thing about being young is that you are not experienced enough to know you can't possibly do the thing you are doing.

Quoted in *Reader's Digest*

Keep true the dreams of thy youth.

Friedrich von Schiller (1759–1805) German poet and writer

Live as long as you may, the first twenty years are the longest half of your life.

Robert Southey (1774–1843) English poet and writer *The Doctor*

Youth is wholly experimental.

Robert Louis Stevenson (1850–94) Scottish novelist and poet

❈ STAYING YOUNG ❈

Birthdays are nice, as long as you don't have too many.

Anon

Stay youthful: watch that posture, dress young, keep your hair on, hold it all in, improve the bad bits, avoid the daylight.

Simon Bond English cartoonist *Success And How To Be One*

Age . . . is a matter of feeling, not of years.

George William Curtis (1824–92) American man of letters

While we've youth in our hearts, we can never grow old.

Oliver Wendell Holmes (1809–94) American physician and writer

About the only way to stay young is to live honestly, eat sensibly, sleep well, work hard, worship regularly, and lie about your age.
E. C. McKenzie American writer and compiler

If you don't want to get old, hang yourself while young.
Leo Rosten's Treasury of Jewish Quotations

The trick is to grow up without growing old.
Frank Lloyd Wright (1867–1959) American architect

❋ ❋ MIDDLE AGE ❋ ❋

Years ago we discovered the exact point, the dead centre of middle age. It occurs when you are too young to take up golf and too old to rush up to the net.
Franklin P. Adams (1881–1960) American journalist *Nods and Becks*

Middle age is terrible – when you start noticing that the people around you are getting it, you know that you've already caught it.
Anon

Middle age is a time of life
That a man first notices his wife.
Richard Armour (1906–) American writer

Women over thirty are at their best, but men over thirty are too old to recognize it.
Jean-Paul Belmondo (1933–) French film actor

Forty years on, growing older and older,
   Shorter in wind, as in memory long,
Feeble of foot, and rheumatic of shoulder,
What will it help you that once you were strong?
Edward Ernest Bowen (1836–1901) Schoolmaster *'Forty Years On'* Harrow School Song

What's a man's age? He must hurry more, that's all;
Cram in a day what his youth took a year to hold.
Robert Browning (1812–89) English poet

A lady of a 'certain age,' which means certainly aged.
George Gordon, Lord Byron (1788–1824) English poet

Middle age: when you start to exchange your emotions for symptoms.
Irvin S. Cobb (1876–1944) American writer

The really frightening thing about middle age is the knowledge that you'll grow out of it.
Doris Day (1924–) American singer and film actress

The years between fifty and

seventy are the hardest. You are always being asked to do things and you are not yet decrepit enough to turn them down.

T. S. Eliot (1888–1965) British poet and critic

The great thing about being thirty is that there are a great deal more available women. The young ones look younger and the old ones don't look nearly as old.

Glenn Frey American rock singer

Middle Age is when your age starts to show around your middle.

Bob Hope (1903–) American comedian

Boys will be boys, and so will a lot of middle-aged men.

Kin Hubbard (1868–1930) American humorist

Forty is the old age of youth; fifty the youth of old age.

Victor Hugo (1802–85) French poet and author

Middle age is when, wherever you go on holiday, you pack a sweater.

Denis Norden (1922–) English scriptwriter and broadcaster

When you've reached a certain age and think that a face-lift or a trendy way of dressing will make you feel twenty years younger, remember – nothing can fool a flight of stairs.

Denis Norden

At 50, everyone has the face he deserves.

George Orwell (1903–50) English novelist

Life begins at forty.

Walter B. Pitkin (1878–1953) *Book Title*

Proust saw his friends, in old age, disguised with white hair; I see mine, in their mid-40s, prudent upon their pedestals, just as young as they were, only older.

Frederic Raphael (1931–) quoted in *The Listener*

One good thing about middle-age spread is that it brings people closer together.

Quoted in *Reader's Digest*

Fair, Fat and Forty.

Walter Scott (1771–1832) Scottish novelist and poet

Every man over forty is a scoundrel.

George Bernard Shaw (1856–1950) Irish dramatist

On the whole, I take it that middle age is a happier period than youth.

Alexander Smith (1830–67) Scottish poet

The youth gets together materials for a bridge to the moon, and at length the middle-aged man decides to make a woodshed with them.

Henry D. Thoreau (1817–62) American essayist and poet

A man enters middle age when he begins to turn down the lights more for economy than mood.
Quoted in *Reader's Digest*

Thirty-five is a very attractive age. London society is full of women of the very highest birth who have, of their own free choice, remained thirty-five for years.
Oscar Wilde (1854–1900) Irish playwright, novelist and wit *The Importance of Being Earnest*

Middle Age: Later than you think and sooner than you expect.
Earl Wilson (1907–87) American columnist

Be wise with speed;
A fool at forty is a fool indeed.
Edward Young (1683–1765) English poet *Love of Fame*

❈ AGE AND THE SIGNS ❈ OF AGEING

When your friends begin to flatter you on how young you look, it's a sure sign you're getting old.
Anon

Age is not important – unless you are a cheese.
Anon

Lately I appear
To have reached that stage
When people look old
Who are only my age.
Richard Armour (1906–)
American writer

Age will not be defied.
Francis Bacon (1561–1626)
English philosopher and statesman *Essays of Regiment of Health*

Whenever a man's friends begin to compliment him about looking young, he may be sure that they think he is growing old.
Washington Irving (1783–1859) American man of letters *Bracebridge Hall, Bachelors*
Also attributed to Mark Twain (1835–1910) with slightly different phraseology.

From birth to eighteen a girl needs good parents. From eighteen to thirty-five she needs good looks. From thirty-five to fifty-five a woman needs personality; and from fifty-five on the old lady needs cash.
Kathleen Norris (1880–1966) American novelist

Growing old is like being increasingly penalised for a crime you haven't committed.
Anthony Powell (1905–) English novelist *A Dance to the Music of Time*

I have always thought that a woman has the right to treat the subject of her age with ambiguity until, perhaps, she passes into the realm of over ninety. Then it is better she be candid with herself and with the world.

Helena Rubinstein (1871–1965) American businesswoman

It's no use growing older if you only learn new ways of misbehaving yourself.

Saki (H. H. Munro) (1870–1916) British novelist

I'm tired of all this nonsense about beauty being only skin deep . . . What do you want – an adorable pancreas?

Herbert Spencer (1820–1903) English philosopher

I'm as old as my tongue and a little older than my teeth.

Jonathan Swift (1667–1745) Anglo-Irish poet and satirist

Grey hair is great. Ask anyone who's bald.

Lee Trevino (1937–) American golfer *Peter Alliss's Bedside Golf*

The old believe everything: the middle-aged suspect everything: the young know everything.

Oscar Wilde (1854–1900) Irish playwright, novelist and wit

GROWING OLDER: ❀ ❀ THE BENEFITS ❀ ❀

The age of a woman doesn't mean a thing.
The best tunes are played on the oldest fiddles.

Sigmund Z. Engel *Newsweek,* 4 July 1949

One of the many things nobody ever tells you about middle age is that it's such a nice change from being young.

Dorothy Canfield Fisher (1879–1958) American novelist

No man is ever old enough to know better.

Holbrook Jackson (1874–1948) English bibliophile and literary historian

The best thing about the future is that it comes only one day at a time.

Abraham Lincoln (1809–65) 16th American President

One of the pleasures of middle age is to find out that one WAS right, and that one was much righter than one knew at say 17 or 23.

Ezra Pound (1885–1972) American poet and critic

No wise man ever wished to be younger.

Jonathan Swift (1667–1745) Anglo-Irish poet and satirist

GROWING OLDER:
❖ THE DRAWBACKS ❖

You never see it coming!
Richard Briers (1934–) British actor *On his Sixtieth Birthday*

If youth only knew; if age only could.
Henri Estienne (1531–98) *Les Prémices*

Men, like peaches and pears, grow sweet a little while before they start to decay.
Oliver Wendell Holmes (1809–94) American physician and writer *The Autocrat of the Breakfast Table*

Fun is like life insurance; the older you get, the more it costs.
Kin Hubbard (1868–1930) American humorist

I think age is a very high price to pay for maturity.
Tom Stoppard (1937–) British playwright

Life would be infinitely happier if we could only be born at the age of eighty and gradually approach eighteen.
Mark Twain (1835–1910) American writer

By the time a man is wise enough to watch his step he's too old to go anywhere.
Earl Wilson (1907–87) American columnist

❖ ❖ ❖ OLD AGE ❖ ❖ ❖

That man never grows old who keeps a child in his heart.
Anon

Old men are children for a second time.
Aristophanes (c.444–380 BC) Greek playwright *The Clouds*

Old age is like everything else. To make a success of it, you've got to start young.
Fred Astaire (1899–1987) American dancer, singer and actor

I refuse to admit that I am more than fifty-two, even if that does make my sons illegitimate.
Nancy Astor (1879–1964) British politician

Ageing seems to be the only available way to live a long time.
Daniel-François-Esprit Auber (1782–1871) French operatic composer

Declining years: Period when you can decline all invitations to dull parties by pretending to be too old and feeble.
Mike Barfield (1962–) *Dictionary For Our Time – 'The Oldie'*

Some folks as they grow older grow wise, but most folks simply grow stubborner,
Josh Billings (1818–85) American humorist

Old age takes away from us what we have inherited and gives us what we have earned.
Gerald Brenan (1894–1987) English travel writer and novelist *Thoughts in a Dry Season*

People ask what I'd most appreciate getting. I'll tell you: a paternity suit.
George Burns (1898–) American humorist *On his Eighty-seventh Birthday*

There's many a good tune played on an old fiddle.
Samuel Butler (1835–1902) English author, painter and musician *The Way Of All Flesh*

The gardener's rule applies to youth and age:
When young 'sow wild oats', but when old, grow sage.
H. J. Byron (1834–84) English playwright

Growing old isn't so bad when you consider the alternative.
Maurice Chevalier (1888–1972) French film actor

Childhood itself is scarcely more lovely than a cheerful, kindly, sunshiny old age.
L. M. Child (1802–80) American abolitionist and author

The happiest time of life is between seventy and eighty, and I advise everyone to hurry up and get there as soon as possible.
Joseph Choate (1832–1917) American diplomat

Old age begins at forty-six years, according to common opinion.
Marcus Cicero (106–43 BC) Roman statesman and orator

Age does not depend upon years, but upon temperament and health. Some men are born old, and some never grow so.
Tyron Edwards (1809–94) American theologian

I love everything that's old; old friends, old times, old manners, old books, old wines.
Oliver Goldsmith (1728–74) Irish playwright, novelist and poet *She Stoops to Conquer*

You will never be old
  With a twinkle in your eye,
With the Springtime in your heart
  As you watch the Winter fly.
You will never be old
  While you have a smile to share,
While you wonder at mankind
  And you find the time to care.
While there's magic in your world
  And a special dream to hold,
While you still can laugh at life,
  You never will be old.
Iris Hellelden: quoted in Francis Gay's *Friendship Book* 1994

To be seventy years young is sometimes far more cheerful and

hopeful than to be forty years old.
  Oliver Wendell Holmes (1809–94) American physician and writer

How beautiful can time with goodness make an old man look.
  Douglas Jerrold (1803–57) English author and dramatist

The evening of a well-spent life brings its lamps with it.
  Joseph Joubert (1754–1824) French writer and moralist

What find you better or more honourable than age? Take the pre-eminence of it in everything: in an old friend, in old wine, in an old pedigree.
  Shackerley Marmion (1603–39) English dramatist *The Antiquary*

Anyone can get old. All you have to do is to live long enough.
  Groucho Marx (1895–1977) American comedian

Life's a tough proposition, and the first hundred years are the hardest.
  Wilson Mizner (1876–1933) American humorist *Saying*

A man not old, but mellow, like good wine.
  Stephen Phillips (1864–1915) English poet *Ulysses*

Age only matters when one is ageing. Now that I have arrived at a great age. I might just as well be twenty.
  Pablo Picasso (1881–1973) Spanish painter

Few people know how to be old.
  François, Duc de la Rochefoucauld (1613–80) French writer *Maxims*

In a dream you are never eighty.
  Anne Sexton (1928–74) American poet *Old*

Old age is the most unexpected of all the things that happen to a man.
  Leon Trotsky (1879–1940) Russian Jewish revolutionary *Diary in Exile*

✻ CELEBRATION AND ✻ DRINKING

If all be true as I do think,
There are five reasons we should
    drink:
Good wine, a friend, or being dry,
Or lest we should be by and by –
Or any other reason why.
  Henry Aldrich (1647–1710) English cleric

Actually, it only takes one drink to get me loaded. Trouble is, I can't remember if it's the thirteenth or fourteenth.
  George Burns (1898–) American humorist

Let us have wine and women,
    mirth and laughter,
Sermons and soda-water the day
    after.
  George Gordon, Lord Byron (1788–1824) English poet

A man hath no better thing under the sun than to eat, and to drink, and to be merry.
  Ecclesiastes 5:15

I always keep a supply of stimulant handy in case I see a snake – which I also keep handy.
  W. C. Fields (1879–1946) American comedian

Eat, drink, and be merry, for tomorrow ye diet.
  William Gilmour (1869–1942) Scottish author

For any ceremonial purpose the otherwise excellent liquid, water, is unsuitable in colour and other respects.
  Alan P. Herbert (1890–1971) English writer and politician

You're not drunk if you can lie on the floor without holding on.
  Dean Martin (1917–) American singer and entertainer

Home is heaven and orgies are vile
But you need an orgy, once in a
  while.
  Ogden Nash (1902–71) American poet

There are two reasons for drinking: one is, when you are thirsty, to cure it; the other, when you are not thirsty, to prevent it . . . Prevention is better than cure.
  Thomas Love Peacock (1785–1866) English novelist and poet *Melincourt*

'Tis not the eating, nor 'tis not the drinking that is to be blamed, but the excess.
  John Selden (1584–1654) English historian

I'm only a beer teetotaller, not a champagne teetotaller.
  George Bernard Shaw (1856–1950) Irish dramatist *Candida*

I hate to advocate drugs, alcohol, violence, or insanity to anyone, but they've always worked for me.
  Hunter S. Thompson (1939–) American journalist and author

CHAPTER THREE

CHRISTMAS AND OTHER HOLIDAYS

❋ ❋ ❋ CHRISTMAS ❋ ❋ ❋

I have often thought, says Sir Roger, it happens very well that Christmas should fall out in the Middle of Winter.

Joseph Addison (1672–1719) English essayist and politician *The Spectator*

The past is past, but I hope the present is what you wanted.
Anon

How the whole round world is brightened
In the ruddy Christmas glow?
Mary Austin (1868–1934) American writer *The Shepherds in Judea*

Fir: Tree which keeps its leaves all year round except during Christmas.
Mike Barfield (1962–) *Dictionary For Our Time – 'The Oldie'*

Xmas: Popular festival made to sound like a skin disease.
Mike Barfield *Dictionary For Our Time – 'The Oldie'*

Christmas itself may be called into question, if carried too far it creates indigestion.
Ralph Bergengren *The Unwise Christmas*

Christmas, *n*: A day set apart and consecrated to gluttony, drunkenness, maudlin sentiment, gift taking, and public dullness and domestic behaviour.
Ambrose Bierce (1842–1914) American journalist *The Enlarged Devil's Dictionary*

Came home at 3.15, not tight, loosened, if anything, one or two joints unbolted, no more than that, perfectly capable of sticking key in letter-box and walking into Christmas tree.
Alan Coren (1938–) British editor and humorist

Christmas has come, let's eat and drink –
This is no time to sit and think.
William H. Davies (1870–1940) Welsh poet

Every idiot who goes about with Merry Christmas on his lips should be boiled with his own pudding, and buried with a stake of holly through his heart.
Charles Dickens (1812–70) English novelist

HUMBUG!
Charles Dickens *A Christmas Carol*

Christ did not say 'Kill Trees for Christmas'.
  Graffiti: Edinburgh

Christmas comes but once a year
Thank God I'm not Christmas.
  Graffiti: Luton

And the angel said unto the shepherds, 'Shove off. This is cattle country.'
  Graffiti: Royal College of Art, London

I am more and more convinced that Scrooge was one of the most sensible men that I have ever read about.
  Michael Green (1947–) British TV executive

If I sent a Christmas card to Gilbert Harding he would add to the words 'from Hubert Gregg' the words 'and Gilbert Harding', and send it to someone else.
  Hubert Gregg (1914–) English actor and writer

'Peace upon earth!' was said. We sing it,
And pay a million priests to bring it.
After two thousand years of mass
We've got as far as poison-gas.
  Thomas Hardy (1840–1928) English novelist, poet and dramatist *Chistmas: 1924*

Glorious time of great Too-Much . . .
Right thy most unthrifty glee,
And Pious thy Mince-Piety.
  Leigh Hunt (1784–1859) English poet and writer *Christmas*

There are some people who want to throw their arms round you simply because it is Christmas; there are other people who want to strangle you simply because it is Christmas.
  Robert Lynd (1879–1949) Anglo-Irish essayist and journalist

It's customarily said that Christmas is done 'for the kids'. Considering how awful Christmas is and how little our society likes children, this must be true.
  P. J. O'Rourke (1947–) American writer

If you send Christmas cards too early it looks as if you are simply soliciting cards in return. If you send them too late it looks more like a Panic Response than a Message of Goodwill.
  Oliver Pritchett (1939–) English writer

Christmas – could Satan in his most malignant mood have devised a worse combination of graft plus bunkum than the system whereby several hundred million people get a billion or so gifts for which they have no use, and some thousands of shop-clerks die of exhaustion while selling them, and

every other child in the western world is made ill from overeating – all in the name of the lowly Jesus?
  Upton Sinclair (1878–1968) American author *Money Writes! Boni*

Those who promote and organize the most riotous Christmas parties are seldom those who have one's best interests at heart. **Christopher Ward** (1942–) English publisher

The first rule in buying Christmas presents is to select something shiny. If the chosen object is of leather, the leather must look as if it had been well greased; if of silver, it must gleam with the light that never was on sea or land. This is because the wariest person will often mistake shininess for expensiveness.
  P. G. Wodehouse (1881–1975) English novelist

❈ ❈ TRADITIONAL ❈ ❈ CHRISTMAS

Christians awake! salute the happy morn,
Whereon the Saviour of the world was born!
  John Byrom (1692–1763) English poet and stenographer *Hymn for Christmas Day*

How many observe Christ's birthday! How few, his precepts!

O! 'tis easier to keep holidays than commandments.
  Benjamin Franklin (1706–90) American statesman *Poor Richard's Almanack*

I heard the bells on Christmas day
Their old, familiar carols play.
And wild and sweet
The words repeat
Of peace on earth, goodwill to men.
  Henry Wadsworth Longfellow (1807–82) American poet

The best Christmas gift of all is the presence of a happy family all wrapped up with one another.
  E. C. McKenzie American writer and compiler

This is the month and this the happy morn.
  John Milton (1608–74) English poet *On the Morning of Christ's Nativity*

'Twas the night before Christmas, when all through the house
Not a creature was stirring, not even a mouse;
The stockings were hung by the chimney with care,
In hopes that St Nicholas soon would be there.
  Professor Clement C. Moore (1779–1863) American author *A Visit from St Nicholas*

Happy Christmas to all, and to all good night.
  Professor Clement C. Moore *A Visit from St Nicholas*

Christmas comes but once a year
But when it comes it brings good
   cheer.
   Proverb

Heap on more wood! the wind is
   chill
But let it whistle as it will.
We'll keep our Christmas merry
   still.
   Walter Scott (1771–1832) Scottish
novelist and poet *Marmion*

At Christmas play and make good
   cheer,
For Christmas comes but once a
   year.
   Thomas Tusser (c.1520–c.1580)
English agricultural writer *Five
Hundred Points of Good Husbandry*

To perceive Christmas through its
wrapping becomes more difficult
with every year.
   Elwyn B. White (1899–1985)
American essayist, children's
novelist and poet *The Second Tree
from the Corner*

So now is come our joyfull'st feast;
Let every man be jolly;
Each room with Ivy leaves is drest,
And every post with Holly.
   George Wither (1588–1667)
English poet *Christmas Carol*

❄ ❄ ❄ NEW YEAR ❄ ❄ ❄

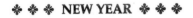

Frenzy yourself into sickness and
dizziness – Christmas is over and

Business is Business.
   Franklin P. Adams (1881–1960)
American journalist *For the Other
364 Days*

One swallow does not make a
summer, but it can certainly break
a New Year's resolution.
   Anon

Year's end is neither an end nor a
beginning but a going on, with all
the wisdom that experience can
instil in us.
   Hal Borland (1900–) American
writer *Sundial of the Seasons*

If you resolve to give up smoking,
drinking and loving, you don't
actually live longer; it just seems
longer.
   Clement Freud (1924–) British
writer, broadcaster and politician

Abstinence is the thin end of the
pledge.
   Graffiti

He who breaks a resolution is a
weakling; the who makes one is a
fool.
   F. M. Knowles *A Cheerful Year
Book*

New Year's Day is every man's
birthday.
   Charles Lamb (1775–1834)
English essayist

Every first of January that we
arrive at is an imaginary milestone
on the turnpike track of human life,

at once a resting place for thought and meditation, and a starting point for fresh exertion in the performance of our journey.
Charles Lamb

The unfortunate thing about this world is that the good habits are much easier to give up than the bad ones.
William Somerset Maugham (1874–1965) British writer

Ring out the old, ring in the new,
Ring, happy bells, across the snow:
The year is going, let him go;
Ring out the false, ring in the true.
Alfred, Lord Tennyson (1809–92) English poet *In Memoriam*

✤ ✤ ✤ ✤ EASTER ✤ ✤ ✤ ✤

Easter: A national celebration of chocolate.
Mike Barfield (1962–) *Dictionary For Our Time – 'The Oldie'*

Easter is cancelled this year.
They've found the body.
Graffiti: Chicago

✤ TRADITIONAL EASTER ✤

I love the gay Eastertide, which brings forth leaves and flowers; and I love the joyous song of the birds, re-echoing through the copse.
Bertrand le Born (Twelfth century) French soldier

'Twas Easter Sunday. The full blossomed trees
Filled all the air with fragrance and with joy.
Henry Wadsworth Longfellow (1807–82) American poet *The Spanish Student*

At Easter let your clothes be new
Or else be sure you will it rue.
Old English Rhyme

Spring bursts to-day,
For Christ is risen and all earth's at play.
Christina Rossetti (1830–94) English poet *Easter Carol*

'Christ the Lord is risen today',
Sons of men and angels say.
Raise your joys and triumphs high,
Sing, ye heavens, and earth reply.
Charles Wesley (1707–88) English hymn writer and evangelist

CHAPTER FOUR

AFFAIRS OF THE HEART

✣ ✣ ✣ HUMOROUS ✣ ✣ ✣

Love is the answer, but while you are waiting for the answer, sex raises some pretty good questions.
Woody Allen (1935–) American film director

My love is like a red, red rose . . .
Expensive and hard to handle!
Anon

I was brought up to believe it was very insulting to sleep with your wife or any lady. A gentleman stays eagerly awake. He sleeps at his work.
Alan Ayckbourn (1939–) English playwright

To woo: See 'To wit'.
Mike Barfield (1962–) *Dictionary For Our Time – 'The Oldie'*

Love, *n*: A temporary insanity curable by marriage or by removal of the patient from the influences under which he incurred the disorder. This disease, like caries and many other ailments, is prevalent only among civilized races living under artificial conditions; barbarous nations breathing pure air and eating simple food enjoying immunity from its ravages. It is sometimes fatal, but more frequently to the physician than to the patient.
Ambrose Bierce (1842–1914) American journalist *The Enlarged Devil's Dictionary*

I feel so miserable without you, It's almost like having you here.
Stephen Bishop American singer and songwriter

A kiss is now attestedly a quite innocuous performance, with nothing very fearful about it one way or the other. It even has its pleasant side.
James Branch Cabell (1879–1958) American novelist and critic

Do you know why God withheld the sense of humour from women? That we may love you instead of laughing at you.
Mrs Patrick Campbell (1865–1940) British actress

I have to be genuinely in love with a girl to make a pass.
George Chakiris (1933–) American actor

The strangest whim has seized me . . . After all
I think I will not hang myself today.
G. K. Chesterton (1874–1936) English critic and novelist

Do you like me more than you don't like me or don't you like me more than you do?

Shelagh Delaney (1939–) English playwright *A Taste of Honey*

You may not be an angel
'Cause angels are so few,
But until the day that one comes along
I'll string along with you.

Al Dublin American songwriter *20 Million Sweethearts*

If you want to kiss me anytime during the evening, just let me know and I'll be glad to arrange it for you. Just mention my name.

F. Scott Fitzgerald (1896–1940) American novelist

Love is like the measles; we all have to go through it.

Jerome K. Jerome (1859–1927) English humorous writer, novelist and playwright *Idle Thoughts of an Idle Fellow, On Being In Love*

Relationship: The civilized conversationalist uses this word in public only to describe a seafaring vessel carrying members of his family.

Fran Lebowitz (1951–) American journalist and photographer

If music be the food of love, let's have a Beethoven butty.

John Lennon (1940–80) British singer and songwriter

What is a promiscuous person? It's usually someone who is getting more sex that you are.

Victor Lownes London Playboy Club manager

He says his lust is in his heart. I hope it's a little lower.

Shirley Maclaine (1934–) American actress and writer

You're the most beautiful woman I've ever seen, which doesn't say much for you.

Groucho Marx (1895–1977) American comedian

In the language of flowers, the yellow rose means friendship, the red rose means love, and the orchid means business.

E. C. McKenzie American writer and compiler

I started out to be a sex fiend, but I couldn't pass the physical.

Robert Mitchum (1917–) American film actor

It has to be admitted that we English have sex on the brain, which is a very unsatisfactory place to have it.

Malcolm Muggeridge (1903–90) British journalist *The Observer*, 'Sayings of the Decade' 1964

Little is known about St Valentine except that he was born in a wood and his twin brother was carried off by a bear. Hence the tradition, begun by greeting card moguls in

the 15th century, of the rest of us sending expensive unsigned messages to each other.
Not The Nine O'Clock News *Not 1983*

I did not sleep. I never do when I am over-happy, over-unhappy, or in bed with a strange man.
Edna O'Brien (1932–) Irish novelist

There are a number of mechanical devices which increase sexual arousal, particularly in women. Chief among these is the Mercedes-Benz 380SL convertible.
P. J. O'Rourke (1947–) American writer

Brevity is the soul of lingerie – as the Petticoat said to the Chemise.
Dorothy Parker (1893–1967) American wit and journalist

I don't believe we've met . . . I'm Mr Right.
Playboy

I used to look out of my bedroom window every morning to observe the postman making his tantalising journey down the street. I do not do that any more because I have discovered this infallible bit of folk wisdom: 'A watched postman never delivers.'
Oliver Pritchett (1939–) English writer

Lord, I wonder what fool it was that first invented kissing!
Jonathan Swift (1667–1745) Anglo-Irish poet and satirist

❋ ❋ ❋ SEX AND LUST ❋ ❋ ❋

I have arranged my etchings in the living room so that you can enjoy them over a nice cup of coffee.
Anon

Englishmen make the best lovers in the world.
Barbara Cartland (1901–) English romantic novelist

But did thee feel the earth move?
Ernest Hemingway (1899–1961) American novelist *For Whom the Bell Tolls*

Lolita, light of my life, fire of my loins.
Vladimir Nabokov (1891–1977) Russian-born American novelist *Lolita*

There are two things a real man likes – danger and play; and he likes woman because she is the most dangerous of playthings.
Friedrich Nietzsche (1844–1900) German philosopher, scholar and writer

Blondes have the hottest kisses.
Ronald Reagan (1911–) Actor
and 40th American President

To err is human – but it feels
divine.
Mae West (1893–1980) American
film actress

When I'm good I'm very very
good, but when I'm bad, I'm better.
Mae West

Between the two evils, I always
pick the one I never tried before.
Mae West

The only way to get rid of
temptation is to yield to it.
Oscar Wilde (1854–1900) Irish
playwright, novelist and wit

❋ ❋ ❋ COURTING ❋ ❋ ❋

I think a lot, of you.
With and without the comma.
Anon

If you cannot inspire a woman
with love of yourself, fill her above
the brim with love of herself; all
that runs over will be yours.
Charles Caleb Colton (1780–1832)
English clergyman and writer

You can't be at a loss for words
while courting –

Women will always give you two
for one.
Elizabeth Inchbald (1753–1821)
English playwright and author

Court a mistress, she denies you;
Let her alone, she will court you.
Ben Jonson (c.1572–1637) English
dramatist

Courtship is that period during
which the female decides whether
or not she can do any better.
E. C. McKenzie American writer
and compiler

She's beautiful and therefore to be
wooed;
She is a woman, therefore to be won.
William Shakespeare (1564–1616)
English playwright and poet
Henry VI Part I

Courtship consists in a number of
quiet attentions, not so pointed as
to alarm, nor so vague as not to be
understood.
Laurence Sterne (1713–68)
Anglo-Irish novelist

❋ ADVICE FOR LOVERS ❋

Hope is a lover's staff.
Anon

The most important thing in life is
to love someone. The second most
important thing in life is to have
someone loving you. The third

most important thing is to have the first two happening at the same time.

Anon quoted in *Reader's Digest*

Love is above all the gift of oneself.
 Jean Anouilh (1910–87) French dramatist

Love and do what you will.
 St Augustine of Hippo (354–430) Latin Church father

Let no one who loves be called altogether unhappy. Even love unreturned has its rainbow.
 J. M. Barrie (1860–1937) Scottish novelist and dramatist *The Little Minister*

Love ceases to be a pleasure when it ceases to be a secret.
 Aphra Behn (1640–89) English playwright and poet

Woman would be more charming if one could fall into her arms without falling into her hands.
 Ambrose Bierce (1842–1914) American journalist *Epigrams*

(But) he that dares not grasp the thorn,
Should never crave the rose.
 Anne Brontë (1820–49) English novelist and poet

Maidens, like moths, are ever caught by glare.
 George Gordon, Lord Byron (1788–1824) English poet

The head does its best but the heart is the boss.
 Wendy Cope (1945–) English poet *Serious Concerns*

Gather ye rosebuds while ye may,
 Old Time is still a-flying,
And this same flower that smiles to-day,
To-morrow will be dying.
 Robert Herrick (1591–1674) English poet *Hesperides*

Love is like quicksilver in the hand. Leave the fingers open and it stays. Clutch it, and it darts away.
 Dorothy Parker (1893–1967) American wit and journalist

Smooth runs the water when the brook is deep.
 William Shakespeare (1564–1616) English playwright and poet *Henry VI Part II*

All strategems are fair in love and war.
 Ellen Wood (1813–87) English playwright

❋ ❋ ❋ FLATTERY ❋ ❋ ❋

Through all Eternity to Thee
A joyful Song I'll raise,
For oh! Eternity's too short
To utter all Thy Praise.
 Joseph Addison (1672–1719) English essayist and politician *The Spectator*

She is neither white nor brown,
    But as the heavens fair;
There is none hath her form divine
    In earth or in the air.
  Anon *As ye came from the Holy Land*

The best part of beauty is that
which a picture cannot express.
  Francis Bacon (1561–1626)
English philosopher and statesman
A Collection of Sentences

A blonde to make a bishop kick a
hole in a stained-glass window.
  Raymond Chandler (1888–1959)
American novelist *Farewell, My
Lovely*

Her very frowns are fairer far
Than smiles of other maidens are.
  Hartley Coleridge (1796–1849)
English man of letters *Song: She is
not Fair*

There's not a Shakespeare sonnet
  Or a Beethoven quartet
That's easier to like than you
  Or harder to forget
I like you more than I would like to
  have a cigarette.
  Wendy Cope (1945–) English
poet *Making Cocoa for Kingsley Amis*

A Face, that's best
By it's own beauty drest,
Can by it's own commend the rest.
  Richard Crashaw (c.1612–49)
English religious poet *Wishes to His
Supposed Mistress*

Things that are lovely
Can tear my heart in two –

Moonlight on still pools,
You.
  Dorothy Dow (1903–) American
poet

Never so happily in one
  Did heaven and earth combine:
And yet 'tis flesh and blood alone
  That makes her so divine.
  Thomas D'Urfey (1653–1723)
English dramatist and songwriter
Chloe Divine

I like your cheeks, I like your nose,
I like the way your lips disclose
The neat arrangement of your teeth
(Half above and half beneath)
In rows.
  John Fuller (1937–) English poet
and novelist *Valentine*

Where beauty is, there will be love.
Nature, that wisely nothing made
  in vain,
Did make you lovely to be loved
  again.
  Robert Heath (c.1617–c.1660) *To
Clarastella*

I dare not ask a kiss;
  I dare not beg a smile;
Lest having that, or this,
  I might grow proud the while.
  Robert Herrick (1591–1674)
English poet *To Electra*

I think nature hath lost the mould
  Where she her shape did take;
Or else I doubt if nature could
  So fair a creature make.
  John Heywood (c.1497–c.1580)
English playwright and musician *A
Praise of his Lady*

O thou art fairer than the evening
air,
Clad in the beauty of a thousand
stars.
Christopher Marlowe (1564–93)
English dramatist and poet *Doctor Faustus*

I ne'er saw true beauty till this
night.
William Shakespeare (1564–1616)
English playwright and poet *Romeo and Juliet*

Shall I compare thee to a summer's
day?
Thou art more lovely and more
temperate.
William Shakespeare *Sonnet 18*

What really flatters a man is that
you think him worth flattering.
George Bernard Shaw (1856–
1950) Irish dramatist *John Bull's Other Island*

Her angel's face,
As the great eye of heaven, shined
bright,
And made a sunshine in the shady
place.
Edmund Spenser (1552–99)
English poet *The Faerie Queene*

When I walk with you I feel as if I
had a flower in my button-hole.
William Thackeray (1811–63)
English novelist

❁ ❁ DECLARATIONS ❁ ❁ OF LOVE

Two things a man cannot hide: that
he is drunk, and that he is in love.
Antiphanes (Fourth century BC)
Athenian playwright

My heart has made its mind up
And I'm afraid it's you.
Wendy Cope (1945–) English
poet *Making Cocoa for Kingsley Amis*

It is probable that every lover,
before he makes his passion
known, exercises his fancy in the
formation of some pretty or
eloquent phrase for conveying the
tremendous secret that masters his
heart; but where one lover
remembers his fine speech at the
critical moment, perhaps a
hundred will forget.
Daphne Dale

For 'twas not into my ear you
whispered
but into my heart;
'Twas not my lips that you kissed
But my soul.
Judy Garland (1922–69) American
singer and actress

I am going to hire a hit man and
have that little wart rubbed out. I
will not have him fouling this
beautiful earth. Do you know
what that little scum has done? He
has wormed his way into my
affection.
Cynthia Heimel American writer

It is difficult to know at what moment love begins; it is less difficult to know that it is begun.
Henry Wadsworth Longfellow (1807–82) American poet *Hyperion*

Do not the most moving moments of our lives find us without words?
Marcel Marceau (1923–) French mime artist *Reader's Digest* 1958

If I speak to thee in Friendship's name,
Thou think'st I speak too coldly;
If I mention Love's devoted flame,
Thou say'st I speak too boldly.
Thomas Moore (1779–1852) Irish poet *How shall I woo?*

I do not love thee! – No! I do not love thee!
And yet when thou art absent I am sad;
And envy even the bright blue sky above thee,
Whose quiet stars may see thee and be glad.
Caroline Norton (1808–77) Irish writer and reformer *A Nameless Poem*

I know I do not love thee! Yet, alas!
Others will scarcely trust my candid heart;
And oft I catch them smiling as they pass,
Because they see me gazing where thou art.
Caroline Norton *I Do Not Love Thee*

Of all forms of caution, caution in love is perhaps the most fatal to true happiness.
Bertrand Russell (1872–1970) Welsh philosopher and writer *The Autobiography of Bertrand Russell*

Who ever loved that loved not at first sight?
William Shakespeare (1564–1616) English playwright and poet *As You Like It*

I do love nothing in the world so well as you: is not that strange?
William Shakespeare *Much Ado About Nothing*

Love conquers all things: let us too give in to love.
Virgil (70–19 BC) Roman poet

I'm not very well today. I can only write prose.
William Butler Yeats (1865–1939) Irish poet *Attributed*

❋ FROM THE HEART ❋ (EXPRESSIONS OF LOVE)

I love you and you alone but most of all I love us together.
Anon

O, would I were where I would be!
There would I be where I am not:
For where I am would I not be,
And where I would be I can not.
Anon *Suspiria*

I'll Love you till the ocean
  Is folded and hung up to dry
And the seven stars go squawking
  Like geese about the sky
  Wystan Hugh Auden (1907–73)
Anglo-American poet and essayist
As I Walked Out One Evening

How I do love thee? Let me count
  the ways.
I love thee to the depth and
  breadth and height
My soul can reach, when feeling
  out of sight
For the ends of beginning and ideal
  grace.
  Elizabeth Barrett Browning
(1806–61) English poet *Sonnets from
the Portuguese*

I love thee with the breath,
Smiles, tears, of all my life! – and, if
  God choose,
I shall but love thee better after
  death.
  Elizabeth Barrett Browning
Sonnets from the Portuguese

If thou must love me, let it be for
  naught
Except for love's sake only.
  Elizabeth Barrett Browning
Sonnets from the Portuguese

Escape Me?
Never–
Beloved!
  Robert Browning (1812–89)
English poet *Life In A Love*

O, my Luve's like a red red rose
That's newly sprung in June:

O my Luve's like a melodie
That's sweetly play'd in tune.
  Robert Burns (1759–96) Scottish
poet *My Luve Is Like A Red Red Rose*

Though poor in gear, we're rich in
love.
  Robert Burns (1759–96) Scottish
poet *The Sodger's Return*

To see her is to love her,
And love but her for ever;
For nature made her what she is,
And never made another!
  Robert Burns *Bonnie Lesley*

She walks in beauty, like the night
Of cloudless climes and starry
  skies;
And all that's best of dark and
  bright
Meet in her aspect and her eyes.
  George Gordon, Lord Byron
(1788–1824) English poet

Give me a thousand kisses, then a
  hundred,
then another thousand, then a
  second hundred,
then yet another thousand, then a
  hundred.
  Gaius Catullus (c.84–c.54 BC)
Roman lyric poet

All day long I love the oaks,
But, at nights, yon little cot,
Where I see the chimney smokes,
Is by far the prettiest spot.
  James Clarke (1810–88) American
theologian

She is not fair to outward view
  As many maidens be;
Her loveliness I never knew
  Until she smiled on me.
Oh! then I saw her eye was bright,
A well of love, a spring of light.
  Hartley Coleridge (1796–1849)
English man of letters *Song: She is
not Fair*

I love thee for a heart that's kind –
Not for the knowledge in thy
  mind.
  William H. Davies (1871–1940)
Welsh poet

Yet 'twas of my mind, seizing thee,
  Though in thee it cannot
  persevere
For I had rather owner be
  Of thee one hour, than all else
  ever.
  John Donne (1572–1631) English
poet *The Undertaking*

I cannot work. I cannot read or
  write.
How can I frame a letter to
  implore.
Eloquence is a lie. The truth is trite.
Nothing I say will make you love
  me more.
  James Fenton (1949–) English
poet *Nothing*

I don't want to live – I want to love
first, and live incidentally.
  Zelda Fitzgerald (1900–47)
Letter to her husband

I love thee, I love thee,
  'Tis all that I can say;

It is my vision in the night,
  My dreaming in the day.
  Thomas Hood (1799–1845)
English poet and humorist
I Love Thee

Like these cool lilies may our loves
  remain,
Perfect and pure, and know not
  any stain.
  Andrew Lang (1844–1912)
Scottish man of letters *A Vow to
Heavenly Venus*

My love is of a birth as rare
As 'tis for object strange and high:
It was begotten by despair
Upon impossibility.
  Andrew Marvell (1621–78)
English poet *The Definition of Love*

When with your arms you hold
  me,
And kisses speak your love
  unspoken,
Then my eyes with tears run over,
And my very heart is broken.
  Robert Nichols (1893–1944)
English poet *Aurelia*

The heart has its reasons which
reason knows nothing of.
  Blaise Pascal (1623–62) French
mathematician and man of letters

Doubt thou the stars are fire;
  Doubt that the sun doth move;
Doubt truth to be a liar;
  But never doubt I love.
  William Shakespeare (1564–1616)
English playwright and poet

I fear thy kisses, gentle maiden,
  Thou needest not fear mine;
My spirit is too deeply laden
  Ever to burden thine.
  Percy Bysshe Shelley (1792–1822)
English poet *I fear thy kisses*

So let us love, dear Love, like as we
  ought,
– Love is the lesson which the Lord
  us taught.
  Edmund Spenser (1552–99)
English poet *Amoretti Sonnet 68*

If love were what the rose is,
And I were like the leaf,
Our lives would grow together
In sad or singing weather,
Blown fields or flowerful closes,
Green pleasure or grey grief.
  Algernon Charles Swinburne
(1837–1909) English poet and critic
A Match

Now folds the lily all her sweetness
  up,
And slips into the bosom of the
  lake:
So fold thyself, my dearest, thou,
  and slip
Into my bosom and be lost in me.
  Alfred, Lord Tennyson (1809–92)
English poet *Now Sleeps The
Crimson Petal*

O that I had a music and a voice
Harmonious as your own, that I
  might tell
What ye have done for me!
  William Wordsworth (1770–1850)
English poet *Prelude Book XII*

I have spread my dreams under
  your feet;
Tread softly because you tread on
  my dreams.
  William Butler Yeats (1865–1939)
Irish Poet *He wishes for the Cloths of
Heaven*

❧ ❧ THE ESSENCE ❧ ❧
OF LOVE

Mysterious Love, uncertain
  treasure,
Hast thou more of pain or
  pleasure!
Endless torments dwell about thee:
Yet who would live, and live
  without thee!
  Joseph Addison (1672–1719)
English essayist and politician
Rosamond

Love isn't the only thing in life but
it's way ahead of whatever is in
second place.
  Anon

Young love is a flame; very pretty,
often very hot and fierce, but still
only light and flickering. The love
of the older and disciplined heart is
as coals, deep-burning,
unquenchable.
  Henry Ward Beecher (1813–87)
American congregationalist
clergyman and writer

Never seek to tell thy love,
Love that never told can be;

For the gentle wind does move
Silently, invisibly.
  William Blake (1757–1827)
English poet and artist *Love's Secret*

All thoughts, all passions, all
    delights,
Whatever stirs this mortal frame,
All are but ministers of Love,
  And feed his sacred flame.
  Samuel Taylor Coleridge (1772–
1834) English poet *Love*

You know exactly what to do;
I think of little else but you.
  Wendy Cope (1945–) English
poet *Making Cocoa for Kingsley Amis*

For love all love of other sights
  controls
And makes one little room an
  everywhere.
  John Donne (1573–1631) English
poet *The Good-morrow*

Love, all alike, no season knows,
  nor clime,
Nor hours, days, months, which
  are the rags of time.
  John Donne *The Sun-Rising*

The devil take me, if I think
anything but love to be the object
of love.
  Henry Fielding (1707–54) English
novelist *Amelia*

It's love that makes the world go
round.
  Translation of a French song

Youth's the season made for joys,
  Love is then our duty.
  John Gay (1685–1732) English
poet *The Beggar's Opera*

Two souls with but a single
    thought,
Two hearts that beat as one.
  Friedrich Halm (1806–71) German
poet and playwright *Der Sohn der
Wildnis*

Love . . . is like a beautiful flower
which I may not touch, but whose
fragrance makes the garden a place
of delight just the same.
  Helen Keller (1880–1968)
American writer

No, there's nothing half so sweet in
life as love's young dream.
  Thomas Moore (1779–1852) Irish
poet *Love's Young Dream*

On life's vast ocean diversely we
  sail,
Reason the card, but passion is the
  gale.
  Alexander Pope (1688–1744)
English poet

There is no pleasure like the pain
  Of being loved, and loving.
  Winthrop M. Praed (1802–39)
English humorous poet *Legend of
the Haunted Tree*

There is only one happiness in life,
to love and be loved.
  George Sand (1804–76) French
novelist

Love does not consist in gazing at each other but in looking together in the same direction.
  Antoine de Saint-Exupery (1900–44) French novelist and airman

Love sought is good, but given unsought is better.
  William Shakespeare (1564–1616) English playwright and poet *Twelfth Night*

In the Spring a young man's fancy lightly turns to thoughts of love
  Alfred, Lord Tennyson (1809–92) English poet *Locksley Hall*

❀ ❀ ❀ PROPOSALS ❀ ❀ ❀

I don't like your surname – why don't we change it?
  Anon

Grow old with me!
The best is yet to be.
  Robert Browning (1812–89) English poet *Rabbi Ben Ezra*

Come live with me, and be my love,
And we will some new pleasures prove
Of golden sands, and crystal brooks,
With silken lines, and silver hooks.
  John Donne (1573–1631) English poet *The Bait*

As you are woman, so be lovely:
As you are lovely, so be various,
Merciful as constant, constant as various,
So be mine, as I yours for ever.
  Robert Graves (1895–1985) English poet and novelist *Pygmalion to Galatea*

Bid me to live, and I will live
  Thy Protestant to be:
Or bid me love, and I will give
  A loving heart to thee.
  Robert Herrick (1591–1674) English poet *Hesperides*

With you I should love to live, with you be ready to die.
  Horace (65–8 BC) Roman poet and satirist

No time like the present.
  Mary Manley (1663–1724) British writer *The Lost Lover*

Come live with me and be my love
And we'll defy the storms above.
We'll lack for food, we'll lack for gold,
No lack of tales when we're old.
  Christopher Marlowe (1564–93) English dramatist and poet

Come live with me and be my love,
And we will all the pleasures prove,
That valleys, groves, hills and fields,
Woods, or steepy mountain yields.
  Christopher Marlowe *The Passionate Shepherd to his Love*

Emily, I've a little confession to make. I really am a horse doctor.

But marry me and I'll never look at another horse.
Groucho Marx (1895–1977) American comedian

She whom I love is hard to catch and conquer,
Hard, but O the glory of the winning were she won!
George Meredith (1828–1909) English novelist *Love in the Valley*

If you are not too long, I will wait for you all my life.
Oscar Wilde (1854–1900) Irish playwright, novelist and wit

❊ LOVE ON THE ROCKS ❊

My life will be sour grapes and ashes without you.
Daisy Ashford (1881–1972) English writer *The Young Visitors*

Alone: in bad company.
Ambrose Bierce (1842–1914) American journalist *The Devil's Dictionary*

The mind has a thousand eyes,
And the heart but one;
Yet the light of a whole life dies,
When love is done.
F. W. Bourdillon (1852–1921) English poet *The Night Has A Thousand Eyes*

But to see her was to love her:
Love but her and love forever.

Had we never loved sae kindly,
Had we never loved sae blindly,
Never met – or never parted –
We had ne'er been broken-hearted.
Robert Burns (1759–96) Scottish poet *Ae Fond Kiss*

Yesterday I loved, today I suffer, tomorrow I die: but I still think fondly, today and tomorrow, of yesterday.
Gotthold E. Lessing (1729–81) German dramatist

Love is dead. We are cured –
But are we happy?
Therese Robinson (1797–1882) German-American poet and novelist

There exist people who would never have been in love, had they never heard of love.
François, Duc de la Rochefoucauld (1613–80) French writer *Maxims*

Love is the whole history of a woman's life,
it is but an episode in a man's.
Madame de Staël (1766–1817) French novelist and critic

Yet leave me not; yet, if thou wilt, be free;
Love me no more, but love my love of thee.
Algernon Charles Swinburne (1837–1909) English poet and critic *Erotion*

'Tis better to have loved and lost
Than never to have loved at all.
  Alfred, Lord Tennyson (1809–92)
English poet *In Memoriam*

O that 'twere possible
After long grief and pain
To find the arms of my true love
Round me once again!
  Alfred, Lord Tennyson *Maud*

Many waters cannot quench love,
neither can floods drown it.
  The Song Of Solomon

Thou art my life – if thou but turn
  away
My life's a thousand deaths. Thou
  art my way –
Without thee Love, I travel but
  stray.
  John Wilmot, Earl of Rochester
(1647–80) English courtier and poet
To his Mistress

CHAPTER FIVE

MATRIMONY

❈ ❈ ❈ HUMOROUS ❈ ❈ ❈

Nothing ever causes a young man greater surprise than to find that someone has fallen in love with his sister.
Around Atlanta quoted in *Reader's Digest*

The test of true love is whether you can endure the thought of cutting your sweetheart's toe-nails.
W. N. P. Barbellion (pseudonym of Bruce F. Cummings) (1889–1919) English diarist

Wedding cake: The major threat to Liz Taylor's diet plans.
Mike Barfield (1962–) *Dictionary For Our Time – 'The Oldie'*

Wedding ring: See 'Wife-swapping circle'.
Mike Barfield *Dictionary For Our Time – 'The Oldie'*

Marriage, *n*: The state or condition of a community consisting of a master, a mistress and two slaves, making in all two.
Ambrose Bierce (1842–1914) American journalist *The Devil's Dictionary*

Marriage is a wonderful invention; but then again so is a bicycle repair kit.
Billy Connolly (1942–) Scottish comedian

Marriage is like strong horseradish. You can praise it and still have tears in your eyes.
Funny Funny World quoted in *Reader's Digest*

Husbands are like fires. They go out when unattended.
Zsa Zsa Gabor (1919–) Hungarian film star

My mother said it was simple to keep a man – you must be a maid in the living-room, a cook in the kitchen and a whore in the bedroom. I said I'd hire the other two and take care of the bedroom bit.
Jerry Hall (1956–) American model

I never knew what real happiness was until I got married. And then it was too late.
Max Kauffmann

Nothing is more distasteful to me than that entire complacency and satisfaction which beams in the countenances of a new-married couple.
Charles Lamb (1775–1834) English essayist *Essays of Elia*

The honeymoon is over when he phones that he'll be late for supper

– and she has already left a note that it's in the refrigerator.

Bill Lawrence (1930–) American newsman

The Japanese have a word for it. It's Judo – the art of conquering by yielding. The western equivalent of Judo is 'yes dear'.

J. P. McEvoy (1895–1958) American writer *Charlie Would Have Loved This*

Kissing don't last. Cooking do!

George Meredith (1828–1909) English novelist *The Ordeal of Richard Feverel*

Dancing is wonderful training for girls; it's the first way you learn to guess what a man is going to do before he does it.

Christopher Morley (1890–1957) American novelist and essayist

Marriage is the alliance of two people, one of whom never remembers birthdays and the other never forgets them.

Ogden Nash (1902–71) American poet

Marriages are best made of dissimilar material.

Theodore Parker (1810–60) American Unitarian clergyman

Marriage is at best a dangerous experiment.

Thomas Love Peacock (1785–1866) English novelist and poet

When I was a young man I vowed never to marry until I found the ideal woman. Well, I found her – but, alas, she was waiting for the ideal man.

Robert Schumann (1810–56) German composer

When I said I would die a bachelor I did not think I should live till I were married.

William Shakespeare (1564–1616) English playwright and poet *Much Ado About Nothing*

The best part of married life is the fights. The rest is merely so-so.

Thornton Niven Wilder (1897–1976) American author and playwright *The Matchmaker*

❈ ❈ ENGAGEMENT ❈ ❈

Pre-marital sex: Now compulsory test of future physical compatibility. However, results can be inconclusive, and the test may need repeating for many years before a couple finally recognise they are incompatible, and the man marries someone younger.

Mike Barfield (1962–) *Dictionary For Our Time – 'The Oldie'*

And her 'Yes', once said to you,
Shall be Yes for evermore.
 Elizabeth Barrett Browning
(1806–61) English poet

When you're a married man,
Samivel, you'll understand a good
many things as you don't
understand now.
 Charles Dickens (1812–70)
English novelist *Pickwick Papers*

Whoever loves, if he do not propose
The right true end of love, he's one
 that goes
To sea for nothing but to make him
 sick.
 John Donne (1573–1631) English
poet *Love's Progress*

Man has his will but woman has
her way.
 Oliver Wendell Holmes (1809–
94) American physician and writer
The Autocrat of the Breakfast Table

The surest way to hit a woman's
heart is to aim kneeling.
 Douglas Jerrold (1803–57)
English author, dramatist and wit

Engaged couples should realize
that marriage will never be as good
as she believes or as bad as he
suspects.
 E. C. McKenzie American writer
and compiler

It is superstition to put one's hopes
in formalities; but it is pride to be
unwilling to submit to them.
 Blaise Pascal (1623–62) French
mathematician and man of letters

Advice to those about to marry . . .
Don't.
 Punch Magazine

Even in civilized mankind faint
traces of monogamous instinct can
be perceived.
 Bertrand Russell (1872–1970)
Welsh philosopher and writer

Of all forms of caution, caution in
love is perhaps the most fatal to
true happiness.
 Bertrand Russell *Marriage and
Morals*

The rose was awake all night for
 your sake,
Knowing your promise to me;
The lilies and roses were all awake,
They sighed for dawn and thee.
 Alfred, Lord Tennyson (1809–92)
English poet

A ring on the finger is worth two
on the phone.
 Harold Thompson English writer
Body, Books and Britches

Long engagements give people the
opportunity of finding out each
other's character before marriage,
which is never advisable.
 Oscar Wilde (1856–1900) Irish
playwright, novelist and wit

MARRIAGE:
❋ THE POSITIVE VIEW ❋

A happy marriage has in it all the
pleasures of a friendship, all the

enjoyments of sense and reason, and, indeed, all the sweets of life.
Joseph Addison (1672–1719) English essayist and politician

Two things doth prolong thy life: A quiet heart and a loving wife.
Anon

Marriage is that relation between man and woman in which the independence is equal, the dependence mutual, and the obligation reciprocal.
Louis K. Anspacher (1878–1947) American dramatist

The most important things to do in this world are to get something to eat, something to drink and somebody to love you.
Brendan Behan (1923–64) Irish author quoted in *Weekend*, 1968

No human relation gives one possession in another – every two souls are absolutely different. In friendship or in love, the two side by side raise hands together to find what one cannot reach alone.
Kahlil Gibran (1883–1931) American writer and artist

You give but little when you give your possessions. It is when you give yourself that you truly give.
Kahlil Gibran *The Prophet*

There is no earthly happiness exceeding that of a reciprocal satisfaction in the conjugal state.
Herbert Giles (1845–1935) English scholar and linguist

The sexes were made for each other, and only in the wise and loving union of the two is the fullness of health and duty and happiness to be expected.
William Hall (1943–) American business executive

Marriage has many pains, but celibacy has no pleasures.
Dr Samuel Johnson (1709–84) English writer and critic *Rasselas*

Love is moral even without legal marriage, but marriage is immoral without love.
Ellen Key (1849–1926) Swedish reformer *Essay, The Morality of Women*

Occasionally in life there are those moments of unutterable fulfilment which cannot be completely explained by those symbols called words. Their meanings can only be articulated by the inaudible language of the heart.
Martin Luther King Jr. (1929–68) American clergyman and civil rights campaigner

To love is to place our happiness in the happiness of another.
Gottfried Wilhelm Leibniz (1646–1716) German philosopher and mathematician

There is no more lovely, friendly and charming relationship, communion or company than a good marriage.
Martin Luther (1483–1546) German Protestant reformer

Marriage is the only known example of the happy meeting of the immovable object and the irresistible force.

Ogden Nash (1902–71) American poet

Marriage is popular because it combines the maximum of temptation with the maximum of opportunity.

George Bernard Shaw (1856–1950) Irish dramatist *'Marriage'*

And if your hearts are bound together by love; if both are yielding and true; if both cultivate the spirit of meekness, forbearance, and kindness, you will be blessed in your home and in the journey of life.

Matthew Hale (1609–76) English judge

Marriage resembles a pair of shears, so joined that they cannot be separated; often moving in opposite directions, yet always punishing anyone who comes between them.

Sydney Smith (1883–1969) New Zealand forensic expert

A Wedding-day! It is a day of rejoicing as it should be; but it is no less a day of life-long merriment.

Charles Titcomb

The bonds of matrimony are like any other bonds – they mature slowly.

Peter de Vries (1910–) American novelist

MARRIAGE: ✷ THE CYNICAL VIEW ✷

The most popular labour saving device today is still a husband with money.

Joey Adams (1911–) American comedian *Cindy & I*

A woman seldom asks advice before she has bought her wedding clothes.

Joseph Addison (1672–1719) English essayist and politician *The Spectator*

If it were not for the presents, an elopement would be preferable.

George Ade (1866–1944) American humorist and playwright

It doesn't matter who you marry, you are sure to find next morning that it was someone else.

Anon

It is a truth universally acknowledged, that a single man in possession of a good fortune must be in want of a wife.

Jane Austen (1775–1817) English novelist *Pride and Prejudice*

Happiness in marriage is entirely a matter of chance.
Jane Austen *Pride and Prejudice*

Human nature is so well disposed towards those who are in interesting situations, that a young person, who either marries or dies, is sure to be kindly spoken of.
Jane Austen *Emma*

Made for each other: Phrase now true only of Frankenstein's monster and his bride.
Mike Barfield (1962–) *Dictionary For Our Time – 'The Oldie'*

Wedlock: Type of lock easily undone nowadays.
Mike Barfield *Dictionary For Our Time – 'The Oldie'*

Marriage is not just spiritual communion and passionate embraces; marriage is also three meals a day and remembering to carry out the trash.
Joyce Brothers (1928–) American psychiatrist and TV presenter *Good Housekeeping*

Brigands demand your money or your life, whereas women require both.
Samuel Butler (1835–1902) English author, painter and musician

Marriage is the result of the longing for the deep, deep peace of the double bed after the hurly-burly of the chaise longue.
Mrs Patrick Campbell (1865–1940) British actress

The trouble with some women is they get all excited about nothing – and then they marry him.
Cher (1946–) American singer and actress

Oh! how many torments lie in the small circle of a wedding-ring!
Colley Cibber (1671–1757) English actor and dramatist *The Double Gallant*

Any intelligent woman who reads the marriage contract, and then goes into it, deserves all the consequences.
Isadora Duncan (1878–1927) American dancer and writer

All marriages are happy. It's the living together afterwards that causes the trouble.
Farmers Almanac

One fool at least in every married couple.
Henry Fielding (1707–54) English novelist

I give you this ring which has no beginning and I don't know when the end comes.
Zsa Zsa Gabor (1919–) Hungarian film star

A man in love is incomplete until he is married. Then he's finished.
Zsa Zsa Gabor

Marrying a man is like buying something you've been admiring for a long time in a shop window. You may love it when you get home, but it doesn't always go with everything else in the house.
Jean Kerr (1923–) American playwright

Marriage is an indissoluble contract in which one party obtains from the other party more than either ever may hope to repay.
O. A. Lattista *Everybody's Weekly*

Many a man in love with a dimple often makes the mistake of marrying the whole girl.
Stephen Leacock (1869–1944) Canadian humorist and economist

Marriage is neither heaven nor hell, it is simply purgatory.
Abraham Lincoln (1809–65) 16th American President

Bachelors know more about women than married men; if they didn't, they'd be married too.
Henry L. Mencken (1880–1965) American journalist and linguist

Marriage is the only actual bondage known to our law. There remain no legal slaves, except the mistress of every house.
John Stuart Mill (1806–73) English philosopher and social reformer *The Subjection of Women*

Before marriage, a man will lie awake thinking about something you said; after marriage, he'll fall asleep before you finish saying it.
Helen Rowland (1875–1950) American journalist

In olden times sacrifices were made at the altar – a practice which is still continued.
Helen Rowland *Violets & Vinegar*

A husband is what is left of the lover after the nerve has been extracted.
Helen Rowland

When a man makes a woman his wife, it's the highest compliment he can pay her, and it's usually the last.
Helen Rowland

To marry is to halve your rights and double your duties.
Arthur Schopenhauer (1788–1860) German philosopher *The World as Will and Idea*

What God hath joined together no man ever shall put asunder: God will take care of that.
George Bernard Shaw (1856–1950) Irish dramatist

It is a woman's business to get married as soon as possible, and a man's to keep unmarried as long as he can.
George Bernard Shaw *Man and Superman*

By all means marry: if you get a good wife you'll become happy; if you get a bad one, you'll become a philosopher.

Socrates (469–399 BC) Greek philosopher

Marriage is like life in this – that it is a field of battle and not a bed of roses.

Robert Louis Stevenson (1850–94) Scottish novelist and poet *Virginibus Puerisque*

The fight that was no fight is over,
The uncontested victory is won;
The conquered sleeping by her
     side,
Forgets already what is done.

Leonard A. G. Strong (1896–1958) English novelist and poet *The Bride*

You have but a very few years to be young and handsome in the eyes of the world; and as few months to be so in the eyes of a husband.

Jonathan Swift (1667–1745) Anglo-Irish poet and satirist *Letter to a Young Lady on her Marriage*

Marriage is the waste-paper basket of the emotions.

Sidney Webb (1859–1947) English social reformer

Woman begins by resisting a man's advances and ends up blocking his retreat.

Oscar Wilde (1854–1900) Irish playwright, novelist and wit

The proper basis for marriage is mutual misunderstanding.

Oscar Wilde

SECOND
❖ ❖ ❖ MARRIAGE ❖ ❖ ❖

Marriage is a lot like the army; everyone complains, but you'd be surprised at the large number that re-enlist.

James Garner (1928–) American actor

He loves his bonds, who when the
     first are broke,
Submits his neck unto a second
     yoke.

Robert Herrick (1591–1674) English poet *To Love*

Wedlock's like wine, not properly judged of till the second glass.

Douglas Jerrold (1803–57) English author and dramatist

Another instance of the triumph of hope over experience.

Dr Samuel Johnson (1709–84) English writer and critic *Referring to a friend's second marriage*

The plural of spouse is spice.

Christopher Morley (1890–1957) American novelist and essayist

---

❖ ❖ ❖ THE BRIDE ❖ ❖ ❖

Women wish to be loved without a why or wherefore; not because they are pretty, or good, or well-bred, or graceful, or intelligent, but

because they are themselves.
Henri Frédéric Amiel (1821–81)
Swiss philosopher and writer

Men who do not make advances to
women are apt to become the
victims of women who make
advances to them.
Walter Bagehot (1826–77) English
writer

Give me my golf clubs, fresh air
and a beautiful partner, and you
can keep my golf clubs and the
fresh air.
Jack Benny (1894–1974) American
comedian

He that still may see your cheeks,
  Where all rareness still reposes,
Is a fool if e'er he seeks
  Other lilies, other roses.
William Browne (1591–1643)
English pastoral poet *Epitaph*

But to see her was to love her,
Love but her, and love for ever.
Robert Burns (1759–96) Scottish
poet *Ae Fond Kiss*

A little still she strove, and much
  repented,
And whispering 'I will ne'er
  consent' – consented.
George Gordon, Lord Byron
(1788–1824) English poet

She was one of the early birds,
And I was one of the worms.
T. W. Connor (Nineteenth
century) *She was a Dear Little
Dickie-Bird*

If you would have a good wife
marry one who has been a good
daughter.
Thomas Fuller (1608–61) English
writer and clergyman

The only way to understand a
woman is to love her – and then it
isn't necessary to understand her.
Sydney J. Harris (1903–76)
American journalist

She plucked from my lapel the
invisible strand of lint (the
universal act of a woman to
proclaim ownership).
O. Henry (1862–1910) American
writer

Blest is the Bride on whom the sun
  doth shine.
Robert Herrick (1591–1674)
English poet *Hesperides*

Man has his will, but woman has
her way.
Oliver Wendell Holmes (1809–
94) American physician and writer
The Autocrat of the Breakfast Table

What winning graces! What
  majestic mien!
She moves a goddess, and looks a
  queen!
Homer (c.850 BC) Greek poet *The
Iliad*

I have learned that only two things are necessary to keep one's wife happy. First, let her think she's having her way. And second, let her have it.

Lyndon B. Johnson (1908–73) 36th American President *At a White House reception*

One should choose for a wife only a woman one would choose for a friend if she were a man.

Joseph Joubert (1754–1824) French writer and moralist

After paying for the wedding, about the only thing a father has left to give away is the bride.

E. C. McKenzie American writer and compiler

My wife, poor wretch.

Samuel Pepys (1633–1703) English diarist *Diary*, September 18 1661

Be to her virtues very kind.
Be to her faults a little blind.

Matthew Prior (1664–1721) English poet and diplomat

My son is my son till he gets him a wife,
But my daughter's my daughter for all her life.

Proverb

Marriage is the only thing that affords a woman the pleasure of company and the perfect sensation of solitude at the same time.

Helen Rowland (1875–1950) American journalist

What's in a name? That which we call a rose
By any other name would smell as sweet.

William Shakespeare (1564–1616) English playwright and poet *Romeo and Juliet*

What's mine is yours, and what is yours is mine.

William Shakespeare *Measure for Measure*

A woman seeking a husband is the most unscrupulous of all beasts of prey.

George Bernard Shaw (1856–1950) Irish dramatist

A happy bridesmaid makes a happy bride.

Alfred, Lord Tennyson (1809–92) English poet *The Bridesmaid*

This ring the Bride-groom did for none provide
But for his bride.

Henry Vaughan (1622–95) Welsh religious poet *The World*

She didn't think he was good enough for her, but she married him because she thought he was too good for any other woman.

Douglas Yates British scientist *Works*

❧ ❧ THE GROOM ❧ ❧

Husband, *n*: One who, having dined, is charged with the care of the plate.
Ambrose Bierce (1842–1914) American journalist *The Enlarged Devil's Dictionary*

On the whole, I haven't found men unduly loath to say, 'I love you.' The real trick is to get them to say, 'Will you marry me?'
Ilka Chase

The male is a domestic animal which, if treated with firmness and kindness, can be trained to do most things.
Jilly Cooper (1937–) English columnist and writer

You say, to me-wards your
    affection's strong;
Pray love me little so you love me
    long.
Robert Herrick (1591–1674) English poet *Love me little, love me long*

No self-made man ever did such a good job that some woman didn't want to make a few alterations.
Kin Hubbard (1868–1930) American humorist

The feller that puts off marryin' till he can support a wife ain't very much in love.
Kin Hubbard

Behind every successful man stands a surprised mother-in-law.
Hubert Humphrey (1911–78) American politician

He kept telling me he was a confirmed bachelor and I thought, at least one knows where one stands.
Princess Anne, The Princess Royal (1950–)

If you have never seen a total eclipse, just watch the groom at a wedding.
Herbert V. Prochnow (1897–) American banker and writer

When a girl marries she exchanges the attentions of many men for the inattention of one.
Helen Rowland (1875–1950) American journalist

The hardest task in a girl's life is to prove to a man that his intentions are serious.
Helen Rowland

My true love hath my heart, and I
    have his,
By just exchange one for another
    given;
I hold his dear, and mine he cannot
    miss,
There never was a better bargain
    driven.
Philip Sidney (1554–86) English poet *Arcadia*

It is one thing to be told that a tall, dark, handsome stranger is shortly

to come into your life; the big trick is to nobble him.
Jack Thomas

He is dreadfully married. He's the most married man I ever saw in my life.
Artemus Ward (Charles Farrar Browne; 1834–67) American humorist

There aren't many left like him nowadays, what with education and whisky the price it is.
Evelyn Waugh (1903–66) English novelist and travel writer

When a confirmed bachelor falls in love, he does it with a wholeheartedness beyond the scope of the ordinary man.
P. G. Wodehouse (1881–1975) English novelist

My husband chased me until I caught him.
Pia Zadora (1956–) American actress

❋ TO THE HAPPY COUPLE ❋

'Enjoy yourselves. It's later on you'll think.'
Telegram sent to the bride and groom at a wedding in Edinburgh quoted in *Reader's Digest*

Today is the first day of the rest of your life.
Anon quoted in G. Bellamy, *The Secret Lemonade Drinker*

Wedding, *n*: A ceremony at which two persons undertake to become one, one undertakes to become nothing, and nothing undertakes to become supportable.
Ambrose Bierce (1842–1914) American journalist *The Enlarged Devil's Dictionary*

Let those love now who never loved before,
And those who always loved now love the more.
Robert Burton (1577–1640) English writer and clergyman

Let there be spaces in your togetherness.
Kahlil Gibran (1883–1931) American writer and artist

Here's to matrimony, the high sea for which no compass has yet been invented.
Heinrich Heine (1797–1856) German poet and essayist

Hail wedded love, mysterious law, true source
Of human offspring, sole propriety
In Paradise of all things common else.
John Milton (1608–74) English poet *Paradise Lost*

Strange to say what delight we married people have to see these poor fools decoyed into our condition.
Samuel Pepys (1633–1703) English diarist *Diary*, 25 Dec. 1665

True love is like ghosts, which everybody talks about and few have seen.
François, Duc de la Rochefoucauld (1613–80) French writer *Maxims*

Best Wishes for a happy and successful first marriage.
Marc Rosen

A married couple are well suited when both partners usually feel the need to quarrel at the same time.
Jean Rostand (1894–1977) French writer

No sooner met but they look'd; no sooner look'd but they lov'd.
William Shakespeare (1564–1616) English playwright and poet *As You Like It*

Those of us who are already married truly love a wedding in the same way that someone who has jumped into an unheated swimming pool is delighted when a friend falls for the old 'come on in the water's fine' gag.
Gareth Sharpe (1965–)

Let endless peace your steadfast
　hearts accord
And blessed plenty wait upon your
　board.
Let your bed with pleasures chaste
　abound
That fruitful issue may to you
　afford

Which may your foes confound;
And make your joys redound upon
　your bridal day, which is not
　long.
Edmund Spenser (1552–99)
English poet

❖ ❖ ❖ BIBLICAL ❖ ❖ ❖

Can two walk together, except they be agreed?
Amos 3:3

It is better to marry than to burn.
1 Corinthians 7:9

Beloved, let us love one another:
　for love is of God; and every one
　that loveth is born of God, and
　knoweth God.
He that loveth not knoweth not
　God; for God is love.
1 John 4:7

He who finds a wife finds what is good and receives favour from the lord.
Proverbs 18:22

ADVICE
❖ ❖ ❖ ❖ TO THE ❖ ❖ ❖ ❖
NEWLY WEDS

Don't over-analyse your marriage; it's like yanking up a fragile indoor

plant every 20 minutes to see how its roots are growing.

The Bill Ballance Hip Handbook quoted in *Reader's Digest*

A good husband is never the first to go to sleep at night or the last to awake in the morning.

Honoré de Balzac (1799–1850) French novelist *The Physiology of Marriage*

No man has ever yet discovered the way to give friendly advice to a woman, not even to his wife.

Honoré de Balzac

To catch a husband is an art, to keep him is a job.

Simone de Beauvoir (1908–86) French novelist and feminist

Being a husband is a whole-time job.

Arnold Bennett (1867–1931) English novelist *The Card*

Marriage and how to manage it: Communicate, decide things together, be kind, and tender, have time for yourself, and together. Be romantic – even foolish, have similar interests, be sensible with money but occasionally be rash. Surprise each other and have humour, and fun, but mostly – ENJOY!

Simon Bond English cartoonist *Success And How To Be One*

Laugh and the world laughs with you, snore and you sleep alone.

Anthony Burgess (1917–) English novelist, critic and composer

In matters of religion and matrimony I never give any advice; because I will not have anybody's torments in this world or the next laid to my charge.

Philip Stanhope, Earl of Chesterfield (1694–1773) English statesman, orator and wit

My wife and I tried to breakfast together, but we had to stop or our marriage would have been wrecked.

Sir Winston Churchill (1874–1965) English statesman *Attributed*

Never go to bed mad. Stay up and fight.

Phyllis Diller (1917–) American TV personality

Keep your eyes wide open before marriage, and half-shut afterwards.

Benjamin Franklin (1706–90) American statesman

The critical period in matrimony is breakfast-time.

Alan P. Herbert (1890–1971) English writer and politician *Uncommon Law*

A marriage works when both parties are prepared to give before the other needs to take.

Philip Loader (1966–) Restaurateur

To keep your marriage brimming
With love in the marriage cup,
Whenever you're wrong, admit it;
Whenever you're right, shut up.
  Ogden Nash (1902–71) American
poet

The great secret of successful
marriage is to treat all disasters as
incidents and none of the incidents
as disasters.
  Harold Nicolson (1886–1968)
British diplomat and writer

There is only one happiness in life,
to love and be loved.
  George Sand (1804–76) French
writer

An ideal wife is any woman who
has an ideal husband.
  Booth Tarkington (1869–1946)
American author *Looking Forward*

CHAPTER SIX

MOVING / NEW HOME

OF HOUSES
❖ ❖ ❖ AND HOME ❖ ❖ ❖

Houses are built to live in, and not to look on; therefore let use be preferred before uniformity, except where both may be had.
Francis Bacon (1561–1626) English philosopher and statesman *Essays: Of Buildings*

House, *n*: A hollow edifice erected for the habitation of man, rat, mouse, beetle, cockroach, fly, mosquito, flea, bacillus and microbe.
Ambrose Bierce (1842–1914) American journalist *The Enlarged Devil's Dictionary*

Well, some people talk of morality, and some of religion, but give me a little snug property.
Maria Edgeworth (1767–1849) Irish novelist *The Absentee*

The ornament of a house is the friends who frequent it.
Ralph Waldo Emerson (1803–82) American poet and essayist

Happiness grows at our own firesides, and is not to be picked in strange gardens.
Douglas Jerrold (1803–57) English author and dramatist

It is better to be a rich tenant than a poor landlord.
Leo Rosten's Treasury of Jewish Quotations

This castle hath a pleasant seat.
William Shakespeare (1564–1616) English playwright and poet *Macbeth*

Home is the girl's prison and the woman's workhouse.
George Bernard Shaw (1856–1950) Irish dramatist *Women in the Home*

Almost any man worthy of his salt would fight to defend his home, but no one ever heard of a man going to war for his boarding house.
Mark Twain (1835–1910) American writer *Mark Twain in Eruption*

Home, nowadays, is a place where part of the family waits till the rest of the family brings the car back.
Earl Wilson (1907–87) American columnist

✿ ✿ ✿ ✿ HOUSE ✿ ✿ ✿ ✿
BUYING

✿ ✿ ✿ ✿ FIRST ✿ ✿ ✿ ✿
HOME

Occasionally a lawyer sends you a legal document covered in kisses, and you really think you're getting somewhere until he tells you he only wants you to sign your name, in three places.

Jilly Cooper (1937–) English columnist and writer

I purchased one of the few tracts of genuine swamp in the New Forest, together with a small cottage sinking picturesquely into it.

Alan Coren (1938–) British editor and humorist

No man acquires property without acquiring with it a little arithmetic also.

Ralph Waldo Emerson (1803–82) American poet and essayist

Private guide to estate agents' jargon . . .

Attractive older-style
  property – A wreck
Cottage-style home – A wreck in
  a terrace
Town house – A modern wreck
  in a terrace

Michael Green (1947–) British TV executive

This is the place!

Brigham Young (1801–77) American Mormon leader *On first seeing the valley of the Great Salt Lake*

When moving into your first home and learning to fend for yourself there is one thing you should know which will make the whole ordeal much less traumatic – only in the fantasy world of TV advertising is it possible to get the grill pan 'spotless'.

Anon

Oh, to have a little house!
To own the hearth and stool and all!

Pádraic Colum (1881–1972) Irish poet and playwright *An Old Woman of the Roads*

Many a man who thinks to found a home discovers that he has merely opened a tavern for his friends.

Norman Douglas (1868–1952) Scottish novelist and essayist

My house, my house, though thou art small, thou art to me the Escurial.

George Herbert (1593–1633) English metaphysical poet and clergyman *Jacula Prudentum*

Private property was the original source of freedom. It still is its main bulwark.

Walter Lippmann (1889–1974) American journalist *The Good Society*

Tomorrow to fresh woods and pastures new.
John Milton (1608–74) English poet *Lycidas*

It is a proud moment in a woman's life to reign supreme within four walls to be the one to whom all questions of domestic pleasure and economy are referred.
Elizabeth Cady Stanton (1815–1902) American historian and writer

But all I could think of, in the darkness and the cold,
Was that I was leaving home and my folks were growing old.
Robert Louis Stevenson (1850–94) Scottish novelist and poet *Christmas at Sea*

HOME OWNERSHIP:
❊ ❊ PLEASURES AND ❊ ❊
PROBLEMS

You think you'll do some little job, perfectly simple . . . Fate isn't going to have it. I once sat down to put some new cotton wool in a cigarette lighter, and before I'd finished I'd got all the floorboards up in the spare bedroom.
J. Basil Boothroyd (1910–) English writer and broadcaster

We make our friends; we make our enemies; but God makes our next-door neighbour.
G. K. Chesterton (1874–1936) English critic and novelist

The house of every one is to him as his castle and fortress.
Edward Coke (1552–1634) English jurist

Never keep up with the Joneses. Drag them down to your level. It's cheaper.
Quentin Crisp (1908–) English author

There was no need to do any housework at all. After the first four years, the dirt doesn't get any worse.
Quentin Crisp

The trouble about housework is that whatever you do seems to lead to another job to do or a mess to clear up.
Monica Dickens (1915–) English author

Property has its duties as well as its rights.
Thomas Drummond (1797–1840) Scottish engineer and statesman *Letter to the Earl of Donoughmore*

The most fortunate of men,
Be he king or commoner, is he
Whose welfare is assured in his own home.
Johann Wolfgang von Goethe (1749–1832) German poet and writer *Iphigenia in Tauris*

We're in the throes of moving –
throwing away everything we can.
  Rev David Reed quoted in
Reader's Digest

A comfortable house is a great
source of happiness. It ranks
immediately after health and a
good conscience.
  Rev Sydney Smith (1771–1845)
English clergyman, essayist and
wit *Letter to Lord Murray*
29 September 1843

❈ BLESS THIS HOUSE ❈

God bless this house from roof to
  floor
God bless the windows and the
  door
God bless us all for evermore
God bless the house with fire and
  light
God bless each room with thy
  might
God with thy hand keep us right
God be with us in this dwelling
  site.
  David Adam English poet *The
Edge of Glory*

Peace be to this house, and to all
that dwell in it.
  Book of Common Prayer

As for me and my house, we will
serve the Lord.
  Joshua 24:15

In the house of the righteous there
is much treasure.
  Proverbs 15:6

Through wisdom a house is built,
and by understanding it is
established, by knowledge the
rooms are filled with all precious
and pleasant riches.
  Proverbs 24:3–4

The generation of the upright will
be blessed. Wealth and riches will
be in his home, and his
righteousness endures for ever.
  Psalms 112:2–3

Unless the Lord builds the house,
they labour in vain who build it.
  Psalms 127:1

CHAPTER SEVEN

HOME & AWAY

❖ ❖ ❖ TRAVEL ❖ ❖ ❖

Travel, in the younger sort, is a part of education; in the elder, a part of experience.
Francis Bacon (1561–1626) English philosopher and statesman *Essays Of Travel*

Why do the wrong people travel
When the right people stay back at
home?
Noël Coward (1899–1973) English actor and dramatist

Our object in travelling should be, not to gratify curiosity, and seek mere temporary amusement, but to learn, and to venerate, to improve the understanding of the heart.
Nigel Gresley (1876–1941) English locomotive engineer

Ever let the fancy roam,
Pleasure never is at home.
John Keats (1795–1821) English poet *Fancy*

He travels the fastest who travels alone.
Rudyard Kipling (1865–1936) English writer *The Winners*

Like most people who don't own Bermuda shorts, I'm bored by travel. See the beautiful Grand Canyon. OK I see it, OK it's beautiful. Now what?
P. J. O'Rourke (1947–) American writer

The compulsive need to travel is a recognised physical condition.
Michael Palin (1943–) English comic writer and actor *Around The World In 80 Days*

No matter what happens, travel gives you a story to tell.
Leo Rosten's Treasury of Jewish Quotations

He who would travel happily must travel light.
Antoine de Saint-Exupery (1900–44) French novelist and airman *Wind, Sand and Stars*

Travel and change of place impart new vigour to the mind.
Seneca (c.55 BC–c. AD 40) Roman rhetorician

Travel is only glamorous in retrospect.
Paul Theroux (1941–) American writer

❖ FOREIGN TRAVEL ❖

Passport, *n*: A document treacherously inflicted upon a

citizen going abroad, exposing him as an alien and pointing him out for special reprobation and outrage.

Ambrose Bierce (1842–1914) American journalist *The Enlarged Devil's Dictionary*

'Abroad', that large home of ruined reputations.

George Eliot (1819–80) English novelist *Felix Holt*

The rule for travelling abroad is to take our common sense with us and leave our prejudices behind.

William Hazlitt (1778–1830) English essayist

The great and recurrent question about abroad is is it worth getting there?

Rose Macaulay (1881–1958) English novelist and essayist

A man's feet must be planted in his country, but his eyes should survey the world.

George Santayana (1863–1952) Spanish philosopher, poet and novelist

A man should know something of his own country, too, before he goes abroad.

Laurence Sterne (1713–68) Anglo-Irish novelist *Tristram Shandy*

If you look like your passport photo, in all probability you need the journey.

Earl Wilson (1907–87) American columnist

FOREIGNERS
❋ ❋ AND FOREIGN ❋ ❋
COUNTRIES

In countries where nature does the most, man does the least.

Charles Caleb Colton (1780–1832) English clergyman and writer *Lacon*

The drawback of all seaside places is that half the landscape is unavailable . . . being covered with useless water.

Norman Douglas (1868–1952) Scottish novelist and essayist

Worth seeing? Yes; but not worth going to see.

Dr Samuel Johnson (1709–84) English writer and critic *referring to the Giant's Causeway*

Continental breakfasts are very sparse, usually just a pot of coffee or tea and a teensy roll that looks like a suitcase handle. My advice is to go right to lunch without pausing.

Miss Piggy *Miss Piggy's Guide to Life*

I loathe abroad, nothing would induce me to live there . . . and, as for foreigners, they are all the same, and they all make me sick.

Nancy Mitford (1904–73) British writer *The Pursuit of Love*

Foreigners may pretend otherwise, but if English is spoken loudly

enough, anyone can understand it, the British included.
P. J. O'Rourke (1947–) American writer

In an underdeveloped country don't drink the water, in a developed country don't breathe the air.
Jonathan Raban (1942–) English writer

I dislike feeling at home when I am abroad.
George Bernard Shaw (1856–1950) Irish dramatist

I've always had a weakness for foreign affairs.
Mae West (1893–1980) American film actress

PARTING
❀ ❀ AND LEAVING ❀ ❀

It is amazing how nice people are to you when they know you are going away.
Michael Arlen (1895–1956) British novelist

Life! we've been long together
Through pleasant and through cloudy weather;
'Tis hard to part when friends are dear;
Perhaps 'twill cost a sigh, a tear.
Anna Letitia Barbauld (1743–1825) English author *Life*

It is never any good dwelling on goodbyes;
It is not the being together that it prolongs,
It is the parting.
Elizabeth Bibesco (1897–1945) English writer and poet

When we two parted
In silence and tears,
Half broken-hearted
To sever for years.
George Gordon, Lord Byron (1788–1824) English poet *When we two parted*

One fond kiss before we part,
Drop a tear and bid adieu.
Robert Dodsley (1704–64) English playwright *The Parting Kiss*

Would the last person to leave the country please switch off the lights.
Graffiti

Weep if you must,
Parting is hell,
But life goes on,
So sing as well.
Joyce Grenfell (1910–79) British comedienne

To leave is to die a little;
To die to what we love.
We leave behind a bit of ourselves
Wherever we have been.
Edmond Haraucourt (1856–1941) *Choix de Poésies*

I have no parting sigh to give, so take my parting smile.
Letitia Elizabeth Landon (1802–38) English poet and author

Kiss me, and say good-bye;
  Good-bye, there is no word to say
but this.
  Andrew Lang (1844–1912)
Scottish man of letters *Good-bye*

I take a long, last, lingering view;
Adieu! my native land, adieu!
  John Logan (1748–88) Scottish
poet and clergyman *The Lovers*

The pain of leaving those you grow
to love is only the prelude to
understanding yourself and others.
  Shirley MacLaine (1934–)
American actress and writer

Could we see when and where we
are to meet again, we would be
more tender when we bid our
friends good-bye.
  Ouida (Marie Louise de la Ramée;
1839–1908) English popular
novelist

If we do meet again, why we shall
    smile!
If we do not, why then, this parting
    was well made.
  William Shakespeare (1564–1616)
English playwright and poet *Julius
Caesar*

Good-night, good-night! parting is
    such sweet sorrow
That I shall say good-night till it be
    morrow.
  William Shakespeare *Romeo and
Juliet*

Adieu! I have too grieved a heart to
take a tedious leave.
  William Shakespeare

I hear a voice you cannot hear,
Which says I must not stay;
I see a hand you cannot see,
Which beckons me away.
  Thomas Tickell (1686–1740)
English poet *Colin and Lucy*

FAREWELL
❖ ❖ ❖ ❖ AND ❖ ❖ ❖ ❖
BON VOYAGE

Once more farewell!
If e'er we meet hereafter, we shall
    meet
In happier climes, and on a safer
    shore.
  Joseph Addison (1672–1719)
English essayist and politician *Cato*

Fare thee well! and if for ever,
Still for ever, fare thee well.
  George Gordon, Lord Byron
(1788–1824) English poet *Fare Thee
Well*

Farewell! a word that must be, and
    hath been,
A sound which makes us linger;
    yet farewell!
  George Gordon, Lord Byron
Childe Harold

Go West, young man, and grow up
with the country.
  Horace Greeley (1811–72)
American editor and politician
Hints toward Reform

Be Good. If You Can't Be Good, Be Careful!
John Harington (1561–1612)
English courtier and writer

Welcome ever smiles, and farewell goes out sighing.
William Shakespeare (1564–1616)
English playwright and poet
Troilus and Cressida

To unpathed waters, undreamed shores.
William Shakespeare *The Winter's Tale*

PLANES,
❀ ❀ TRAINS AND ❀ ❀
AUTOMOBILES

There are two classes of travel – first class, and with children.
Robert Benchley (1889–1945)
American humorist and critic *Inside Benchley*

Children on a night boat seem to be built of harder stock . . . They stay awake later, get up earlier, and are heavier on their feet.
Robert Benchley

Airline travel is hours of boredom interrupted by moments of stark terror.
Al Boliska from *Quotations for our Time*

There was a 'Punch' joke about a caterpillar saying to a butterfly,

'You'll never get me up in one of those things!'
J. Basil Boothroyd (1910–)
English writer and broadcaster

A capital ship for an ocean trip
  Was the 'Walloping Window-
  blind.'
No gale that blew dismayed her crew
  Or troubled the Captain's mind.
Charles E. Carryl (1841–1920)
American author *Davy and the Goblin, a Nautical Ballad*

The only way to be sure of catching a train is to miss the one before it.
G. K. Chesterton (1874–1936)
English critic and novelist

A third-class carriage is a community, while a first-class carriage is a place of wild hermits.
G. K. Chesterton

There's nothing like an airport for bringing you down to earth.
Richard Gordon (1921–) British doctor and writer

– Breakfast in London
– Lunch in New York
– Luggage in Bermuda
Graffiti: British Airways poster

The best things in life are duty free.
Graffiti: Heathrow airport

There is nothing – absolutely nothing – half so much worth doing as simply messing about in boats.

Kenneth Grahame (1859–1932) Scottish children's writer *The Wind in the Willows*

Beware of men on airplanes.

The minute a man reaches 30,000 feet, he immediately becomes consumed by distasteful sexual fantasies which involve doing uncomfortable things in those tiny toilets. These men should not be encouraged, their fantasies are sadly low-rent and unimaginative. Affect an aloof, cool demeanour as soon as any man tries to draw you out. Unless, of course, he's the pilot.

Cynthia Heimel American writer

I feel about airplanes the way I feel about diets. It seems to me they are wonderful things for other people to go on.

Jean Kerr (1923–) American playwright

It is better to travel hopefully than to arrive, Robert Louis Stevenson assures us . . . I doubt if R.L.S. ever had to sit for an hour outside Didcot station while British Rail, reluctant to admit that in winter our weather tends to be wintry, struggled to unfreeze the points.

Samuel, Lord Mancroft (1914–87) English politician and writer

My heart is warm with the friends I make
And better friends I'll not be knowing;
Yet there isn't a train I wouldn't take
No matter where it's going.

Edna St Vincent Millay (1892–1950) American poet

The scientific theory I like best is that the rings of Saturn are composed entirely of lost airline luggage.

Mark Russell quoted in *Reader's Digest*

Old and young, we are all on our last cruise.

Robert Louis Stevenson (1850–94) Scottish novelist and poet

We had crossed the International dateline and the waiters were even more mutinous because they were working an eight–day week.

Hugo Williams (1942–) British writer

CLIMATE
 ❋ ❋ ❋ ❋ AND ❋ ❋ ❋ ❋
WEATHER

To sit in the shade on a fine day and look upon verdure is the most perfect refreshment.

Jane Austen (1775–1817) English novelist *Mansfield Park*

What dreadful hot weather we have! It keeps me in a continual state of inelegance.
Jane Austen *Letter, 18 September 1796*

If it's heaven for climate, it's hell for company.
J. M. Barrie (1860–1937) Scottish novelist and dramatist *The Little Minister*

The English Winter – ending in July
To recommence in August.
Gordon George, Lord Byron (1788–1924) English poet

At twelve noon the natives swoon
And no further work is done.
But mad dogs and Englishmen
Go out in the midday sun.
Noël Coward (1899–1973) English actor and dramatist *Mad Dogs and Englishmen*

No weather is bad.
When you're suitably clad.
Arthur Guiterman (1871–1943) American author *A Poet's Proverbs*

Thank heavens, the sun has gone in, and I don't have to go out and enjoy it.
Logan Pearsall Smith (1865–1946) British writer *Last Words*

There is no such thing as bad weather in Cornwall: It's all spectacular.
Dudley Sutton English actor

For a feeling that makes you very much alive, sensitive to every movement of your being and aware of the vibrations of your environment, there's nothing like a good sunburn.
Paul Sweeney *The Quarterly* quoted in *Reader's Digest*

There are seven ways to warm your feet in February. Dipping them in the Caribbean is one. If you can afford that, forget the other six.
The Kiplinger Magazine quoted in *Reader's Digest*

Some people wore summer clothes in a hopeful, goosepimpled way.
Paul Theroux (1941–) American writer

Everybody talks about the weather, but nobody does anything about it.
Charles Dudley Warner (1829–1900) American writer *The Hartford Couran*

I must get out of these wet clothes and into a dry Martini.
Alexander Woolcott (1887–1943) American journalist and writer *Attributed*

❖ ❖ ❖ **ABSENCE** ❖ ❖ ❖

Absence makes the heart grow fonder,
Isle of Beauty, Fare thee well!
Thomas H. Bayly (1797–1839) *Isle of Beauty*

Absence, *n*: That which 'makes the heart grow fonder' – of absence.
Ambrose Bierce (1842–1914) American journalist *The Enlarged Devil's Dictionary*

Absence is to love what wind is to fire; it extinguishes the small, it enkindles the great.
Comte de Bussy-Rabutin (1618–93) French soldier and writer *Histoire Amoureuse des Gaules* (*'Maximes d'Amours'*)

Love reckons hours for months, and days for years; and every little absence is an age.
John Dryden (1631–1700) English poet

The Lord watch between me and thee, when we are absent one from another.
Genesis 31:49

Absence diminishes mediocre passions and increases great ones, as the wind blows out candles and fans fires.
François, Duc de la Rochefoucauld (1613–80) French writer *Maxims*

HOMESICKNESS
❈ (MISSING FRIENDS ❈ AND RELATIVES)

The more foreigners I saw, the more I loved my homeland.
P. L. B. Du Belloy (1725–75) French poet *Le Siège de Calais*

Homesick, *adj*: Dead broke abroad.
Ambrose Bierce (1842–1914) American journalist *The Enlarged Devil's Dictionary*

They say such tears as children weep
Will soon be dried away;
That childhood's grief, however strong,
Is only for a day;
And parted friends, how dear so e're,
Will soon forgotten be;
It may be so with other hearts;
It is not so with me.
Anne Brontë (1820–49) English novelist and poet

If I should meet thee
After long years,
How should I greet thee? –
With silence and tears.
George Gordon, Lord Byron (1788–1824) English poet *When we two parted*

'Tis distance lends enchantment to the view,
And robes the mountain in its azure hue.
Thomas Campbell (1777–1844) Scottish poet and journalist *Pleasures of Hope*

Where'er I roam, whatever realms to see,
My heart, untravelled, fondly turns to thee.
Oliver Goldsmith (1728–74) Irish playwright, novelist and poet *The Traveller*

No distance breaks the tie of blood; brothers are brothers evermore.
John Keble (1792–1866) English churchman and poet

As cold waters to a thirsty soul, so is good news from a far country.
Proverbs 25:25

The accent of one's birthplace lingers in the mind and in the heart as it does in one's speech.
François, Duc de la Rochefoucauld (1613–80) French writer *Maxims*

There is a divine covenant in everyone's heart: to love his native soil – despite its climate.
Leo Rosten's Treasury of Jewish Quotations

Absence from those we love is self from love – a deadly banishment.
William Shakespeare (1564–1616) English playwright and poet

The proper means of increasing the love we bear to our native country is to reside some time in a foreign one.
William Shenstone (1714–63) English poet

HOLIDAYS
❖ ❖ AND TOURISM ❖ ❖

The rainy days a man saves for usually seem to arrive during his vacation.
Anon

Leisure, *n*: Lucid intervals in disordered life.
Ambrose Bierce (1842–1914) American journalist *The Enlarged Devil's Dictionary*

A good place to visit but a poor place to stay.
Josh Billings (1818–85) American humorist

The traveller sees what he sees, the tourist sees what he has come to see.
G. K. Chesterton (1874–1936) English critic and novelist

There's sand in the porridge and sand in the bed,
And if this is pleasure we'd sooner be dead!
Noël Coward (1899–1973) English actor and dramatist

Arthur Watts (illustrator) kept asking me to 'look more dejected'. As if, he explained, I was really having a holiday with my family.
E. M. Delafield (1890–1943) English novelist

A toothbrush and a nightdress and a couple of little bedside books never seem to me to weigh very much. But the moment one puts them in a suitcase they become extraordinarily heavy.
E. M. Delafield

Why does it take so much luggage to get away from it all
Doug Larson quoted in *Reader's Digest*

I shall need to sleep three weeks on end to get rested from the rest I've had.

Thomas Mann (1875–1955)
German novelist

Why is it that a tourist will travel thousands of miles to get away from people – just so he can send cards saying, 'Wish you were here'?

E. C. McKenzie American writer and compiler

A day in such serene enjoyment spent
Is worth an age of splendid discontent.

James Montgomery (1771–1854)
Scottish poet *Greenland*

One of the symptoms of approaching nervous breakdown is the belief that one's work is terribly important, and that to take a holiday would bring all sorts of disaster. If I were a medical man, I should prescribe a holiday to any patient who considered his work important.

Bertrand Russell (1872–1970)
Welsh philosopher and writer

If all the year were playing holidays,
To sport would be as tedious as to work.

William Shakespeare (1564–1616)
English playwright and poet

Man has pursued a lot of dreams – The Golden Fleece, the alchemist's

stone, and the idea that the car can be packed for a family holiday so that only one suitcase need be brought into the hotel at night.

Bill Vaughan quoted in *Reader's Digest*

❇ TOWN AND COUNTRY ❇

Breathless, we flung us on the windy hill,
Laughed in the sun, and kissed the lovely grass.

Rupert C. Brooke (1887–1915)
English poet *The Hill*

If you would be known, and not know, vegetate in a village; if you would know, and not be known, live in a city.

Charles Caleb Colton (1780–1832)
English clergyman and writer

Take nothing but pictures; leave nothing but footprints; kill nothing but time.

Hunter Davies quoted in *Francis Gay's Friendship Book* 1994

Give me the dear blue sky over my head, and the green turf beneath my feet, a winding road before me and a three hours march to dinner.

William Hazlitt (1778–1830)
English essayist *Table Talk*

When I am in the country I wish to vegetate like the country.

William Hazlitt *Table Talk*

The two divinest things this world
   has got,
A lovely woman in a rural spot!
   Leigh Hunt (1784–1859) English
poet and writer *The Story of Rimini*

To one who has been long in city
   spent,
'Tis very sweet to look into the fair
And open face of heaven.
   John Keats (1795–1821) English
poet *To one who has been long*

It is good to be out on the road,
and going one knows not where,
going through meadow and
village, one knows not whither or
why.
   John Masefield (1878–1967)
English poet and novelist
Tewkesbury Road

One day in the country
Is worth a month in town.
   Christina Rossetti (1830–94)
English poet

HOME AND HOMECOMING

Happy he who like Ulysses has
made a great journey.
   Joachim du Bellay (1522–60)
French poet

Home, *n*: The place of last resort –
open all night.
   Ambrose Bierce (1842–1914)
American journalist *The Enlarged
Devil's Dictionary*

Hold the fort, for I am coming
   Philip Paul Bliss (1838–76)
American evangelist and hymn
writer

To know after absence the familiar
street and road and village and
house is to know again the
satisfaction of home.
   Hal Borland (1900–) American
writer *Sundial of the Seasons*

England, home and beauty.
   John Braham (1774–1856) British
tenor

God! I will pack, and take a train,
and get me to England once again!
   Rupert C. Brooke (1887–1915)
English poet

The whole object of travel is not to
set foot on a foreign land. It is at
last to set foot one one's own
country as a foreign land.
   G. K. Chesterton (1874–1936)
English critic and novelist

Had Cain been Scot, God would
   have changed his doom:
Nor forced him wander, but
   confined him home.
   John Cleveland (1613–58) English
satirist

Sweet Stay-at-Home, sweet Well-
content.
   William H. Davies (1871–1940)
Welsh poet *Sweet Stay-at-Home*

Come in the evening, or come in
the morning;
Come when you're looked for, or
come without warning.
  Thomas Osborne Davis (1814–45)
Irish poet *The Welcome*

Home is the place where, when
you have to go there, they have to
take you in.
  Robert Frost (1874–1963)
American lyric poet

The home we first knew on this
beautiful earth
The friends of our childhood, the
place of our birth
In the heart's inner chamber sung
always will be
As the shell ever sings of its home
in the sea.
  Francis Gage (1808–84) American
poet and social reformer

It's odd how people waiting for
you stand out far less clearly than
the people you are waiting for.
  Jean Giraudoux (1882–1944)
French writer

Just like home, minus the Poll Tax.
  Mr P. Godfrey *Comment: visitor's
book*

Home is where the television is.
  Graffiti

There's no place like home, and
many a man is glad of it.
  F. M. Knowles *A Cheerful Year
Book*

Stay, stay at home my heart and
rest;
Home-keeping hearts are happiest.
  Henry Wadsworth Longfellow
(1807–82) American poet

He travels best that knows when to
return.
  Thomas Middleton (c.1570–1627)
English dramatist *The Old Law*

Home, the spot of earth supremely
blest,
A dearer, sweeter spot than all the
rest.
  Robert Montgomery (1807–55)
English preacher and poet

A man travels the world over in
search of what he needs and
returns home to find it.
  George Moore (1852–1933) Irish
novelist *The Book Kerith*

Mid pleasures and places through
we may roam,
Be it ever so humble, there's no
place like home.
  John Howard Payne (1791–1852)
American actor *Home Sweet Home*

Home is where the heart is.
  Pliny the Elder (23–79) Roman
naturalist

East or west, home is best.
  Proverb

Things can be good anywhere, but
they're even better at home.
  *Leo Rosten's Treasury of Jewish
Quotations*

The sight of you is good for sore eyes.
  Jonathan Swift (1667–1745) Anglo-Irish poet and satirist *A Tale of a Tub*

Seek home for rest,
For home is best.
  Thomas Tusser (1524–80) English agricultural writer *Five Hundred Points of Good Husbandry*

Each step hath its value while homeward we move;–
O joy, when the girdle of England appears!
  William Wordsworth (1770–1850) English poet *Memorials of a Tour on the Continent*

ENGLAND
❉ ❉ ❉ AND THE ❉ ❉ ❉
ENGLISH

There are no countries in the world less known by the British
than these selfsame British Islands.
  George Henry Borrow (1803–81) English author *Lavengro*

When Adam and Eve were dispossessed
  Of the garden hard by Heaven,
They planted another one down in the west,
'Twas Devon, glorious Devon!
  Harold E. Boulton (1859–1935) English poet *Glorious Devon*

For England's the one land, I know,
Where men with Splendid Hearts may go.
  Rupert C. Brooke (1887–1915) English poet *The Old Vicarage, Grantchester*

Oh, to be in England
Now that April's there.
  Robert Browning (1812–89) English poet *Home Thoughts, from Abroad*

Be England what she will,
With all her faults, she is my country still.
  Charles Churchill (1731–64) English satirical poet *The Farewell*

Very flat, Norfolk.
  Noël Coward (1899–1973) English actor and dramatist *Private Lives*

England, with all thy faults, I love thee still –
My country!
  William Cowper (1731–1800) English poet *The Timepiece*

I don't hold with abroad, and think that foreigners speak English when our backs are turned.
  Quentin Crisp (1908–) English author *The Naked Civil Servant*

British hotels prefer you to write Mr and Mrs even if you are sinning.
  Len Deighton (1929–) English thriller writer

I love thee, Cornwall, and will
ever,
and hope to see thee once again!
For why? – thine equal knew I
never
For honest minds and active men.
Thomas Freeman (c.1614–?)
Epigrammatist *Encomion Cornubiae*

What is our task? To make Britain
a fit country for heroes to live in.
David Lloyd George (1863–1945)
Welsh Liberal statesman

The stately homes of England,
How beautiful they stand!
Amidst their tall ancestral trees,
O'er all the pleasant land.
Felicia D. Hemans (1793–1835)
English poet *The Homes of England*

If you want to eat well in England,
eat three breakfasts.
William Somerset Maugham
(1874–1965) British writer

Remember that you are an
Englishman, and have
consequently won first prize in the
lottery of life.
Cecil Rhodes (1853–1902) South
African statesman

I travelled among unknown men
In lands beyond the sea;
Nor England! did I know till then
What love I bore to thee.
William Wordsworth (1770–1850)
English poet

SCOTLAND, ❀ ❀ WALES AND ❀ ❀ IRELAND

Scotland: Nowhere beats the heart
so kindly
As beneath the tartan plaid.
William Edmonstoune Aytoun
(1813–65) Scottish poet and
humorist *Charles Edward at
Versailles*

In Ireland the inevitable never
happens and the unexpected
constantly occurs.
John Pentland Mahaffy (1839–
1919) Irish classical scholar

Ireland is a fatal disease, fatal to
Englishmen and doubly fatal to
Irishmen.
George Moore (1852–1933) Irish
novelist

Rain certainly falls in Scotland
(there are no recorded instances of
it rising), but it also has a trick of
hanging about in the air at about
ear level . . . In the Highlands it is
referred to as a 'Scotch mist'.
Frank Muir (1920–) English
writer and broadcaster

I look upon Switzerland as an
inferior sort of Scotland.
Rev Sydney Smith (1771–1845)
English clergyman, essayist and
wit *Letter to Lord Holland*, 1815

There are still parts of Wales where the only concession to gaiety is a striped shroud.

Gwyn Thomas (1913–81) *Article in Punch*, 18 June 1958

Stately Edinburgh throned on crags.

William Wordsworth (1770–1850) English poet *The Excursion*

 **FRANCE**

They are short, blue-vested people who carry their own onions when cycling abroad, and have a yard which is 3.37 inches longer than other people's.

Alan Coren (1938–) British editor and humorist *All You Need to Know about Europe*

Never go to France
Unless you know the lingo,
If you do, like me,
You will repent, by jingo.

Thomas Hood (1799–1845) English poet and humorist *French and English*

What I gained by being in France was, learning to be better satisfied with my own country.

Dr Samuel Johnson (1709–84) English writer and critic *Boswell's Life of Johnson*

It's always a mistake trying to speak French to the Frogs. As Noël

Coward once remarked when he was sustaining a role at the Comédie Française, 'They don't understand their own language.'

Robert Morley (1908–92) English actor and dramatist

The last time I see Paris will be on the day I die. The city was inexhaustible, and so is its memory.

Elliot Paul (1891–1958) American writer *The Last Time I Saw Paris*

You who have ever been to Paris know;
And you have never been to Paris – Go!

John Ruskin (1819–1900) English author and art critic *A Tour Through France*

France is a country where the money falls apart in your hands and you can't tear the toilet paper.

Billy Wilder (1906–) American film maker

 **ITALY**

When in Rome, live as the Romans do; when elsewhere, live as they live elsewhere.

St Ambrose (337–397) Roman churchman *Advice to St Augustine*

Open my heart and you will see Graved inside of it, 'Italy'.

Robert Browning (1812–89) English poet *De Gustibus*

I stood in Venice, on the Bridge of
Sighs;
A palace and a prison on each
hand.
  George Gordon, Lord Byron
(1788–1824) English poet *Childe
Harold*

Venice is like eating an entire box
of chocolate liqueurs at one go.
  Truman Capote (1924–84)
American author *Remark,*
November 1961

A man who has not been to Italy is
always conscience of an inferiority,
from his not having seen what it is
expected a man should see.
  Dr Samuel Johnson (1709–84)
English writer and critic

They spell it Vinci and pronounce
it Vinchy; foreigners always spell
better than they pronounce.
  Mark Twain (1835–1910)
American writer *The Innocents
Abroad*

❋ OTHER EUROPEAN ❋ COUNTRIES

Germany: It is untrue that
Germans are bad drivers. They hit
everything they aim at.
  Joey Adams (1911–) American
comedian *Cindy and I*

Greece: The isles of Greece, the
isles of Greece!

Where burning Sappho loved and
sung.
  George Gordon, Lord Byron
(1788–1824) English poet *Don Juan*

Greece: Fair Greece! Sad relic of
departed worth! Immortal, though
no more; though fallen, great!
  George Gordon, Lord Byron
Childe Harold

Spain: Oh, lovely Spain! renowned
romantic land.
  George Gordon, Lord Byron
Childe Harold

Russia: A riddle wrapped in a
mystery inside an enigma.
  Sir Winston Churchill (1874–
1965) English statesman *Radio
Broadcast*

Switzerland: Since both its national
products, snow and chocolate,
melt, the cuckoo clock was
invented solely in order to give
tourists something solid to
remember it by.
  Alan Coren (1938–) British editor
and humorist *And Though They Do
Their Best*

Austria: Austria is Switzerland,
speaking pure German and with
history added.
  J. E. Morpurgo (1918–) British
writer *The Road to Athens*

Switzerland: In Italy for thirty
years under the Borgias they had
warfare, terror, murder, bloodshed
– they produced Michelangelo,

Leonardo da Vinci and the Renaissance. In Switzerland they had brotherly love, five hundred years of democracy and peace, and what did they produce . . . ? The cuckoo clock.

Orson Welles (1915–85) American film director and actor *The Third Man*

 **AMERICA**

We found Florida beautiful and balmy. I could say the same thing about my wife.

Joey Adams (1911–) American comedian *Cindy and I*

America is the country where you buy a lifetime supply of aspirin for one dollar and use it up in two weeks.

John Barrymore (1882–1942) American actor

America is the only nation in history which miraculously has gone directly from barbarism to degeneration without the usual interval of civilization.

Georges Clemenceau (1841–1929) French statesman *Attributed*

Why, if you're not in New York you are camping out.

Thomas W. Dewing (1851–1938) American artist

Honolulu: it's got everything. Sand for the children, sun for the wife, sharks for the wife's mother.

Ken Dodd (1929–) English stand-up comedian

In the United States, there one feels free . . . Except from the Americans – but every pearl has its oyster.

Randall Jarrell (1914–65) American poet and critic *Pictures from an Institution*

America is a country that doesn't know where it is going but is determined to set a speed record getting there.

Laurence J. Peter (1918–) Canadian writer

And now, dear God, farewell: I am going to America.

Leo Rosten's Treasury of Jewish Quotations

In the United States there is more space where nobody is than where anybody is. That is what makes America what it is.

Gertrude Stein (1874–1946) American writer *The Geographical History of America*

 **CANADA**

I saw a notice which said 'Drink Canada Dry' and I've just started.

Brendan Behan (1923–64) Irish author *Attributed*

Canada is a country so square that even the female impersonators are women.
From the film *Outrageous*

INDIA AND
❀ ❀ THE FAR EAST ❀ ❀

India: One voyage to India is enough; the others are merely repletion.
Sir Winston Churchill
(1874–1965) English statesman *My Early Life*

Far East: Asia is not going to be civilised after the methods of the West. There is too much Asia and she is too old.
Rudyard Kipling (1865–1936) English writer *Life's Handicap*

India: In India 'cold weather' is merely a conventional phrase and has come into use through the necessity of having some way of distinguishing between weather which will melt a brass door-knob and weather which will only make it mushy.
Mark Twain (1835–1910) American writer

AUSTRALIA AND
❀ ❀ NEW ZEALAND ❀ ❀

Australia, *n*: A country lying in the South Sea, whose industrial and commercial development has been unspeakably retarded by an unfortunate dispute among geographers as to whether it is a continent or an island.
Ambrose Bierce (1842–1914) American journalist *The Enlarged Devil's Dictionary*

New Zealand: The United States has Ronald Reagan, Johnny Cash, Bob Hope and Stevie Wonder. New Zealand has Rob Muldoon, no cash, no hope, and no bloody wonder.
Graffiti: Auckland

Australia: Where men are men, and sheep are nervous.
Graffiti

CHAPTER EIGHT

BABIES AND CHILDREN

❖ ❖ ❖ ❖ BIRTH ❖ ❖ ❖ ❖

Two's company. Three's the result!
Anon

'Nappy Birthday.'
Anon

We have never understood the fear of some parents about babies getting mixed up in a hospital. What difference does it make as long as you get a good one?
Heywood Brown (1888–1939)
American journalist and critic

I just noticed that more twins are being born these days. Maybe it's because kids lack the courage to come into this world alone.
Stan Burns *Parade Magazine*
9 April 1967

Ah, the patter of little feet around the house. There's nothing like having a midget for a butler.
W. C. Fields (1879–1946)
American comedian

The family you come from isn't as important as the family you're going to have.
Ring Lardner (1885–1933)
American humorist and short story writer

Who can foretell for what high cause
This darling of the Gods was born?
Andrew Marvell (1621–78)
English poet *A Prospect of Flowers*

There is nothing like a start, and being born, however pessimistic one may become in later years, is undeniably a start.
William McFee (1881–1966)
English writer

Small traveller from an unseen shore,
By mortal eye ne'er seen before,
To you, good-morrow.
(William) Cosmo Monkhouse
English poet *To a New-Born Child*

Congratulations. We all knew you had it in you.
Dorothy Parker (1893–1967)
American wit and journalist

Behold the child, by nature's kindly law.
Alexander Pope (1688–1744)
English poet *An Essay on Man*

No child is born a criminal: no child is born an angel: he's just born.
Sydney Smith (1883–1969) New Zealand forensic expert

Her birth was of the wombe of
  morning dew
And her conception of the joyous
  prime.
  Edmund Spenser (1552–99)
English poet *Faerie Queene Book III*

Families, when a child is born
Want it to be intelligent.
I, through intelligence,
Having wrecked my whole life,
Only hope the baby will prove
Ignorant and stupid.
Then he will crown a tranquil life
By becoming a Cabinet Minister.
  Su Tung-P'O (1036–1101) Chinese
painter, poet and politician *On the
Birth of his Son*

We have become a grandmother.
  Margaret Thatcher (1925–)
English Conservative stateswoman

❊ ❊ BIRTH RHYMES ❊ ❊

JANUARY
Birthstone: Garnet

By her who in this month is born,
No gems save garnets should be
  worn;
They will insure her constancy,
True friendship and fidelity.
  Anon

FEBRUARY
Birthstone: Amethyst

The February born will find
Sincerity and peace of mind;

Freedom from passion and from
  care
If they the amethyst will wear.
  Anon

MARCH
Birthstone: Aquamarine or
Bloodstone

Who in this world of ours their
  eyes
In March first open shall be wise;
In days of peril firm and brave,
And wear a bloodstone to their
  grave.
  Anon

APRIL
Birthstone: Diamond

She who from April dates her
  years,
Diamonds should wear, lest bitter
  tears
For vain repentance flow; this
  stone,
Emblem of innocence is known.
  Anon

MAY
Birthstone: Emerald

Who first beholds the light of day
In Spring's sweet flowery month of
  May
And wears an emerald all her life,
Shall be a loved and happy wife.
  Anon

JUNE
Birthstone: Agate, Pearl,
Moonstone or Alexandrite

Who comes with Summer to this
    earth
And owes to June her day of birth
With ring of agate on her hand,
Can health, wealth, and long life
    command.
Anon

JULY
Birthstone: Ruby

The glowing ruby should adorn
Those who in warm July are born,
Then will they be exempt and free
From love's doubt and anxiety.
Anon

AUGUST
Birthstone: Peridot or Sardonyx

Wear a sardonyx or for thee
No conjugal felicity.
The August-born without this
    stone
'Tis said must live unloved and
    lone.
Anon

SEPTEMBER
Birthstone: Sapphire

A maiden born when Autumn
    leaves
Are rustling in September's breeze,
A sapphire on her brow should
    bind,
'Twill cure diseases of the mind.
Anon

OCTOBER
Birthstone: Opal or Pink
Tourmaline

October's child is born for woe,
And life's vicissitudes must know;
But lay an opal on her breast,
And hope will lull those woes to
    rest.
Anon

NOVEMBER
Birthstone: Topaz or Citrine

Who first comes to this world
    below
With drear November's fog and
    snow
Should prize the topaz's amber
    hue –
Emblem of friends and lovers true.
Anon

DECEMBER
Birthstone: Turquoise or Zircon

If cold December gave you birth,
The month of snow and ice and
    mirth,
Place on your hand a turquoise
    blue,
Success will bless whate'er you do.
Anon

Monday's child is fair of face,
Tuesday's child is full of grace,
Wednesday's child is full of woe,
Thursday's child has far to go,
Friday's child is loving and giving,
Saturday's child works hard for a
    living,
And the child that is born on the
    Sabbath day
Is bonny and blithe, and good and
    gay.
Nursery Rhyme

Born on Monday, fair in the face;
Born on Tuesday, full of God's
grace;
Born on Wednesday, sour and sad;
Born on Thursday, merry and glad;
Born on Friday, worthily given;
Born on Saturday, work hard for
your living;
Born on Sunday, you will never
know want.
Anon

❖

❖ ❖ **BABIES** ❖ ❖

❖

A perfect example of minority rule
is a baby in the house.
Anon

Babies are bits of stardust blown
from the hand of God. Lucky the
woman who knows the pangs of
birth for she has held a star.
Larry Barretto American writer
The Indiscreet Years

Babe or Baby, *n*: A misshapen
creature of no particular age, sex,
or condition, chiefly remarkable for
the violence of the sympathies and
antipathies it excites in others.
Ambrose Bierce (1842–1914)
American journalist *The Enlarged
Devil's Dictionary*

Infancy, *n*: The period of our lives
when, according to Wordsworth,
'Heaven lies about us'. The world
begins lying about us pretty soon
afterward.
Ambrose Bierce *The Enlarged
Devil's Dictionary*

Not merely a chip off the old
'block', but the old block itself.
Edmund Burke (1729–97) Irish
statesman and philosopher

People who say they sleep like a
baby usually don't have one.
Leo. J. Burke from *Quotations for
our Time*

Every baby born into the world is a
finer one than the last.
Charles Dickens (1812–70)
English author *Nicholas Nickleby*

I know a lot about children. Not
being an author, I'm a good critic.
Finley P. Dunne (1867–1936)
American humorist *Mr Dooley
Remembers*

Here we have a baby. It is
composed of a bald head and a
pair of lungs.
Eugene Field (1850–95) American
poet

At six weeks Baby grinned a grin
That spread from mouth to eyes to
chin,
And Doc, the smartie, had the brass
To tell me it was only gas!
Margaret Fishback (1904–85)
American poet

Now why did you name your baby
'John'? Every Tom, Dick and Harry
is named 'John'.
  Samuel Goldwyn (1882–1974)
American film producer

Babies haven't any hair;
Old men's heads are just as bare;
Between the cradle and the grave
Lies a haircut and a shave.
  Samuel Hoffenstein (1890–1947)
Lithuanian writer and humorist
Songs of Faith in the Year After Next

Sleep, my boy, my dearest boy!
I will rock you to sleep and guard
  you.
  Henrik Ibsen (1828–1906)
Norwegian dramatist *Solveig's song*

Give an average baby a fair chance,
and if it doesn't do something it
oughtn't to, a doctor should be
called in at once.
  Jerome K. Jerome (1859–1927)
English humorous writer, novelist
and playwright

Baby: A loud noise at one end and
no sense of responsibility at the
other.
  Ronald Knox (1888–1957) English
theologian and writer

A baby is something you carry
inside you for nine months, in your
arms for three years and in your
heart till the day you die.
  Monica Mason (1941–) Ballet
dancer

Sleep, baby, Sleep!
Thy father's watching the sheep,
Thy mother's shaking the
  dreamland tree,
and down drops a little dream for
  thee.
Sleep, baby, Sleep.
  Elizabeth Prentiss (1818–78)
American writer and poet

He's a chip o' th' old block.
  William Rowley (c.1585–c.1642)
English actor and playwright
A Match at Midnight

A mother's pride, a father's joy!
  Sir Walter Scott (1771–1832)
Scottish novelist and poet

I can't tell you if genius is
hereditary, because heaven has
granted me no offspring.
  James Whistler (1834–1903)
American artist

❀

❀ ❀ **PARENTHOOD** ❀ ❀

❀

Motherhood: A career hazard.
  Mike Barfield (1962–) *Dictionary
For Our Time – 'The Oldie'*

New man: One who has read
enough babycare books to annoy
women by telling them what they
are doing wrong.
  Mike Barfield *Dictionary For Our
Time – 'The Oldie'*

Except that right side up is best, there is not much to learn about holding a baby. There are 152 distinctly different ways – and all are right! At least all will do.

Heywood Brown (1888–1939) American journalist and critic

Womanliness means only motherhood;
All love begins and ends there.

Robert Browning (1812–89) English poet *The Inn Album*

The hand that rocks the cradle is usually attached to someone who isn't getting enough sleep.

Jim Fiebig

Your children are not your children. They are the sons and daughters of Life's longing for itself . . . you may strive to be like them, but seek not to make them like you.

Kahlil Gibran (1883–1931) American writer and artist *The Prophet*, 'Of Children'

How many hopes and fears, how many ardent wishes and anxious apprehensions are twisted together in the threads that connect the parent with the child.

Samuel G. Goodrich (1793–1860) American publisher

There is no such thing as the pursuit of happiness, but there is the discovery of joy.

Joyce Grenfell (1910–79) British comedienne *The Observer* 1976
To be a successful father there's

one absolute rule: when you have a kid, don't look at it for the first two years.

Ernest Hemingway (1899–1961) American novelist

The most important thing a father can do for his children is to love their mother.

Theodore M. Hesburgh (1917–) American university president

You can learn many things from children. How much patience you have, for instance.

Franklin P. Jones

Before marriage the average man takes little notice of prams. It's only after he's been married for nearly a year that he begins to think as much about prams as he does about cars.

John Kenyon (1874–1959) American phonetician and educator

Ask your child what he wants for dinner only if he's buying.

Fran Lebowitz (1951–) American journalist and photographer

Contraceptives should be used on all conceivable occasions.

Spike Milligan (1918–) British comedian

The family is one of nature's masterpieces.

George Santayana (1863–1952) Spanish philosopher, poet and novelist

Parentage is a very important profession; but no test of fitness for it is ever imposed in the interest of children.

George Bernard Shaw (1856–1950) Irish dramatist

How to fold a diaper depends on the size of the baby and the diaper.

Dr Benjamin Spock (1903–) American paediatrician

The more people have studied different methods of bringing up children the more they have come to the conclusion that what good mothers and fathers instinctively feel like doing for their babies is the best after all.

Dr Benjamin Spock *The Common Sense Book of Baby and Child Care*

Who of us is mature enough for offspring before the offspring themselves arrive? The value of marriage is not that the adults produce children but that children produce adults.

Peter de Vries (1910–) American novelist *Tunnel of Love*

Of all the rights of women, the greatest is to be a mother.

Lin Yutang (1895–) Chinese author and philologist

CHILDREN:
❋ ❋ **THE POSITIVE** ❋ ❋
VIEW

Before I married I had six theories about bringing up children, but no children; now I have six children and no theories.

Anon

I love to gaze upon a child;
 A young bud bursting into
 blossom.

Charles S. Calverley (1831–84) Poet *Gemini and Virgo*

The youth of a nation are the trustees of posterity.

Benjamin Disraeli (1804–81) British statesman and novelist

A thing of beauty is a joy forever:
It's loveliness increases.

John Keats (1795–1821) English poet *Endymion*

Land of our birth, we pledge to
 thee
Our love and toil in the years to be;
When we are grown and take our
 place,
As men and women with our race.

Rudyard Kipling (1865–1936) English writer *The Children's Song*

Children are a bridge to heaven.

Proverb

Happy is he that is happy in his children.

Proverb

One good thing about children is that they never pull out photographs of their grandparents.
Quoted in *Reader's Digest*

A child is not a vase to be filled, but a fire to be lit.
François Rabelais (c.1494–c.1553) French satirist

The smallest children are nearest to God, as the smallest planets are nearest the sun.
Jean Paul Richter (1763–1825) German novelist

The role of Mother is probably the most important career a woman can have.
Janet Riley (1915–) American lawyer

Call not that man wretched who, whatever ills he suffers, has a child to love.
Robert Southey (1774–1843) English poet and writer

Wait, thou child of hope, for time shall teach thee all things.
Martin Farquhar Tupper (1810–89) English writer *Of Good in Things Evil*

A babe in a house is a well-spring of pleasure, a messenger of peace and love.
Martin Farquhar Tupper *Of Education*

CHILDREN: ❊ ❊ THE NEGATIVE ❊ ❊ VIEW

Having children is like investing in fine wines to lay down – some believe you are storing up great rewards and pleasures for the future, while others would say that it never really improves, it just gets more expensive.
Anon

He that hath wife and children hath given hostages to fortune.
Francis Bacon (1561–1626) English philosopher and statesman *Essays Of Marriage and Single Life*

Far from cementing a marriage, children more frequently disrupt it. Child rearing is on the whole an expensive and unrewarding bore.
Nigel Balchin (1908–70) English author

Children! You bring them into the world, and they drive you out of it.
Honoré de Balzac (1799–1850) French novelist

Cleaning your house while your kids are still growing
Is like shovelling the walk before it stops snowing.
Phyllis Diller (1917–) American TV personality *Housekeeping Hints*

It is only rarely that one can see in a little boy the promise of a man, but one can almost always see in a little girl the threat of a woman.

Alexandre Dumas (1824–95) French writer

Notoriously insensitive to subtle shifts in mood, children will persist in discussing the colour of a recently sighted cement-mixer long after one's own interest in the topic has waned.

Fran Lebowitz (1951–) American journalist and photographer

I love children. Especially when they cry, for then someone takes them away.

Nancy Mitford (1904–73) British writer

Oh, what a tangled web do parents weave
When they think that their children are naïve.

Ogden Nash (1902–71) American poet

Men are generally more careful of the breed of their horses and dogs than of their children.

William Penn (1644–1718) English Quaker reformer *Reflections and Maxims*

Both the aunt and the children were conversational in a limited, persistent way. Most of the aunt's remarks seemed to begin with 'Don't', and nearly all of the children's remarks began 'Why?'

Saki (H. H. Munro) (1870–1916) British novelist

Not to be born is best. The second best is to have seen the light and then to go back quickly whence we came.

Sophocles (496–406 BC) Athenian tragedian

Children begin by loving their parents. After a time they judge them. Rarely, if ever, do they forgive them.

Oscar Wilde (1854–1900) Irish playwright, novelist and wit

In my Rogues' Gallery of repulsive small boys I suppose he would come about third.

P. G. Wodehouse (1881–1975) English novelist

CHAPTER NINE

MOTHER'S DAY / FATHER'S DAY

❉ ❉ ❉ MOTHERS ❉ ❉ ❉

A mother who is really a mother is never free.
Honoré de Balzac (1799–1850) French novelist

Some are kissing mothers and some are scolding mothers, but it is love just the same (most mothers kiss and scold together).
Pearl S. Buck (1892–1973) American novelist *To My Daughters, With Love*

Mother Stands For Comfort
Kate Bush (1958–) British singer and songwriter *Song Title: Hounds of Love*

A mother is a mother still, The holiest thing alive.
Samuel Taylor Coleridge (1772–1834) English poet *The Three Graves*

As for murmurs, mother, we grumble a little now and then, to be sure. But there's no love lost between us.
Oliver Goldsmith (1728–74) Irish playwright, novelist and poet *She Stoops to Conquer*

What is home without a Mother?
Alice Hawthorne (1827–1902) American songwriter *Title of a poem*

God could not be everywhere and therefore he made mothers.
Hebrew proverb

There is in all this cold and hollow world no fount of deep, strong, deathless love, save that within a mother's heart.
Felicia D. Hemans (1793–1835) English poet

If I were hanged on the highest hill,
Mother o' mine, O Mother o' mine!
I know whose love would follow me still,
Mother o' mine, O Mother o' mine!
If I were damned of body and soul
I know whose prayers would make me whole, Mother o' mine,
O mother o' mine!
Rudyard Kipling (1865–1936) English writer *Mother O' Mine*

All that I am, or hope to be, I owe to my angel mother.
Abraham Lincoln (1809–65) 16th American President

In the heavens above
The angels, whispering to one another,
Can find, amid their burning terms of love,
None so devotional as that of 'mother'.
Edgar Allan Poe (1809–49) American poet and short story writer *To my Mother*

No matter how old a mother is she watches her middle-aged children for signs of improvement.
   Florida Scott-Maxwell *Measure of my Days*

O how this mother swells up toward my heart!
   William Shakespeare (1564–1616) English playwright and poet *King Lear*

All women become like their mothers. That is their tragedy. No man does. That's his.
   Oscar Wilde (1854–1900) Irish playwright, novelist and wit *The Importance of Being Earnest*

MOTHERS AND
❀ YOUNG CHILDREN ❀

One is not born a woman, one becomes one.
   Simone de Beauvoir (1908–86) French novelist and feminist *The Second Sex*

The mother's heart is the child's school room.
   Henry Ward Beecher (1813–87) American Congregationalist clergyman and writer *Proverbs from Plymouth Pulpit*

So for the mother's sake the child was dear,

And dearer was the mother for the child.
   Samuel Taylor Coleridge (1772–1834) English poet

You may have tangible wealth untold;
Caskets of jewels and coffers of gold.
Richer than I you can never be –
I had a mother who read to me.
   Strickland Gillilan (1869–?) American publicist *The Reading Mother*

Now in memory comes my Mother
As she used, in years agone,
To regard the darling dreamers
Ere she left them till the dawn.
   Coates Kinnay (1826–1904) American journalist *Rain on the Roof*

Stories first heard at a mother's knee are never wholly forgotten – a little spring that never quite dries up in our journey through scorching years.
   Giovanni Ruffini (1807–81) Italian writer

Who ran to help me when I fell,
And would some pretty story tell,
Or kiss the place to make it well?
My Mother.
   Ann Taylor (1782–1866) English poet *My Mother*

FATHERS

Anyone can be a father, but it takes someone special to be a dad.
Anon

Father, *n*: A quarter-master and commissary of subsistence provided by nature for our maintenance in the period before we have learned to live by prey.
Ambrose Bierce (1842–1914) American journalist *The Enlarged Devil's Dictionary*

You're a kind of father figure to me, Dad.
Alan Coren (1938–) British editor and humorist

More boys would follow in their father's footsteps if they weren't afraid of being caught.
E. C. McKenzie American writer and compiler

The worst misfortune that can happen to an ordinary man is to have an extraordinary father.
Austin O'Malley (1858–1932) American oculist and writer

My Heart Belongs to Daddy.
Cole Porter (1891–1964) American composer *Song: Leave It To Me*

One father is more than a hundred school masters.
Proverb

One father can support ten children, but ten children seem unable to support one father.
Leo Rosten's Treasury of Jewish Quotations

It is a wise father that knows his own child.
William Shakespeare (1564–1616) English playwright and poet *The Merchant of Venice*

No man is responsible for his father. That is entirely his mother's affair.
Margaret Turnball (1890–1942) American writer and politician

When I was a boy of fourteen, my father was so ignorant I could hardly stand to have the old man around. But when I got to be twenty-one, I was astonished at how much he had learned in seven years.
Mark Twain (1835–1910) American writer

PARENTS

The dear and kindly paternal image.
Dante Alighieri (1265–1321) Italian poet

Having a child makes you a mother/father, but loving and caring makes you a mum/dad.
Anon

There is no friendship no love, like
that of the parent for the child.
 Henry Ward Beecher (1813–87)
American Congregationalist
clergyman and writer *Proverbs from
Plymouth Pulpit*

We never know the love of the
parent till we become parents
ourselves.
 Henry Ward Beecher *Proverbs
from Plymouth Pulpit*

Never throw stones at your
    mother,
You'll be sorry for it when she's
    dead,
Never throw stones at your
    mother,
Throw bricks at your father
    instead.
 Brendan Behan (1923–64) Irish
author *The Hostage*

Lovers grow cold, men learn to
    hate their wives,
And only parents' love can last our
    lives.
 Robert Browning (1812–89)
English poet

The thing that impresses me most
about America is the way parents
obey their children.
 Edward VIII (1894–1972) Duke of
Windsor

Father, Mother, and Me,
Sister and Auntie say
All the people like us are We,
And everyone else is They.
 Rudyard Kipling (1865–1936)
English writer *Mother O' Mine*

I owe a lot to my parents,
especially my mother and father.
 Greg Norman (1955–) Australian
golfer

It is all that the young can do for
the old, to shock them and keep
them up to date.
 George Bernard Shaw (1856–
1950) Irish dramatist

Parents are the bones on which
children sharpen their teeth.
 Peter Ustinov (1921–) British
actor and writer *Dear Me*

My father got me strong and
    straight and slim,
And I give thanks to him.
My mother bore me glad and
    sound and sweet,
I kiss her feet!
 Marguerite Wilkinson (1883–
1928) American poet *The End*

GRANDMOTHERS
❋ AND ❋
GRANDFATHERS

A selection from *Grandmas and
Grandpas* by Richard and Helen
Exley, Exley Publications

Grandmas say that the title makes
them feel old – like a Grand piano,
I suppose. As an alternative, how
about Supermum?
 Isobel Blaber (Age 14)

A grandad is a person you never forget, never.

I'm proud that he's my grandad.

And I'll never forget his hand in mine as we walk down the street together.

Suzanne Cairns (Age 13)

A Granny is jolly and when she laughs a warmness spreads over you.

J. Hawksley (Age 11)

My Grandad is a safety shield against an angry mum.

Rebecca Smith (Age 11)

If we get bored with our Mum and Dad telling us what to do, there's always someone waiting for us with her arms out.

Helen Tidy (Age 9)

Grandmother: a person who will always have time to see you when the rest of the world is busy.

Gill Webb

Grandpas are delightful things they date back to the last century.

Simon Welch (Age 10)

A grandma is old on the outside and young on the inside.

John Wright (Age 7)

CHAPTER TEN

TOGETHERNESS

❋ ❋ ❋ HUMOROUS ❋ ❋ ❋

An archaeologist is the best husband any woman can have. The older she gets, the more interested he is in her.
Agatha Christie (1890–1976) English author

Drama is life with dull bits cut out.
Alfred Hitchcock (1899–1980) English film maker

You had no taste when you married me.
Richard Brinsley Sheridan (1751–1816) Irish dramatist *The School for Scandal*

❋ ❋ ANNIVERSARY ❋ ❋

There is a lady, sweet and kind
As any lady you will find.
I've known her nearly all my life;
She is, in fact, my present wife.
Reginald Arkell (1882–1959) English journalist and playwright *Green Fingers*

Diamond jubilee: Celebration of 60 years of not having your jewelry stolen.
Mike Barfield (1962–) *Dictionary For Our Time – 'The Oldie'*

(Said of Sidney and Beatrice Webb) – two nice people if ever there was one.
Alan Bennett (1934–) English dramatist and actor

Even in these days of marital musical chairs many third fingers still go through life wearing the same old bashed-up ring.
J. Basil Boothroyd (1910–) English writer and broadcaster

Let us be as strange (aloof) as if we had been married a great while; and as well-bred as if we were not married at all.
William Congreve (1670–1729) English dramatist and poet

If twenty years were to be erased and I were to be presented with the same choice again under the same circumstances I would act precisely as I did then.
Edward VIII (1894–1972) Duke of Windsor

There is no more lovely, friendly and charming relationship, communion or company than a good marriage.
Martin Luther (1483–1546) German Protestant reformer

A wife can often surprise her husband on their wedding anniversary by merely mentioning it.

E. C. McKenzie American writer and compiler

When Time, who steals our years
  away,
  Shall steal our pleasures too,
The memory of the past will stay,
  And half our joys renew.

Thomas Moore (1779–1852) Irish poet *Song*

Times change, and we change with them too.

John Owen (c.1560–1622) Welsh epigrammatist

To me, fair friend, you never can be
  old,
For as you were when first your
  eye I eyed,
Such seems your beauty still.

William Shakespeare (1564–1616) English playwright and poet *Sonnet No. 104*

Now are the days both full and
  sweet
With the fruit of happiness mine to
  eat.

R. L. Sharpe (1928–) *card to his Wife on their wedding anniversary*

Love is not a matter of counting the years . . . it's making the years count.

Wolfman Jack Smith American disc jockey

A little in drink, but at all times your faithful husband.

Richard Steel (1672–1729) Irish essayist, dramatist and politician *Midnight letter to his wife*

❉ ENDURING LOVE ❉

O, true love is a durable fire,
  In the mind ever burning,
Never sick, never dead, never cold,
  From itself never turning.

Anon

A dance never seems too long when you have the right partner.

Anon

I'll love you, dear, I'll love you
  Till China and Africa meet,
And the river jumps over the
  mountain
And the salmon sing in the street.

Wystan Hugh Auden (1907–73) Anglo-American poet and essayist *As I Walked Out One Evening*

No one has ever written a romance better than we have lived it.

Lauren Bacall (1924–) American actress *By Myself, on her marriage to Humphrey Bogart*

I love thee with a love I seem to
  lose
  With my lost saints – I love thee
  with the breath,
  Smiles, tears, of all my life! – and, if
  God choose,

I shall but love thee better after
death.
Elizabeth Barrett Browning
(1806–61) English poet *Sonnets from
the Portuguese*

I have lived long enough to know
that the evening glow of love has
its own riches and splendour.
Benjamin Disraeli (1804–81)
British statesman and novelist

All other things to their destruction
draw,
Only our love hath no decay;
This, no tomorrow hath, nor
yesterday,
Running it never runs from us
away,
But truly keeps his first, last,
everlasting day.
John Donne (1573–1631) English
poet *The Anniversary*

We do not necessarily improve
with age; for better or for worse we
become more like ourselves.
Peter Hall (1930–) Opera and
film director *The Observer*
24 January 1988

Love is a circle that doth restless
move
In the same sweet eternity of love.
Robert Herrick (1591–1674)
English poet *Love What It Is*

Love prefers twilight to daylight.
Oliver Wendell Holmes (1809–
94) American physician and writer

Love doesn't make the world go
'round. Love is what makes the
ride worthwhile.
Franklin P. Jones

I shall love you in December
With the love I gave in May!
John Alexander Joyce (1842–
1915) *Question and Answer*

I know of no better definition of
love than the one given by Proust –
'Love is space and time measured
by the heart.'
Gian-Carlo Menotti (1911–)
American composer *Notebook
jottings for 'Maria Golovin'*

To plod on and still keep the
passion fresh.
George Meredith (1828–1909)
English novelist *The Egoist*

My debt to you, Beloved,
Is one I cannot pay
In any coin of any realm
On any reckoning day.
Jessie Rittenhouse (1869–1948)
American poet

We go right enough, darling, if we
go wrong together!
George Santayana (1863–1952)
Spanish philosopher, poet and
novelist *My Host The World*

Happiness is not having what you
want, but wanting what you have.
Hyman Judha Schachtel
American clergyman *The Real
Enjoyment of Living*

Love alters not with his brief hours
and weeks,
But bears it out even to the edge of
doom.
William Shakespeare (1564–1616)
English playwright and poet
Sonnet 116

When you loved me I gave you the
whole sun and stars to play with. I
gave you eternity in a single
moment, strength of the mountains
in one clasp of your arms, and the
volume of all the seas in one
impulse of your soul.
George Bernard Shaw (1856–
1950) Irish dramatist

May I be looking at you when my
last hour has come,
and dying may I hold you with my
weakening hand.
Albius Tibullus (c.50–19 BC)
Roman elegiac poet

A love so violent, so strong so sure,
As neither age can change, nor art
can cure.
Virgil (70–19 BC) Roman poet
Aeneid

When, wearied with a world of
woe,
  To thy safe bosom I retire
Where love, and peace, and truth
does flow,
  May I contented there expire!
John Wilmot, Earl of Rochester
(1647–80) English courtier and poet
Return

HAPPY
❋ ❋ ❋ MEMORIES ❋ ❋ ❋

Perfect happiness, even in
memory, is not common.
Jane Austen (1775–1817) English
novelist *Emma*

I cannot sing the old songs
I sang long years ago,
For heart and voice would fail me,
And foolish tears would flow.
Mrs C. A. Barnard (1840–69)
Fireside Thoughts

God gave us memory so that we
might have roses in December.
J. M. Barrie (1860–1937) Scottish
novelist and dramatist *Rectorial
address at St Andrews*

I have more memories than if I
were a thousand years old.
Charles Baudelaire (1821–67)
French Symbolist poet

I am grown peaceful as old age
tonight;
I regret a little, I would change still
less.
Robert Browning (1812–89)
English poet *Andrea del Sarto*

O my own, my beautiful, my blue-
eyed!
  To be young once more, and bite
my thumb
At the world and all its cares with
you, I'd
  Give no inconsiderable sum.
Charles S. Calverley (1831–84)
Poet *First Love*

There is no time like the old time,
when you and I were young.
Oliver Wendell Holmes (1809–94) American physician and writer *No Time Like the Old Time*

To be able to enjoy one's past life is to live twice.
Martial (c.AD 43–c.104) Roman poet

All to myself I think of you,
Think of the things we used to do,
Think of the things we used to say,
Think of each happy bygone day,
Sometimes I sigh and sometimes I smile,
But I keep each olden, golden while
All to myself.
Wilber D. Nesbit (1871–1927) American poet *All to Myself*

Reminiscences make one feel so deliciously aged and sad.
George Bernard Shaw (1856–1950) Irish dramatist

❧ ❧ ❧ OF WIVES ❧ ❧ ❧

Every man who is high up likes to think he has done it all himself, and the wife smiles and lets it go at that.
J. M. Barrie (1860–1937) Scottish novelist and dramatist

Man's best possession is a loving wife.
Robert Burton (1577–1640) English writer and clergyman

My most brilliant achievement was my ability to be able to persuade my wife to marry me.
Sir Winston Churchill (1874–1965) English statesman

I . . . chose my wife, as she did her wedding gown, not for a fine glossy surface, but such qualities as would wear well.
Oliver Goldsmith (1728–74) Irish playwright, novelist and poet *The Vicar of Wakefield, Preface*

Of all the home remedies, a good wife is best.
Kin Hubbard (1868–1930) American humorist

Sole partner, and sole part of all my joys, dearer thyself than all.
John Milton (1608–74) English poet

A good wife and health are a man's best wealth.
Proverb

A wife is essential to great longevity; she is the receptacle of half a man's cares, and two-thirds of his ill-humor.
Charles Reade (1814–84) English novelist and playwright

Teacher, tender, comrade, wife,
A fellow-farer true through life.
Robert Louis Stevenson (1850–94) Scottish novelist and poet *My Wife*

She who dwells with me, whom I
    have loved
With such communion, that no
    place on earth
Can ever be a solitude to me.
  William Wordsworth (1770–1850)
English poet *There is an Eminence*

✿ ✿ OF HUSBANDS ✿ ✿

Men are like wines: most turn
vinegary as they get older, but the
good ones improve with age.
  Anon

The road to success is filled with
women pushing their husbands
along.
  Thomas, Lord Dewar (1864–1930)
British distiller and writer *Epigram*

Most husbands remember where
and when they got married. What
stumps them is why.
  E. C. McKenzie American writer
and compiler

Husbands never become good.
They merely become proficient.
  Henry L. Mencken (1880–1956)
American journalist and linguist

A married man must shed many
skins before he outgrows the
bachelor in him.
  Romanian proverb: quoted in
Reader's Digest

CHAPTER ELEVEN

RETIREMENT

RETIREMENT:
❋ ❋ EARLY, LATE ❋ ❋ OR NOT AT ALL

Early retirement: Option now available to school-leavers.
Mike Barfield (1962–) *Dictionary For Our Time – 'The Oldie'*

Retirement at sixty-five is ridiculous. When I was sixty-five I still had pimples.
George Burns (1898–) American humorist

When a man falls into his anecdotage, it's a sign for him to retire.
Benjamin Disraeli (1804–81) British statesman and novelist

We would all be idle if we could.
Dr Samuel Johnson (1709–84) English writer and critic

Don't think of retiring from the world until the world will be sorry that you retire. I hate a fellow whom pride or cowardice or laziness drive into a corner, and who does nothing when he is there

but sit and growl. Let him come out as I do, and bark.
Dr Samuel Johnson

When the end of the world comes, I want to be living in retirement.
Karl Kraus (1874–1936) Austrian critic and dramatist *Aphorism*

I am not one of those people who would rather act than eat. Quite the reverse. My own desire as a boy was to retire. That ambition has never changed.
George Sanders (1906–72) English film actor

Retirement, we understand, is great if you are busy, rich and healthy. But then, under those conditions, work is great too.
Bill Vaughan quoted in *Reader's Digest*

❋ ❋ WELL-EARNED ❋ ❋ REST

Retirement is a wonderful time; nothing to do all day and if you leave it half done it doesn't matter.
Anon

The end of labour is to gain leisure.
  Aristotle (384–322 BC) Greek
philosopher and scientist

The end and the reward of toil is
rest.
  James Beattie (1735–1803)
Scottish Poet *The Minstrel*

His was the sort of career that
made the Recording Angel think
seriously about taking up
shorthand.
  Nicolas Bentley (1907–78) English
writer and illustrator *Attributed*

If people really liked to work, we'd
still be ploughing the land with
sticks and transporting goods on
our backs.
  William Feather (1889–)
American businessman

It is very grand to 'die in harness'
but it is very pleasant to have the
tight straps unbuckled and the
heavy collar lifted from the neck
and shoulders.
  Oliver Wendell Holmes (1809–
94) American physician and writer
Over the Teacups

One machine can do the work of
fifty ordinary men. No machine
can do the work of one
extraordinary man.
  Elbert Hubbard (1856–1915)
American author *Roycroft
Dictionary and Book of Epigrams*

They talk of the dignity of work.
Bosh. The dignity is in leisure.
  Herman Melville (1819–91)
American novelist

Rest: the sweet sauce of labour.
  Plutarch (c.46–c.120) Greek
historian

This is the true joy in life, the being
used for a purpose recognised by
yourself as a mighty one; the being
thoroughly worn out before you
are thrown on the scrap heap.
  George Bernard Shaw (1856–
1950) Irish dramatist

QUITTING
❖ ❖ WHILE YOU'RE ❖ ❖
AHEAD

I want to get out with my greatness
intact.
  Muhammad Ali (1942–)
American boxer quoted in the
Observer 4 July 1974

Leave them while you're looking
good.
  Anita Loos *Gentlemen Prefer
Blondes*

One change leaves the way open
for the introduction of others.
  Niccolò Machiavelli (1469–1527)
Italian statesman

Few men of action have been able to make a graceful exit at the appropriate time.
Malcolm Muggeridge (1903–90)
British journalist

To judge rightly of our own worth we should retire from the world so as to see both its pleasures and pains in the proper light and dimensions.
Laurence Sterne (1713–68)
Anglo-Irish novelist

❈ LIVING WITH LEISURE ❈ (BUSILY DOING NOTHING)

So now you have all the time in the world to waste . . . but of course time you can enjoy wasting is never wasted time.
Anon

Retired is being tired twice, I've thought,
First tired of working,
Then tired of not.
Richard Armour (1906–)
American writer

The dreadful burden of having to do nothing.
Nicolas Boileau (1636–1711)
French poet and critic

He whom God hath gifted with the love of retirement, possesses, as it were, an extra sense.
Edward Bulwer-Lytton (1803–73)
English novelist, playwright and politician

Absence of occupation is not rest,
A mind quite vacant is a mind distressed.
William Cowper (1731–1800)
English poet *Retirement*

What is this life if, full of care,
We have no time to stand and stare.
William H. Davies (1871–1940)
Welsh Poet *Leisure*

He that can take rest is greater than he that can take cities.
Benjamin Franklin (1706–90)
American statesman

The greatest luxury is not to be hurried.
Don Herold quoted in *Reader's Digest*

It is impossible to enjoy idling thoroughly unless one has plenty of work to do.
Jerome K. Jerome (1859–1927)
English humorist writer, novelist and playwright *Thoughts of an Idle Fellow*

There is no pleasure in having nothing to do; the fun is having lots to do and not doing it.
Mary Wilson Little

Time is like having an extra cupboard – you always find something to fill it.
Janet Palmer quoted in *Reader's Digest*

I am interested in leisure the way that a poor man is interested in money. I can't get enough of it.
Prince Philip (1921–) Duke of Edinburgh

What is liberty? Leisure. What is leisure? Liberty.
George Bernard Shaw (1856–1950) Irish dramatist

When a man retires and time is no longer a matter of urgent importance, his colleagues generally present him with a watch.
R. C. Sherriff (1896–1975) English playwright and novelist

LIFE
❋ ❋ ❋ BEYOND ❋ ❋ ❋
RETIREMENT

While one finds company in himself and his pursuits, he cannot feel old, no matter what his years may be.
Amos Bronson Alcott (1799–1888) American teacher

It is strange that the one thing that every person looks forward to, namely old age, is the one thing for which no preparation is made.
John Dewey (1859–1952) American philosopher *Attributed*

Happy the man, and happy he alone,

He who can call to-day his own:
John Dryden (1631–1700) English poet *Imitation of Horace*

Don't wait for pie in the sky when you die! Get yours now, with ice-cream on top!
Frederick J. Eikerenkoetter (1935–) American evangelist

You can rise when you want,
  Do as you please,
Work in the garden,
  Or just sit at ease.
Your options are many,
  Everyday will inspire,
For a new life begins
  On the day you retire.
Phyllis Ellison quoted in *Francis Gay's Friendship Book* 1994

Man is so made that he can only find relaxation from one kind of labour by taking up another.
Anatole France (1844–1924) French novelist and poet *The Crime of Sylvestre Bonnard*

The devil finds some mischief still for hands that have not learnt how to be idle.
Geoffrey Madan (1895–1947)

When we are young, we are slavishly employed in procuring

something whereby we may live comfortably when we grow old; and when we are old, we perceive it is too late to live as we proposed.

Alexander Pope (1688–1744) English poet

If a man has important work, and enough leisure and income to enable him to do it properly, he is in possession of as much happiness as is good for any of the children of Adam.

Richard Henry Tawney (1880–1962) English economic historian

Iron rusts from disuse, stagnant water loses its purity, and in cold weather becomes frozen; even so does inaction sap the vigors of the mind.

Leonardo da Vinci (1452–1519) Italian painter and inventor *Notebooks*

CHAPTER TWELVE

ILL HEALTH (GET WELL)

❋ MEDICINE: CURES ❋ AND REMEDIES

It is time, and not medicine, that cures the disease.
Anon

The remedy is worse than the disease.
Francis Bacon (1561–1626)
English philosopher and statesman
Essays of Seditions and Troubles

Everyone knows how to get rid of this cold but me.
J. Basil Boothroyd (1910–)
English writer and broadcaster

Patience is the best medicine.
John Florio (c.1533–1625) The translator of Montaigne *First Frutes*

A cheerful face is nearly as good for an invalid as healthy weather.
Benjamin Franklin (1706–90)
American statesman

There is no medicine like hope.
O. S. Marden (1850–1924)
American journalist

One of the chief objects of medicine is to save us from the natural consequences of our vices and follies.
Henry L. Mencken (1880–1956)
American journalist and linguist

A disease known is half cured.
Proverb

It is part of the cure to wish to be cured.
Lucius Annaeus Seneca (c.55 BC– c. AD 40) Roman rhetorician quoted in *Reader's Digest*

The art of medicine consists of amusing the patient while Nature cures the disease.
Voltaire (1694–1788) French author *Attributed*

❋ ❋ ❋ SICKNESS ❋ ❋ ❋

There was no influenza in my young days. We called a cold a cold.
Arnold Bennett (1867–1931)
English novelist *The Card*

I reckon being ill is one of the great pleasures of life.
Samuel Butler (1835–1902)
English author, painter and musician

When you don't have any money, the problem is food. When you

have money, it's sex. When you have both, it's health.
James Patrick Donleavy (1926–) Irish author

When you're lying awake with a dismal headache, and repose is tabooed by anxiety,
I conceive you may use any language you choose to indulge in without impropriety.
William S. Gilbert (1836–1911) English comic opera and verse writer *Iolanthe*

Life's not just being alive, but being well.
Martial (c. AD 40–c. AD 104) Roman poet

Nobody is sicker than the man who is sick on his day off.
E. C. McKenzie American writer and compiler

Listen, someone's screaming in agony – fortunately I speak it fluently.
Spike Milligan (1918–) British comedian

From winter, plague and pestilence, good Lord, deliver us!
Thomas Nashe (1567–1601) English dramatist and satirist *Summer's Last Will and Testament*

'There is a bug going around', we tell each other. It conjures up a picture of a rather caddish eight-legged character driving around

the place in a sports car, causing trouble wherever he goes.
Oliver Pritchett (1939–) English writer

While there is life, there is hope.
Proverb

One good thing about laryngitis is that the people who have it can't tell you how miserable they are.
Quoted in *Reader's Digest*

Better ten times sick than once dead.
Leo Rosten's Treasury of Jewish Quotations

There was never yet a philosopher that could endure the toothache patiently.
William Shakespeare (1564–1616) English playwright and poet *Much Ado About Nothing*

We are so fond of one another, because our ailments are the same.
Jonathan Swift (1667–1745) Anglo-Irish poet and satirist

I am dying beyond my means.
Oscar Wilde (1854–1900) Irish playwright, novelist and wit

❀ ❀ ❀ ACCIDENTS ❀ ❀ ❀

My only solution for the problem of habitual accidents and, so far, nobody has asked me for my solution, is to stay in bed all day. Even then, there is always the chance that you will fall out.

Robert Benchley (1889–1945) American humorist and critic *Chips off the old Benchley*

Self-decapitation is an extremely difficult, not to say dangerous, thing to attempt.

William S. Gilbert (1836–1911) English comic opera and verse writer

I ran for a catch
With the sun in my eyes, sir . . .
Now I wear a black patch
And a nose such a size, sir!

Coulson Kernahan (1858–1943) English writer

Some hospitals are so crowded that the only way you can get in is by accident.

E. C. McKenzie American writer and compiler

❋ ❋ ❋ HOSPITALS ❋ ❋ ❋

After two days in hospital, I took a turn for the nurse.

W. C. Fields (1879–1946) American comedian

I had never seen a sister close to before. This unexpected proximity had the effect of being in a rowing-boat under the bows of the 'Queen Mary'.

Richard Gordon (1921–) British doctor and writer

Before undergoing a surgical operation, arrange your temporal affairs. You may live.

Rémy de Gourmont (1858–1915) French novelist and critic

It may seem a strange principle to enunciate as the very first requirement in a hospital that it should do the sick no harm.

Florence Nightingale (1820–1910) English nurse *Notes on Hospitals*

❋ ❋ DOCTORS AND ❋ ❋ PHYSICIANS

If a doctor or nurse uses the phrase 'This won't hurt a bit', be sure to ask to whom they are referring.

Anon

Physician, *n*: One upon whom we set our hopes when ill and our dogs when well.

Ambrose Bierce (1842–1914) American journalist *The Enlarged Devil's Dictionary*

Nature, time and patience are the three greatest physicians.
Bulgarian proverb

I don't know much about his ability, but he's got a very good bedside manner.
George L. du Maurier (1834–96) British artist and novelist *Punch* 15 March 1884

Virus is a Latin word used by doctors, meaning, 'Your guess is as good as mine.'
E. C. McKenzie American writer and compiler

God and the doctor we alike adore
But only when in danger, not
    before;
The danger o'er, both alike requited,
God is forgotten, and the Doctor
    slighted.
John Owen (c.1560–1622) Welsh epigrammatist *Epigrams*

Die, my dear Doctor, that's the last thing I shall do.
Henry, Lord Palmerston (1784–1865) English statesman *Attributed last words*

Sleep is the best doctor.
Leo Rosten's Treasury of Jewish Quotations

in such weather, and out of hospital.
Samuel Beckett (1906–89) Irish author and playwright *All that Fall*

Lying in bed would be an altogether perfect and supreme experience if only one had a coloured pencil long enough to draw on the ceiling.
G. K. Chesterton (1874–1936) English critic and novelist *Tremendous Trifles*

Every day, in every way, I am getting better and better.
Emile Coute (1857–1926) *Formula in his clinic*

No more wine and women – sing all the songs you want.
Quoted in *Reader's Digest*

Take rest; a field that has rested gives a beautiful crop.
Ovid (43 BC–AD 17) Roman poet

I enjoy convalescence. It is the part that makes illness worth while.
George Bernard Shaw (1856–1950) Irish dramatist *Back to Methuselah*

❈ CONVALESCENCE ❈

What sky! What light! Ah in spite of all it is a blessed thing to be alive

CHAPTER THIRTEEN

DEATH AND BEREAVEMENT

❋ ❋ REMEMBRANCE ❋ ❋

There is no greater sorrow
Than to be mindful of the happy time
In misery.
Dante Alighieri (1265–1321)
Italian poet *The Divine Comedy*

The song is ended; but the melody lingers on.
Irving Berlin (1888–1989)
American composer *Song Title*

They shall grow not old, as we that are left grow old:
Age shall not weary them, nor the years condemn.
At the going down of the sun and in the morning
We will remember them.
Laurence Binyon (1869–1943)
English poet and art critic *For the Fallen (1914–18)*

To die completely, a person must not only forget but be forgotten, and he who is not forgotten is not dead.
Samuel Butler (1835–1902)
English author, painter and musician *Note Books*

To live in hearts we leave behind
Is not to die.
Thomas Campbell (1777–1844)
Scottish poet and journalist
Hallowed Ground

Though the past haunt me as a spirit, I do not ask to forget.
Felicia D. Hemans (1793–1835)
English poet

I shall not altogether die.
Horace (65–8 BC) Roman poet and satirist

What will survive of us is love.
Philip Larkin (1922–85) English poet *An Arundel Tomb*

Recollection is the only paradise from which we cannot be turned out.
Jean Paul Richter (1763–1825)
German novelist

Remember me when I am gone away,
Gone far away into the silent land.
Christina Rossetti (1830–94)
English poet *Remember*

Yet leaving here a name, I trust, that will not perish in the dust.
Robert Southey (1774–1843)
English poet and writer

Rose leaves, when the rose is dead,
Are heap'd for the beloved's bed;
And so thy thoughts, when thou
    art gone,
Love itself shall slumber on.
Percy Bysshe Shelley (1792–1822)
English poet *An Unnamed Poem*

Sorrow's crown of sorrow is
remembering happier things.
Alfred, Lord Tennyson (1809–92)
English poet

Though lovers be lost love shall
    not;
And death shall have no dominion.
Dylan Thomas (1914–53) Welsh
poet *And Death Shall Have No
Dominion*

We shall meet, but we shall miss
    him,
There will be one vacant chair.
Henry S. Washburn (1813–1903)
American author *The Vacant Chair*

Memories, images, and precious
    thoughts
That shall not die, and cannot be
    destroyed.
William Wordsworth (1770–1850)
English poet *The Excursion*

❖ ❖ CONSOLATION ❖ ❖

See in what peace a Christian can
die.
Joseph Addison (1672–1719)
English essayist and politician
Dying words

Give not thy heart to despair.
No lamentation can lose
Prisoners of death from the grave.
Matthew Arnold (1822–88)
English poet and critic *Merope*

Heaven gives its favourites – early
death.
George Gordon, Lord Byron
(1788–1824) English poet *Childe
Harold*

Far happier are the dead, methinks,
    than they
Who look for death and fear it
    every day.
William Cowper (1731–1800)
English poet

We sometimes congratulate
ourselves at the moment of waking
from a troubled dream; it may be
so the moment after death.
Nathaniel Hawthorne (1804–64)
American novelist

Death is nothing at all. I have only
slipped away into the next room. I
am I and you are you. Whatever
we were to each other, that we are
still . . . What is death but
negligible accident? Why should I
be out of mind because I am out of
sight? I am waiting for you, for an
interval, somewhere very near just
around the corner. All is well.
Henry Scott Holland (1847–1918)
English clergyman and theologian

It matters not how a man dies, but how he lives. The act of dying is not of importance, it lasts so short a time.

Dr Samuel Johnson (1709–84) English writer and critic

The gods conceal from men the happiness of death, that they may endure life.

Lucan (AD 39–65) Roman poet

We can know there is nothing to be feared in death, that one who is not, cannot be made unhappy and that it matters not a scrap whether one might ever have been born at all, when death that is immortal has taken over one's mortal life.

Lucretius (c.94–55 BC) Roman poet and philosopher

God is closest to those with broken hearts.

Leo Rosten's Treasury of Jewish Quotations

Death is for many of us the gate of hell; but we are inside on the way out, not outside on the way in.

George Bernard Shaw (1856–1950) Irish dramatist *Parents and Children*

We understand death for the first time when he puts his hand upon one whom we love.

Madame de Staël (1766–1817) French novelist and critic

After the first death, there is no other.

Dylan Thomas (1914–53) Welsh poet *A refusal to mourn the death, by fire, of a child in London*

OF A
❋ ❋ ❋ BETTER ❋ ❋ ❋
PLACE

Behind is life and its longing,
Its trial, its trouble, its sorrow:
Beyond is Infinite Morning
Of a day without a to-morrow.
Wenonah S. Abbott (1865–?) *A Soul's Soliloquy*

But when the sun, in all his state,
   Illumed the eastern skies,
She passed through Glory's
   morning gate,
And walked in Paradise.
James Aldrich (1810–56) *A Death-bed*

He's gone to join the majority.
Petronius Arbiter (First century) Latin satirical writer

We go to the grave of a friend, saying, 'A man is dead', but angels throng about him, saying, 'A man is born'.
Henry Ward Beecher (1813–87) American Congregationalist clergyman and writer

So he passed over, and all the trumpets sounded for him on the other side.

John Bunyan (1628–88) *The Pilgrim's Progress* English writer and preacher

The path of sorrow, and that path alone,
Leads to the land where sorrow is unknown.

William Cowper (1731–1800) English poet *An Epistle to a Protestant Lady in France*

Parting is all we know of heaven,
And all we need of hell.

Emily Dickinson (1830–86) American poet *Poems, Part 1, Life*

One short sleep past, we wake eternally.
And death shall be no more; death, thou shalt die!

John Donne (1573–1631) English poet *Holy Sonnets VII*

To die is landing on some distant shore.

John Dryden (1631–1700) English poet

The world is the land of the dying; the next is the land of the living.

Tyron Edwards (1809–94) American theologian

In the depths of your hopes and desires lies your silent knowledge of the beyond; and like seeds dreaming beneath the snow your heart dreams of spring. Trust the dreams. for in them is hidden the gate to eternity.

Kahlil Gibran (1883–1931) American writer and artist *The Prophet*

There is no death! the stars go down
To rise upon some other shore,
And bright in heaven's jeweled crown,
They shine for ever more.

John L. McCreery (1835–1906) American journalist and writer *There is no Death*

For death and life, in ceaseless strife,
Beat wild on this world's shore,
And all our calm is in that balm –
Not lost but gone before.

Caroline Norton (1808–77) Irish writer and reformer *Not Lost but Gone Before*

Grandpa has gone to heaven and I'm sure God is finding him very useful.

Princess Margaret (1930–) Countess of Snowdon

Heaven is the place where the donkey at last catches up with the carrot.

Quoted in *Pontius the Pilot, edited by Richard Huggett*

Each departed friend is a magnet that attracts us to the next world.

Jean Paul Richter (1763–1825) German novelist

. . . Who would fardels bear,
To grunt and sweat under a weary
   life,
But that the dread of something
   after death,
The undiscovered country, from
   whose bourn
No traveller returns, puzzles the
   will.
   William Shakespeare (1564–1616)
English playwright and poet
Hamlet

To that high Capital, where kingly
   Death
Keeps his pale court in beauty and
   decay,
He came.
   Percy Bysshe Shelley (1792–1822)
English poet *Adonais*

But Love is indestructible.
Its holy flame for ever burneth,
From Heaven it came, to Heaven
   returneth.
   Robert Southey (1774–1843)
English poet and writer *Curse of
Kehama*

TRIBUTES
❋ ❋ TO THE GOOD ❋ ❋
AND GREAT

He thought as a sage, though he
felt as a man.
   James Beattie (1735–1803)
Scottish poet *The Hermit*

When the sun goes below the
horizon, he is not set; the heavens
glow for a full hour after his
departure. And when a great and
good man sets, the sky of this
world is luminous long after he is
out of sight.
   Henry Ward Beecher (1813–87)
American Congregationalist
clergyman and writer

Any relic of the dead is precious,
if they were valued living.
   Emily Brontë (1818–48) English
novelist and poet

The friend of man, the friend of
   truth,
The friend of age, the guide of
   youth;
If there's another world, he lives in
   bliss;
If there is none, he made the best of
   this.
   Robert Burns (1759–96) Scottish
poet *Epistle to the Rev. John McMath*

No great man lives in vain. The
history of the world is but the
biography of great men.
   Thomas Carlyle (1795–1881)
Scottish historian and essayist
Heroes and Hero Worship

His faith, perhaps, in some nice
   tenets might
Be wrong; his life, I'm sure, was in
   the right.
   Abraham Cowley (1618–67)
English author and poet *On the
Death of Mr. Crashaw*

The best of men cannot suspend
   their fate:

The good die early, and the bad die late.
Daniel Defoe (1660–1731) English author and adventurer

Green be the turf above thee,
Friend of my better days!
None knew thee but to love thee,
Nor named thee but to praise.
Fitz-Greene Halleck (1790–1867) American poet *On the Death of Joseph Rodman Drake*

Great lives never go out. They go on.
Benjamin Harrison (1833–1901) 23rd American President

Forever honour'd, and forever mourn'd.
Homer (Eighth century BC) Greek epic poet *Iliad*

Farewell! I did not know thy worth;
But thou art gone, and now 'tis prized;
So angels walked unknown to earth,
But when they flew were recognised.
Thomas Hood (1799–1845) English poet and humorist *To an Absentee*

He was not of an age, but for all time!
Ben Jonson (c.1572–1637) English dramatist *To the Memory of . . . Shakespeare*

Lives of great men all remind us
We can make our lives sublime,

And, departing, leave behind us
Footprints on the sands of time.
Henry Wadsworth Longfellow (1807–82) American poet *A Psalm of Life*

Whom the gods love dies young.
Menander (c.341–c.291 BC) Greek poet

Death and love are the two wings that bear the good man to heaven.
Michelangelo (1475–1564) Italian sculptor and painter

It is foolish and wrong to mourn the men who died. Rather we should thank God that such men lived.
George S. Patton Jr. (1885–1945) American soldier *Speech*, 7 June 1945

The universe is so vast and so ageless that the life of one man can only be justified by the measure of his sacrifice.
Pilot Officer V. A. Rosewarne (1916–40)

He was a man, take him for all in all,
I shall not look upon his like again.
William Shakespeare (1564–1616) English playwright and poet *Hamlet*

Death lies on her like an untimely frost
Upon the sweetest flower of all the field.
William Shakespeare *Romeo and Juliet*

Life levels all men: death reveals the eminent.
  George Bernard Shaw (1856–1950) Irish dramatist

The bad end unhappily, the good unluckily. That is what tragedy means.
  Tom Stoppard (1937–) British playwright *Rosencrantz and Guildenstern are Dead*

I held it truth, with him who sings
To one clear harp in divers tones,
That men may rise on stepping-
    stones
Of their dead selves to higher
    things.
  Alfred, Lord Tennyson (1809–92)
English poet *In Memoriam*

Forgive my grief for one removed,
Thy creature, whom I found so fair.
I trust he lives in Thee, and there
I find him worthier to be loved.
  Alfred, Lord Tennyson *In
Memoriam*

❋ ❋ ❋ **GRIEF** ❋ ❋ ❋

Strew on her roses, roses,
  And never a spray of yew.
In quiet she reposes:
  Ah! would that I did too.
  Matthew Arnold (1822–88)
English poet and critic *Requiescat*

I ask not each kind soul to keep
Tearless, when of my death he
    hears.

Let those who will, if any, weep!
There are worse plagues on earth
    than tears.
  Matthew Arnold *A Wish*

The shatter'd bowl shall know
    repair; the
  riven lute shall sound once more;
But who shall mend the clay of
    man, the
  stolen breath to man restore?
  Richard Burton (1821–90) English
orientalist and explorer *Kasidah*

No grief is so acute but that time
ameliorates it.
  Marcus Cicero (106–43 BC) Roman
statesman and orator

Grief is itself a med'cine.
  William Cowper (1731–1800)
English poet *Charity*

Nothing speaks our grief so well
As to speak nothing.
  Richard Crashaw (c.1613–49)
English religious poet *Upon the
Death of a Gentleman*

At night, when heavenly peace is
    flying
Above the world that sorrow mars,
Ah, think not of my grave with
    sighing!
For then I greet you from the stars.
  **Annette Elisabeth von Droste-
Hülshoff** (1797–1848) German poet
and novelist

The greatest griefs shall find
    themselves inside the smallest
    cage,

It's only then that we can hope to tame their rage.

D. J. Enright (1920–) English poet

Between grief and nothing I will take grief.

William Faulkner (1897–1962) American novelist *The Wild Palms*

Bid me weep, and I will weep
  While I have eyes to see:
And, having none, yet will I keep
  A heart to weep for thee.

Robert Herrick (1591–1674) English poet *To Anthea, who may command him Anything*

A man never sees all that his mother has been to him till it's too late to let her know that he sees it.

William D. Howells (1837–1920) American novelist and poet

The bitterest tears shed over graves are for words left unsaid and deeds left undone.

Harriet Stowe (1811–96) American novelist *Little Foxes*

Speak not of comfort where no comfort is.

James Thomson (1834–82) Scottish poet *The City of Dreadful Night*

Where there is sorrow there is holy ground.

Oscar Wilde (1854–1900) Irish playwright, novelist and wit *De Profundis*

❋ ❋ ❋ FINAL ❋ ❋ ❋ REST

If thou wilt ease thine heart
Of love and all its smart,
Then sleep, dear, sleep.

T. L. Beddoes (1798–1851) *Death's Jest Book*

That peace which the world cannot give.

Book of Common Prayer

Life's race well run,
Life's work well done,
Life's victory won,
Now cometh rest.

Dr Edward H. Parker (1823–96) American doctor

(Also attributed to **John Mills,** a Manchester baker.)

The fever call'd 'Living'
Is conquered at last.

Edgar Allan Poe (1809–49) American poet and story writer

After life's fitful fever he sleeps well.

William Shakespeare (1564–1616) English playwright and poet *Macbeth*

Journey's End.

R. C. Sherriff (1896–1975) English playwright and novelist *Play Title*

❈ ❈ AN END TO ❈ ❈ SUFFERING

We all labour against our own cure, for death is the cure of all diseases.
Thomas Browne (1605–82)
English author and physician
Religio Medici

For the unhappy man death is the commutation of a sentence of life imprisonment.
Alexander Chase American journalist *Perspectives*

Oh, write of me, not 'Died in bitter pains,
But 'Emigrated to another star!'
Helen Friske Hunt (1830–85)
American writer and poet

He who sleeps feels not the toothache.
William Shakespeare (1564–1616)
English playwright and poet
Cymbeline

From the contagion of the world's slow stain
He is secure.
Percy Bysshe Shelley (1792–1822)
English poet *Adonais*

Every man desires to live long; but no man would be old.
Jonathan Swift (1667–1745)
Anglo-Irish poet and satirist

God's finger touched him, and he slept.
Alfred, Lord Tennyson (1809–92)
English poet

❈ ❈ IN THE LINE ❈ ❈ OF DUTY

What a pity it is that one can die but once to serve our country.
Joseph Addison (1672–1719)
English essayist and politician

If I should die, think only this of me:
That there's some corner of a foreign field
That is for ever England.
Rupert C. Brooke (1887–1915)
English poet *The Soldier*

How sleep the brave, who sink to rest
By all their country's wishes blest!
William Collins (1721–59)
English poet *Ode written in the Year 1746*

Lovely and honourable it is to die for one's country.
Horace (65–8 BC) Roman poet and satirist

I have a rendezvous with Death
At some disputed barricade.
Alan Seeger (1888–1916)
American poet

. . . Gave his body to that pleasant country's earth,

And his pure soul unto his captain
Christ,
Under whose colours he had
fought so long.
William Shakespeare (1564–1616)
English playwright and poet
Richard II

To sacrifice oneself is the height of bliss – for some people.
Ivan Turgenev (1818–83) Russian novelist

✤ ✤ ✤ THE BIBLE ✤ ✤ ✤

As in Adam all die, even so in Christ shall all be made alive.
1 Corinthians 15:22

Weeping may endure for a night, but joy cometh in the morning.
Psalms 30:5

Be strong and of a good courage.
Joshua 1:6

Blessed are they that mourn: for they shall be comforted.
Matthew 5:4

The Lord bless thee and keep thee:
The Lord make his face shine upon
thee,
and be gracious unto thee:
The Lord lift up his countenance
upon thee,
and give thee peace.
Numbers 6:24

Death hath no more dominion over him.
Romans 6:9

✤ ✤ ✤ OF DEATH ✤ ✤ ✤

I do not believe that any man fears to be dead, but only the stroke of death.
Francis Bacon (1561–1626)
English philosopher and statesman
An Essay on Death 3

Men fear death as children fear the dark; and as that natural fear in children is increased with tales, so is the other.
Francis Bacon *Of Death*

To die will be an awful big adventure.
James M. Barrie (1860–1937)
Scottish novelist and dramatist
Peter Pan

Death comes along like a gas bill one can't pay – and that's all one can say about it.
Anthony Burgess (1917–)
English novelist, critic and composer

It is important what a man still plans at the end. It shows the measure of injustice in his death.
Elias Canetti (1905–) Bulgarian man of letters

It seems that we were born to misery,
And when we are too happy, can but die.
Marceline Desbordes-Valmore (1786–1859) French actress and poet

Because I could not stop for Death –
He kindly stopped for me –
The carriage held but just ourselves –
And immortality.
Emily Dickinson (1830–86) American poet *Because I could not stop for Death*

It hath been often said, that it is not death, but dying, which is terrible.
Henry Fielding (1707–54) English novelist

Pale Death, with impartial foot, strikes at poor men's hovels and the towers of kings.
Horace (65–8 BC) Roman poet and satirist

The cemetery is an open space among the ruins, covered in winter with violets and daisies. It might make one in love with death, to think that one should be buried in so sweet a place.
Percy Bysshe Shelley (1792–1822) English poet *Adonais*

❋ THE INEVITABILITY ❋ OF DEATH

Time goes, you say? Ah no!
Alas, Time stays, we go.
Henry Austin Dobson (1840–1921) English author and poet *The Paradox of Time*

For all must go where no wind blows,
And none can go for him that goes;
None, none return whence no one knows.
Ebenezer Elliott (1781–1849) English industrialist, radical and poet *Plaint*

Someone said that life is a party. You join after it's started and you leave before it's finished.
Elsa Maxwell (1883–1963) American columnist and songwriter *How To Do It*

Anyone can stop a man's life, but no one his death; a thousand doors open on to it.
Marcus Seneca (c.55 BC–c. AD 40) Roman rhetorician

Every minute dies a man, every minute one is born.
Alfred, Lord Tennyson (1809–92) English poet

I know death hath ten thousand several doors
For men to take their exits.
John Webster (c.1580–c.1625) English dramatist *The Duchess of Malfi*

I saw him even now going the way of all flesh.

John Webster *Westward Hoe*

❋ LIFE AND DEATH ❋

It is as natural to die as to be born; and to a little infant, perhaps, the one is as painful as the other.

Francis Bacon (1561–1626) English philosopher and statesman *Essays*

In three words I can sum up everything I've learned about life. It goes on.

Robert Frost (1874–1963) American lyric poet

Weep if you must,
Parting is hell,
But life goes on,
So sing as well.

Joyce Grenfell (1910–79) British comedienne

Life has given of me its best –
Laughter and weeping, labour and rest;
Little of gold, but lots of fun,
Shall I then sigh that all is done?

Norah M. Holland (1876–1925) American poet

And life is given to none freehold, but it is leasehold for all.

Lucretius (c.94–55 BC) Roman poet and philosopher

'Tis not the whole of life to live, Nor all of death to die.

James Montgomery (1771–1854) Scottish poet *Issues of Life and Death*

Death is the veil which those who live call life:
They sleep, and it is lifted.

Percy Bysshe Shelley (1792–1822) English poet *Prometheus Unbound*

Men may live fools, but fools they cannot die.

Edward Young (1683–1765) English poet

❋ BLACK HUMOUR ❋

It's not that I'm afraid to die, I just don't want to be there when it happens.

Woody Allen (1935–) American film director

On the plus side, death is one of the few things that can be done as easily lying down.

Woody Allen

I don't want to achieve immortality through my work . . . I want to achieve it by not dying.

Woody Allen

I am ready to meet my Maker. Whether my Maker is prepared for the ordeal of meeting me is another matter.

Sir Winston Churchill (1874–1965) English statesman

Don't ask me about heaven or hell,
I have friends in both places.
Jean Cocteau (1889–1963) French
poet, playwright and film director

Death is nature's way of telling
you to slow down.
Graffiti

Death is the greatest kick of all –
that's why they save it till last.
Graffiti

He had decided to live forever or
die in the attempt.
Joseph Heller (1923–) American
novelist

If after I depart this vale you ever
remember me and have thought to
please my ghost, forgive some
sinner and wink your eye at some
homely girl.
Henry L. Mencken (1880–1956)
American journalist and linguist

I cannot forgive my friends for
dying: I do not find these
vanishing acts of theirs at all
amusing.
Logan Pearsall Smith (1865–1946)
British writer *All Trivia*

❋ ❋ ❋ **EPITAPHS** ❋ ❋ ❋

Beneath this silent stone is laid
A noisy, talkative old maid,

Whose tongue was only stayed by
death,
And ne'er before was out of breath.
Anon

Warm summer sun shine kindly
here:
Warm summer wind blow softly
here:
Green sod above lie light, lie light:
Goodnight Dear Heart: goodnight,
goodnight.
Anon

Here lie I by the chancel door;
They put me here because I was
poor.
The further in, the more you pay,
But here lie I as snug as they.
Anon – *on a Devon tombstone.*

My fire's extinct, my forge
decayed,
And in the Dust my Vice is laid
My coals are spent, my iron's gone
My Nails are Drove, my Work is
done.
William Strange (?–1746) *Epitaph*

His time was come; he ran his race;
We hope he's in a better place.
Jonathan Swift (1667–1745)
Anglo-Irish poet and satirist *On the
Death of Dr Swift*

Cast a cold Eye
On Life, on Death.
Horseman, pass by!
William Butler Yeats (1865–1939)
Irish poet *Epitaph*

CHAPTER FOURTEEN

GOOD LUCK

❋ ❋ HUMOROUS ❋ ❋

The best thing about the future is that it only comes one day at a time.
Dean Acheson (1893–1971) American politician *Quote and Unquote*

Optimists are wrong just as often as pessimists, but they enjoy life.
Anon

Never give a sucker an even break.
W. C. Fields (1879–1946) American comedian *His punchline*

If at first you don't succeed, try again. Then quit. No use being a damn fool about it.
W. C. Fields *quoted in Leslie Halliwell, The Filmgoer's Book of Quotes*

The meek shall inherit the earth but not its mineral rights.
John Paul Getty (1892–1976) American oil magnate

There's no problem so big or complicated that it can't be run away from.
Graffiti

I don't want any yes-men around me. I want everybody to tell me the truth even if it costs them their jobs.
Samuel Goldwyn (1882–1974) American film producer

I intended to give you some advice but now I remember how much is left over from last year unused.
George Harris (1844–1922) American Congressman

Depend upon it, Sir, when a man knows he is to be hanged in a fortnight, it concentrates his mind wonderfully.
Dr Samuel Johnson (1709–84) English writer and critic *Boswell's Life of Johnson*

One good thing about being young is that you are not experienced enough to know you can't possibly do the thing you are doing.
Quoted in *Reader's Digest*

If you can't invent a really convincing lie, it's often better to stick to the truth.
Angela Thirkell (1891–1961) English novelist

There is no sadder sight than a young pessimist, except an old optimist.
Mark Twain (1835–1910) American writer

ADVICE

Distrust yourself, and sleep before
you fight.
'Tis not too late tomorrow to be
brave.
John Armstrong (1709–79)
Scottish physician and poet *The Art
of Preserving Health*

There is no such thing as a great
talent without great willpower.
Honoré de Balzac (1799–1850)
French novelist

The difference between
perseverance and obstinacy is, that
one often comes from a strong will,
and the other from a strong won't.
Henry Ward Beecher (1813–87)
American Congregationalist
clergyman and writer

Hope for the best, and expect the
worst.
Margaret Bieber (1879–1978)
German educator and
archaeologist

Do what thy manhood bids thee to
do, from
None but self expect applause;
He noblest lives and noblest dies
who makes
and keeps his self-made laws
Richard Burton (1821–90) English
orientalist and explorer *Kasidah*

I never think of the future. It comes
soon enough.
Albert Einstein (1879–1955)
German-Swiss-American
mathematical physicist

Try not to become a man of success
but rather try to become a man of
value.
Albert Einstein *Life*, 2 May 1955
(Personal memoir of William Miller)

In skating over thin ice, our safety
is in our speed.
Ralph Waldo Emerson (1803–82)
American poet and essayist

If you wish in this world to
advance
Your merits you're bound to
enhance;
You must stir it and stump it,
And blow your own trumpet.
Or trust me, you haven't got a
chance.
William S. Gilbert (1836–1911)
English comic opera and verse
writer *Ruddigore*

It is not doing the thing we like to
do, but liking the thing we have to
do, that makes life blessed.
Johann Wolfgang von Goethe
(1749–1832) German poet and
writer

Do not be afraid of enthusiasm.
You need it. You can do nothing
effectually without it.
François Guizot (1787–1874)
French historian and statesman

To have begun is half the job:
be bold and be sensible.
   Horace (65–8 BC) Roman poet and
satirist

Happiness is like coke – something
you get as a by-product in the
process of making something else.
   Aldous Huxley (1894–1963)
English novelist and essayist

Winning isn't everything, but
wanting to win is.
   Vince Lombardi (1913–70)
American football coach *Attributed*

He that would govern others, first
   should be
The master of himself.
   Philip Massinger (1583–1640)
English playwright

The world is divided into people
who do things and people who get
the credit. Try, if you can, to belong
to the first group. There's less
competition.
   Dwight W. Morrow (1873–1931)
American lawyer and diplomat

Courage in danger is half the battle.
   Plautus (c.250–184 BC) Roman
comic writer

A merry heart maketh a cheerful
countenance.
   Proverbs 15:13

Pay no attention to what the critics
say. No statue has ever been put
up to a critic.
   Jean Sibelius (1865–1957) Finnish
composer *Attributed*

The shortest way to do many
things is to do only one thing at
once.
   Samuel Smiles (1812–1904)
Scottish writer and social reformer
Self-Help

Necessity is the mother of
invention.
   Jonathan Swift (1667–1745)
Anglo-Irish poet and satirist

❖ ❖ OPPORTUNITY ❖ ❖

A wise man will make more
opportunities than he finds.
Francis Bacon (1561–1626) English
philosopher and statesman *Essays
Of Ceremonies and Respects*

Opportunity: a favourable occasion
for grasping a disappointment.
   Ambrose Bierce (1842–1914)
American journalist *The Devil's
Dictionary*

New roads: new ruts.
   G. K. Chesterton (1874–1936)
English critic and novelist
Attributed

There is no security in this life.
There is only opportunity.
   Douglas MacArthur (1880–1964)
American soldier

When fortune knocks, open the
door.
   Proverb

Grab a chance and you won't be sorry for a might-have-been.
Arthur Ransome (1884–1967) English journalist and writer of children's books *We didn't Mean to Go to Sea*

It is the greatest of all advantages to enjoy no advantage at all.
Henry David Thoreau (1817–62) American essayist and poet

❋ FAITH AND TRUST ❋

Achieving starts with believing.
Anon

Put your trust in God, but keep your powder dry.
Oliver Cromwell (1599–1658) English soldier and statesman

For they conquer who believe they can.
John Dryden (1631–1700) English poet

There is only one real failure in life that is possible, and that is, not to be true to the best one knows.
Frederic Farrar (1831–1903) English clergyman and writer

To accomplish great things, we must not only act but also dream, not only plan but believe.
Anatole France (1844–1924) French novelist and poet

It matters not how strait the gate,
How charged with punishments the scroll,
I am the master of my fate:
I am the captain of my soul.
William Ernest Henley (1849–1903) English poet and playwright *Invictus*

It is a blessed thing that in every age someone has had the individuality enough and courage enough to stand by his own convictions.
Robert Greene Ingersoll (1833–99) American lawyer and orator

Self-confidence is the first requisite to great undertakings.
Dr Samuel Johnson (1709–84) English writer and critic

Where there's a will, there's a way.
Proverb

The world continues to offer glittering prizes to those who have stout hearts and sharp swords.
Frederick E. Smith (1872–1930) English lawyer and statesman *Rectorial Address* 7 Nov. 1923

They can because they think they can.
Virgil (70–19 BC) Roman poet *Aeneid*

I am an optimist. But I am an optimist who takes his raincoat
Harold Wilson (1916–) English Labour statesman

✤ ✤ ✤ ✤ **LUCK** ✤ ✤ ✤ ✤

I never knew an early-rising, hard-working, prudent man, careful of his earnings, and strictly honest, who complained of bad luck.
Joseph Addison (1672–1719) English essayist and politician

Of course I don't believe in it (referring to a lucky charm). But I understand that it brings you luck whether you believe in it or not.
Niels Bohr (1885–1962) Danish physicist *Attributed*

I'm a great believer in luck, and I find the harder I work the more I have of it.
Thomas Jefferson (1743–1826) 3rd American President

Fortune is a woman, and therefore friendly to the young, who command her with audacity.
Niccolò Machiavelli (1469–1527) Italian statesman *Principal*

✤ ✤ ✤ ✤ **HOPE** ✤ ✤ ✤ ✤

Pray with me,
Luck sway the scale.
Aeschylus (525–c.456 BC) Greek playwright *Agamemnon*

Hope is a good breakfast, but it is a bad supper.
Francis Bacon (1561–1626) English philosopher and statesman

It is not necessary to hope in order to undertake, nor to succeed in order to persevere.
Charles the Bold (1433–77) Duke of Burgundy

Hope for the best, but prepare for the worst.
Proverb

✤ **WORRY AND FEAR** ✤

There are two days about which nobody should every worry, and these are yesterday and today.
Robert Jones Burdette (1844–1914) American humorist

When I look back on all these worries I remember the story of the old man who said on his deathbed that he had had a lot of trouble in his life, most of which had never happened.
Sir Winston Churchill (1874–1965) English statesman *Their Finest Hour Vol. II*

As a cure for worrying, work is better than whisky.
Thomas Alva Edison (1845–1931) American inventor and physicist

You're only here for a short visit. Don't hurry. Don't worry. And be sure to smell the flowers along the way.
Walter C. Hagen (1892–1969) American professional golfer *The Walter Hagen Story*

There is no terror in a bang – only in the anticipation of it.
Alfred Hitchcock (1899–1980) English film maker *The Filmgoer's Companion*

Worry is interest paid on trouble before it falls due.
William R. Inge (1860–1954) English prelate and theologian

We should not let our fears hold us back from pursuing our hopes.
John F. Kennedy (1917–63) 35th American President

Courage is not the absence of fear, but the conquest of it.
E. C. McKenzie American writer and compiler

Courage is doing what you're afraid to do. There can be no courage unless you're scared.
Eddie Rickenbacker (1890–1973) American World War I fighter pilot *New York Times* 1963

Our doubts are traitors,
And make us lose the good we oft might win,
By fearing to attempt.
William Shakespeare (1564–1616) English playwright and poet

❖ SUCCESS AND HOW ❖ TO ACHIEVE IT

He that would make sure of success should keep his passion cool, and his expectation low.
Jeremy Collier (1650–1726) English clergyman

The secret of success is constancy to purpose.
Benjamin Disraeli (1804–81) British statesman and novelist

If a man write a better book, preach a better sermon, or make a better mouse-trap than his neighbour, tho' he build his house in the woods, the world will make a beaten path to his door.
Ralph Waldo Emerson (1803–82) American poet and essayist

Don't aim for success if you want it; just do what you love and believe in, and it will come naturally.
D. Frost quoted in *Reader's Digest*

My formula for success? Rise early, work late, strike oil.
John Paul Getty (1892–1976) American oil magnate

Do your work with your whole heart and you will succeed – there is so little competition.
Elbert Hubbard (1856–1915) American author *The Note Book*

There's no secret about success.
Did you ever know a successful
man that didn't tell you about it.
  Kin Hubbard (1868–1930)
American humorist

The quality of a person's life is in
direct proportion to their
commitment to excellence,
regardless of their chosen field of
endeavour.
  Vince Lombardi (1913–70)
American football coach

Half the things that people do not
succeed in, are through the fear of
making the attempt.
  James Northcote (1746–1831)
English painter

Commit to the Lord whatever you
do, and your plans will succeed.
  Proverbs 16:3

The only place where success
comes before work is in a
dictionary.
  Vidal Sassoon (1928–) British
hairstylist

I cannot give you the formula for
success, but I can give you the
formula for failure – which is: Try
to please everybody.
  Herbert Bayard Swope (1882–
1958) American newspaper editor

All you need in this life is
ignorance and confidence, and
then success is sure.
  Mark Twain (1835–1910)
American writer

❋ TAKING THE PLUNGE ❋

Don't stare up the steps – step up
the stairs.
  Anon

One should try everything once,
except incest and folk-dancing.
  Arnold Bax (1883–1953) English
composer

Be always sure you're right – then
go ahead!
  David Crockett (1786–1836)
American soldier *Autobiography*

The distance doesn't matter; it is
only the first step that is difficult.
  Marquise du Deffand (1697–
1780) French salon hostess

A journey of a thousand mile must
begin with a single step.
  Lao-tze (Sixth century BC) Chinese
philosopher and sage *Tao Te Ching*

Well begun is half done.
  Proverb

You never know till you have tried.
  Proverb

❋ ❋ AIMING HIGH ❋ ❋

No bird soars too high if he soars
with his own wings.
  William Blake (1757–1827)
English poet and artist *Proverbs of
Hell*

Large streams from little fountains
 flow,
Tall oaks from little acorns grow.
David Everett (1770–1813)
English author *Lines written for a
School Declamation*

Don't be afraid to take a big step if
one is indicated; you can't cross a
chasm in two small jumps.
David Lloyd George (1863–1945)
Welsh Liberal statesman

Aim at the sun, and you may not
reach it; but your arrow will fly far
higher than if you aimed at an
object on a level with yourself.
Judy Hawes (1913–) American
children's writer

If you would hit the mark, you
must aim a little above it.
Henry Wadsworth Longfellow
(1807–82) American poet

The road is hard to climb, but glory
gives me strength.
Sextus Propertius (c.48–c.15 BC)
Roman poet *Elegies*

They built too low who build
beneath the skies.
Edward Young (1683–1765)
English poet

❋ ❋ ❋ NEW JOB ❋ ❋ ❋

A smart coat is a good letter of
introduction.
Anon

Vocation: Defined as any badly
paid job which someone has taken
out of choice.
Mike Barfield (1962–) *Dictionary
For Our Time – 'The Oldie'*

I am a young executive.
No cuffs than mine are cleaner;
I have a Slimline brief-case
and I use the firm's Cortina.
John Betjeman (1906–84) British
poet

Interview; How to and what to:
Arrive nice and clean, be friendly
but not too familiar, speak clearly
(and in the right language). Be
decisive, answer clearly and
concisely, if you don't know . . . say
so. Try to enjoy the interview, leave
the interview with a good
impression ('Whom do I make the
cheque out to?').
Simon Bond English cartoonist
Success And How To Be One

O let us love our occupations,
Bless the squire and his relations,
Live upon our daily rations,
And always know our proper
 stations.
Charles Dickens (1812–70)
English novelist *The Chimes*

All work and no play makes Jack a
 dull boy,
All play and no work makes Jack a
 mere toy.
Maria Edgeworth (1767–1849)
Irish novelist

Plough deep while sluggards sleep.
  Benjamin Franklin (1706–90)
American statesman

About the only job left that a
woman can beat a man in is female
impersonator in vaudeville.
  O. Henry (1862–1910) American
writer *The Hand that Rules the World*

Yonder see the morning blink:
  The sun is up, and up must I,
To wash and dress and eat and
    drink
And look at things and talk and
    think
  And work, and God knows why.
  Alfred E. Houseman (1859–1936)
English poet and scholar *XI Last
Poems*

For the labourer is worthy of his
hire.
  Mark 10:7

Be nice to people on your way up
because you'll meet 'em on your
way down.
  Wilson Mizner (1876–1933)
American humorist

Never turn down a job because you
think it's too small, you don't
know where it can lead.
  Julia Morgan (1872–1957)
American architect

Work expands so as to fill the time
available for its completion.
  Cyril Northcote Parkinson
(1909–)

Lazy hands make a man poor, but
diligent hands bring wealth.
  Proverbs 10:4

The closest to perfection a person
ever comes is when he fills out a
job application form.
  Stanley J. Randall from
Quotations for our Time

Climbing is performed in the same
posture as creeping.
  Jonathan Swift (1667–1745)
Anglo-Irish poet and satirist

Nobody likes hard work more than
the person who pays for it.
  The Houghton Line quoted in
Reader's Digest

Employees make the best dates.
You don't have to pick them up
and they're always tax deductible.
  Andy Warhol (1926–87) American
pop artist and film maker

The best careers advice to give to
the young is 'Find out what you
like doing best and get someone to
pay you for doing it.'
  Katharine Whitehorn (1926–)
British columnist *The Observer*, 1975

Whatever women do they must do twice as well as men to be thought half as good. Luckily, this is not difficult.

Charlotte Whitton quoted in *The Book of Insults*

MAJOR
❖ ❖ CHALLENGE ❖ ❖

Pure and ready to mount the stars.
Dante Alighieri (1265–1321)
Italian poet

For England, home, and beauty.
Samuel J. Arnold (1774–1852)
English dramatist *The Death of Nelson*

He most prevails who nobly dares.
Rev. William Broome (1689–1745)
English scholar *Courage in Love*

The humblest citizen of all the land, when clad in the armour of a righteous cause, is stronger than all the hosts of Error.

William J. Bryan (1860–1925)
American statesman *Speech at the National Democratic Convention, Chicago*, 10 July 1896

You cannot choose your battlefield,
The gods do that for you,
But you can plant a standard
Where a standard never flew.
Nathalia Crane (1913–)
American poet *The Colors*

A desperate disease requires a dangerous remedy.
Guy Fawkes (1570–1606) English conspirator

Adversity is the state in which a man most easily becomes acquainted with himself, being especially free from admirers then.
Dr Samuel Johnson (1709–84)
English writer and critic

Either I will find a way, or I will make one.
Sir Philip Sidney (1554–86)
English soldier and poet

If you will observe, it doesn't take
A man of giant mould to make
A giant shadow on the wall;
And he who in our daily sight
Seems but a figure mean and small,
Outlined in Fame's illusive light,
May stalk, a silhouette sublime,
Across the canvas of time.
J. T. Trowbridge (1827–1916)
American author

EDUCATION
❖ ❖ ❖ AND ❖ ❖ ❖
STUDY

Natural abilities are like natural plants; they need pruning by study.
Francis Bacon (1561–1626)
English philosopher and statesman

There is a great deal of difference between the eager man who wants to read a book, and the tired man who wants a book to read.

Gilbert K. Chesterton (1874–1936) English critic and novelist *Charles Dickens*

Genius is one per cent inspiration and ninety-nine per cent perspiration.

Thomas Alva Edison (1845–1931) American inventor and physicist *Quoted in Life* 1932

If a man empties his purse into his hand, no one can take it away from him. An investment in knowledge always pays the best interest.

Benjamin Franklin (1706–90) American statesman

It is the greatest nuisance that knowledge can be acquired only by hard work.

William Somerset Maugham (1874–1965) British writer

In cheerfulness is the success of our studies.

Pliny the Elder (23–79) Roman naturalist

The noblest exercise of the mind within doors, and most befitting a person of quality, is study.

William Ramsay

What we want is to see the child in pursuit of knowledge, and not knowledge in pursuit of the child.

George Bernard Shaw (1856–1950) Irish dramatist

❧ ❧ ❧ EXAMS ❧ ❧ ❧

Write down the thoughts of the moment. Those that come unsought for are commonly the most valuable.

Francis Bacon (1561–1626) English philosopher and statesman

Try to know everything of something, and something of everything.

Henry Peter, Lord Brougham (1779–1868) Scottish jurist and politician

There is no such word as 'fail'.

Edward Bulwer-Lytton (1803–73) English novelist, playwright and politician *Richelieu*

Examinations are formidable even to the best prepared, for the greatest fool may ask more than the wisest man can answer.

Charles Caleb Colton (1780–1832) English clergyman and writer *Lacon*

It is nonsense to say there is not enough time to be fully informed . . . Time given to thought is the greatest time-saver of all.

Norman Cousins (1915–) American professor of medicine

The significance of a man is not in what he attains, but rather in what he longs to attain.
Kahlil Gibran (1883–1931) American writer and artist

Examinations – Nature's laxative.
Graffiti: City of London Polytechnic

Do not on any account attempt to write on both sides of the paper at once.
W. C. Sellar (1898–1951) and **R.J. Yeatman** (1897–1968) *1066 And All That*

✿ ✿

CHAPTER FIFTEEN

SUCCESS AND HAPPINESS

❖ ❖ ❖ HUMOROUS ❖ ❖ ❖

The penalty of success is to be bored by people who used to snub you.
Nancy Astor (1879–1964) British politician *Sunday Express*, 12 January 1956

Back of every achievement is a proud wife and a surprised mother-in-law.
Brooks Hays (1898–) American congressman and writer

We never eat anybody's health, always drink it. Why should we not stand up now and then eat a tart to somebody's success?
Jerome K. Jerome (1859–1927) English humorous writer, novelist and playwright

If one mhides one's talent under a bushel one must be careful to point out to everyone the exact bushel under which it is hidden.
Saki (H. H. Munro) (1870–1916) British novelist and short-story writer

The usual drawback to success is that it annoys one's friends so.
P. G. Wodehouse (1881–1975) English novelist *The Man Upstairs*

❖ ❖ ACHIEVEMENT ❖ ❖ (ACKNOWLEDGEMENT OF)

A work of real merit finds favour at last.
Amos Bronson Alcott (1799–1888) American teacher

The toughest thing about success is that you've got to keep on being a success.
Irving Berlin (1888–1989) American composer

Look Ma! Top of the world.
James Cagney (1899–1986) American film actor *Film: White Heat*

Almost everything that is great has been done by youth.
Benjamin Disraeli (1804–81) British statesman and novelist *Coningsby*

Mediocrity knows nothing higher than itself, but talent instantly recognizes genius.
Sir Arthur Conan Doyle (1856–1930) Scottish writer

The reward of a thing well done is to have done it.
Ralph Waldo Emerson (1803–82) American poet and essayist *Essays, New England Reformers*

See the conquering hero comes!
Sound the trumpets, beat the
drums!
Dr Thomas Morell (1703–84)
English classical scholar *Libretto of
Handel's 'Joshua'*

Sound, sound the clarion, fill the
fife!
To all the sensual world proclaim,
One crowded hour of glorious life
Is worth an age without a name.
Sir Walter Scott (1771–1832)
Scottish novelist and poet *Old
Mortality*

Anyone can sympathize with the
sufferings of a friend, but it
requires a fine nature to
sympathize with a friend's success.
Oscar Wilde (1854–1900) Irish
playwright, novelist and wit

GOOD
❄ ❄ ❄ FORTUNE ❄ ❄ ❄

Every dog has his day.
Miguel de Cervantes (1547–1616)
Spanish novelist *Don Quixote*

Whenever you see a successful
business, someone once made a
courageous decision.
Peter Drucker (1909–) American
management consultant

All is well that ends well.
John Heywood (1497–c.1580)
English playwright and musician

Don't keep it quiet, but share it,
And pass it round about –
Good news is always welcome
So say it – with a shout!
Anne Kreer: *quoted in Francis
Gay's Friendship Book 1994*

A cheerful look brings joy to the
heart, and good news gives health
to the bones.
Proverbs 15:32

Money can't buy friends, but you
can get a better class of enemy.
Spike Milligan (1918–) British
comedian

I seen my opportunities and I took
'em
George Washington Plunkitt
(1842–1924) *Definition of 'honest
graft'.*

It takes greater character to handle
good fortune than bad.
**François, Duc de la
Rochefoucauld** (1613–80) French
writer *Maxims*

There is a tide in the affairs of men,
Which, taken at the flood, leads on
to fortune.
William Shakespeare (1564–1616)
English playwright and poet *Julius
Caesar*

Be not afraid of greatness: some
men are born great, some achieve
greatness and some have greatness
thrust upon them.
William Shakespeare *Twelfth
Night*

❀ ❀ PERSEVERANCE ❀ ❀

All rising to Great Place is by a winding stair.
Francis Bacon (1561–1626) English philosopher and statesman

Consider the postage stamp; its usefulness consists in the ability to stick to one thing till it gets there.
Josh Billings (1818–85) American humorist

To finish is both a relief and a release from an extraordinarily pleasant prison.
Robert Burchfield (1923–) English scholar and lexicographer *On completing the supplements to the Oxford English Dictionary*

Good luck often has the odour of perspiration about it.
E. C. McKenzie American writer and compiler

So far, so good.
Proverb

I have learned that success is to be measured not so much by the position that one has reached in life as by the obstacles which one has overcome while trying to succeed.
Booker T. Washington (1856–1915) American black reformer *Up from Slavery*

❀ ❀ THE GOOD LIFE ❀ ❀

Every man's life is a fairy tale written by God's fingers.
Hans Christian Andersen (1805–75) Danish author

All this and heaven too.
Matthew Henry (1662–1714) English clergyman and writer *Attributed*

Sweet Smell of Success.
Earnest Lehman (1920–) *Title of a Novel and Film*

Too much of a good thing is simply wonderful.
Liberace (1919–87) American entertainer

You can always tell luck from ability by its duration.
E. C. McKenzie

❀ CONGRATULATIONS ❀ (BEGRUDGED)

Even a stopped clock is right twice a day.
Anon

In defeat unbeatable; in victory unbearable.
Sir Winston Churchill (1874–1965) English statesman

A fool must now and then be right by chance.
William Cowper (1731–1800) English poet

He has not a single redeeming defect.
  Benjamin Disraeli (1804–81) British statesman and novelist

Wonders will never cease.
  Henry Dudley (1745–1824) Clergyman and journalist *Letter to Garrick* 13 September 1776

To the victor belong the spoils of the enemy.
  William Marcy (1786–1857) American statesman *Speech*, 1832

A man is tested by the praise he receives.
  Proverbs 27:21

We can't all be heroes because someone has to sit on the curb and clap as they go by.
  Will Rogers (1879–1935) American humorist-philosopher

Whenever a friend succeeds a little something in me dies.
  Gore Vidal (1925–) American novelist

CHAPTER SIXTEEN

THANKS AND FOND REGARDS

❁ ❁ GRATITUDE ❁ ❁

Modern science is still unable to produce a better tranquillizer than a few kind words.
Anon

What soon grows old? Gratitude.
Aristotle (384–322 BC) Greek philosopher and scientist

They say late thanks are ever best.
Francis Bacon (1561–1626) English philosopher and statesman *Letter to Robert, Lord Cecil*

Blessed is he who expects no gratitude, for he shall not be disappointed.
W. C. Bennett (1820–95) English songwriter

I don't deserve this, but then, I have arthritis and I don't deserve that either.
Jack Benny (1894–1974) American comedian

Little deeds of kindness, little words of love,

Help to make earth happy, like the heaven above.
Julia Carney (1823–1908) American teacher *Little Things*

No metaphysician ever felt the deficiency of language so much as the grateful.
Charles Caleb Colton (1780–1832) English clergyman and writer

When I had money, money, O!
  My many friends proved all untrue;
But now I have no money, O!
  My friends are real, though very few.
William H. Davies (1871–1940) Welsh poet *Money*

Wise sayings often fall on barren ground; but a kind word is never thrown away.
Arthur Helps (1813–75) English historian

The heart of the giver makes the gift dear and precious.
Martin Luther (1483–1546) German Protestant reformer

You can always tell a real friend: when you've made a fool of yourself he doesn't feel you've done a permanent job.
Laurence J. Peter (1918–) Canadian writer

For this relief much thanks.
William Shakespeare *Hamlet*

Beggar that I am, I am even poor in thanks.

William Shakespeare (1564–1616) English playwright and poet *Hamlet*

FRIENDSHIP

Among those whom I like or admire, I can find no common denominator, but among those I love, I can: all of them make me laugh.

Wystan Hugh Auden (1907–73) Anglo-American poet and essayist

The greatest trust, between man and man, is the trust of giving counsel.

Francis Bacon (1561–1626) English philosopher and statesman *Essays of Counsel*

The principal fruit of friendship, is the ease and discharge of the fulness and swellings of the heart.

Francis Bacon *Essays of Friendship*

Love is like the wild rose-briar;
Friendship like the holly-tree.
The holly is dark when the rose-
   briar blooms,
But which will bloom most
   constantly.

Emily Brontë (1818–48) English novelist and poet

The light of friendship is like the light of phosphorus, even plainest when all around is dark.

Grace Crowell (1877–1969) American poet

A faithful friend is the medicine of life.

Ecclesiasticus 6:16

A Friend may well be reckoned the masterpiece of Nature.

Ralph Waldo Emerson (1803–82) American poet and essayist *Friendship*

The only reward of virtue is virtue; the only way to have a friend is to be one.

Ralph Waldo Emerson *Friendship*

Of all the things which provides to make life entirely happy, much the greatest is the possession of friendship.

Epicurus (341–270 BC) Greek philosopher

Some paint lovely pictures,
   Others write good books,
Some make peaceful gardens,
   Others are fine cooks.
But the talent that endureth,
   That matters in the end,
Is the tenderness and caring
   That makes a faithful friend.

Jean Harris: quoted in *Francis Gay's Friendship Book* 1994

The longer we live, and the more we think, the higher value we learn to put on the friendship and tenderness of parents and of friends. Parents we can have but once; and he promises himself too much, who enters life with the expectation of finding many friends.

Dr Samuel Johnson (1709–84) English writer and critic *Boswell's Life of Johnson*

A true friend is one who sticks by you even when he gets to know you real well.

E. C. McKenzie American writer and compiler

A friend in need is a friend indeed.
Plautus (c.250–184 BC) Roman comic writer *Epidicus*

But if the while I think on thee,
  dear friend,
All losses are restored, and sorrows
  end.
William Shakespeare (1564–1616) English playwright and poet *Sonnet 30*

I am wealthy in my friends.
William Shakespeare *Timon of Athens*

❁ ❁ HOSPITALITY ❁ ❁

Sweet courtesy has done its most
If you have made each guest forget
That he himself is not the host.
Thomas Bailey *Aldrich Hospitality*

The longest day is in June, they
  say,
  The shortest in December.
They did not come to me that
  way;
  The shortest I remember –
You came a day with me to stay,
  And filled my heart with
    laughter;
The longest day – you were away –
  The very next day after.
George Birdseye: quoted in *Francis Gay's Friendship Book* 1994

Welcome as kindly showers to the long parched earth.
John Dryden (1631–1700) English poet

'I feel a very unusual sensation,' said Mr St Barbe, after dining. 'If it's not indigestion, I think it must be gratitude.'
Benjamin Disraeli (1804–81) British statesman and novelist

Happy is the house that shelters a friend!
Ralph Waldo Emerson (1803–82) American poet and essayist *Friendship*

There is an emanation from the heart in genuine hospitality which cannot be described but is immediately felt, and puts the stranger at once at his ease.
Washington Irving (1783–1859) American man of letters

We may live without poetry,
    music, and art;
We may live without conscience,
    and live without heart;
We may live without friends; we
    may live without books;
But civilized man cannot live
    without cooks.
Edward, Lord Lytton (1831–91)
English poet and statesman

I've had a wonderful evening, but
this wasn't it.
Groucho Marx (1895–1977)
American comedian

Small cheer and great welcome
makes a merry feast.
William Shakespeare (1564–1616)
English playwright and poet *The
Comedy of Errors*

❋ ❋ COMPLIMENTS ❋ ❋

Admiration, *n*: Our polite
recognition of another's
resemblance to ourselves.
Ambrose Bierce (1842–1914)
American journalist *The Enlarged
Devil's Dictionary*

If a good face is a letter of
recommendation, a good heart is a
letter of credit.
Edward Bulwer-Lytton (1803–73)
English novelist, playwright and
politician *What Will He Do With It*

A man does not have to be an
angel in order to be a saint.
Albert Schweitzer (1875–1965)
Alsatian medical missionary

Of this blest man, let his just praise
    be given,
Heaven was in him, before he was
    in heaven.
Izaak Walton (1593–1683) English
writer *Referring to Dr Richard Sibbes*

❋ ❋ GENEROSITY ❋ ❋

Happiness is the one thing we can
give without having.
Anon

A man there was, and they called
    him mad;
The more he gave, the more he
    had.
John Bunyan (1628–88) English
writer and preacher

To the generous mind the heaviest
debt is that of gratitude, when it is
not in our power to repay it.
Benjamin Franklin (1706–90)
American statesman

It's better to give than to lend, and
it costs about the same.
Philip Gibbs (1877–1962) British
author and journalist

Once in a century a man may be
ruined or made insufferable by

praise. But surely once in a minute
something generous dies for want
of it.

John Masefield (1878–1967)
English poet and novelist

If there be any truer measure of a
man than by what he does, it must
be by what he gives.

Robert South (1634–1716) English
High Church theologian and
preacher

CHAPTER SEVENTEEN

MISFORTUNE

❋ ❋ HUMOROUS ❋ ❋

Calamity, *n*: A more than commonly plain and unmistakable reminder that the affairs of this life are not of our own ordering. Calamities are of two kinds: misfortune to ourselves, and good fortune to others.
Ambrose Bierce (1842–1914) American journalist *The Enlarged Devil's Dictionary*

Misfortune, *n*: The kind of fortune that never misses.
Ambrose Bierce *The Devil's Dictionary*

The rain it raineth on the just
 And also on the unjust fella:
But chiefly on the just, because
 The unjust steals the just's umbrella.
Charles S. C. Bowen (1835–94) English judge *Sichel, Sands of Time*

If there were any justice in this world, people would occasionally be permitted to fly over pigeons.
Gene Brown quoted in *Reader's Digest*

The speed at which boiling milk rises from the bottom of the pan to any point beyond the top is greater than the speed at which the human brain and hand can combine to snatch the confounded thing off.
H. F. Ellis (1907–) English writer and humorist

If at first you don't succeed, try, try again. Then quit. No use being a damn fool about it.
W. C. Fields (1879–1946) American comedian

The Lord said to Moses, come forth – but he came fifth and got a rubber duck.
Graffiti: Leicester

When I hear somebody sigh, 'Life is hard,' I am always tempted to ask, 'Compared to what?'
Sydney J. Harris (1903–76) American journalist

The right to be heard does not include the right to be taken seriously.
Hubert Humphrey (1911–78) American politician

Cheer up! The worst is yet to come!
Philander Johnson (1866–1939) American journalist

You don't seem to realize that a poor person who is unhappy is in a better position than a rich person who is unhappy. Because the poor person has hope. He thinks money would help.

Jean Kerr (1923–) American playwright

There cannot be a crisis next week. My schedule is already full.

Henry Alfred Kissinger (1923–) American politician

Everything is funny as long as it happens to someone else.

Will Rogers (1879–1935) American humorist-philosopher

When angry, count four; when very angry, swear.

Mark Twain (1835–1910) American writer *Pudd'nhead Wilson's Calendar*

❈ ❈ PHILOSOPHICAL ❈ ❈ THOUGHTS

Even God cannot change the past.

Agathon (446–401 BC) Athenian tragic poet

The best thing one can do when it's raining is to let it rain.

Anon

He that is down need fear no fall.

John Bunyan (1628–88) English writer and preacher

Sorrows are our best educators. A man can see further through a tear than a telescope.

Grief should be the instructor of the wise: sorrow is knowledge; they who know the most must mourn the deepest o'er the fatal truth, – the tree of knowledge is not that of life.

George Gordon, Lord Byron (1788–1824) English poet

One sees great things from the valley; only small things from the peak.

G. K. Chesterton (1874–1936) English critic and novelist *The Hammer of God*

For everything you have missed, you have gained something else.

Ralph Waldo Emerson (1803–82) American poet and essayist *Compensation*

Golf without bunkers and hazards would be lame and monotonous. So would life.

B. C. Forbes (1880–1954) American author

We could never learn to be brave and patient, if there were only joy in the world.

Helen Keller (1880–1968) American writer

If you're going to be able to look back on something and laugh about it, you might as well laugh about it now.

Marie Osmond (1959–) American pop singer quoted in *Reader's Digest*

The only way to be absolutely safe is never to try anything for the first time.

Magnus Pyke (1908–) English scientist and TV personality

It's possible to own too much. A man with one watch knows what time it is; a man with two watches is never quite sure.

Lee Segall from *Quotations for our Time*

The truly poor man is not he who has little but he wishes for more.

Lucius Annaeus Seneca (c.55 BC–c. AD 40) Roman rhetorician

Maybe one day we shall be glad to remember even these things.

Virgil (70–19 BC) Roman poet

Individual misfortunes give rise to the general good; so that the more individual misfortunes exist, the more all is fine.

Voltaire (1694–1778) French author

❋ ENCOURAGEMENT ❋

When we are flat on our backs there is no way to look but up.

Roger W. Babson (1875–1967) American statistician and economist

A stout man's heart breaks bad luck.

Miguel de Cervantes (1547–1616) Spanish novelist *Don Quixote*

What's lost upon the roundabouts
We pulls up on the swings!

Patrick Reginald Chalmers (1872–1942) *Green Days And Blue Days – Roundabouts And Swings*

For, when all joy seemed well-nigh fled,
God gave the gift of hope instead,
A precious, kindly, living spark,
That pierces every kind of dark.

Margaret Dixon: quoted in *Francis Gay's Friendship Book* 1994

My centre is giving way, my right is retreating. Situation excellent. I shall attack.

Ferdinand Foch (1851–1929) French soldier and marshal of France *Message to Joffre*

It matters not how strait the gate,
How charged with punishments the scroll;
I am the master of my fate:
I am the captain of my soul.

William Ernest Henley (1849–1903) English poet and playwright

It is worth a thousand pounds a year to have the habit of looking on the bright side of things.

Dr Samuel Johnson (1709–84) English writer and critic

Don't despair, not even over the fact that you don't despair.

Franz Kafka (1883–1924) Austrian novelist

Although the world is very full of suffering, it is also full of the overcoming of it.
Helen Keller (1880–1968) American writer

Don't give up the ship.
Commander James Lawrence (1781–1813) Naval Commander *Order quoted in The Story of the United States Navy*

Being a man, ne'er ask the gods for life set free from grief, but ask for courage that endureth long.
Menander (c.341–291 BC) Greek poet *Fragments No. 549*

After all, tomorrow is another day.
Margaret Mitchell (1900–49) American novelist *closing words of Gone With The Wind, 1936*

What fails to kill me makes me only stronger.
Friedrich Nietzsche (1844–1900) German philosopher, scholar and writer *Hitler youth slogan*

Pain means Progress.
Arnold Schwarzenegger (1947–) American actor

Once more unto the breach, dear friends, once more . . .
William Shakespeare (1564–1616) English playwright and poet *Henry V*

If winter comes, can spring be far behind?
Percy Bysshe Shelley (1792–1822) English poet *Ode to the West Wind*

Oh yet we trust that somehow good will be the final goal of ill.
Alfred, Lord Tennyson (1809–92) English poet

Fortune helps the brave.
Terence (195–159 BC) Roman dramatist *Phormio*

❋ ❋ ❋ ADVICE ❋ ❋ ❋

Patience, and shuffle the cards.
Miguel de Cervantes (1547–1616) Spanish novelist *Don Quixote*

Swear not at all, for, for thy curse Thine enemy is none the worse.
Arthur Hugh Clough (1819–61) English poet

In trouble to be troubl'd Is to have your trouble doubl'd
Daniel Defoe (1660–1731) English author and adventurer *Robinson Crusoe, The Farther Adventures*

Don't get mad, get even.
Everett Dirksen (1896–1969) American senator

Smile first thing in the morning. Get it over with.
W. C. Fields (1879–1946) American comedian

It is a good thing to follow the first law of holes; if you are in one, stop digging.
Dennis Healey (1917–) English Labour politician

While we're talking, time will have meanly run on: pick today's fruits, not relying on the future in the slightest.

Horace (65–8 BC) Roman poet and satirist

Regret is an appalling waste of energy; you can't build on it; it's only good for wallowing in.

Katherine Mansfield (1888–1923) Short-story writer

Peace of mind is much better than giving them a piece of your mind.

J. P. McEvoy (1895–1958) American writer

Better by far you should forget and smile
Than that you should remember and be sad.

Christina Rossetti (1830–94) English poet

Things without all remedy
Should be without regard: what's done, is done.

William Shakespeare (1564–1616) English playwright and poet *Macbeth*

And, above all things, never think that you're not good enough yourself. A man should never think that. My belief is that in life people will take you very much at your own reckoning.

Anthony Trollope (1815–82) English novelist *The Small House At Allington*

❋
❋ SYMPATHY ❋
❋

There is no greater sorrow than to recall a time of happiness
in sorrow.

Dante Alighieri (1265–1321) Italian poet

If there were no clouds, we should not enjoy the sun.

Anon

Life certainly is a warfare for all of us.

Marceline Desbordes-Valmore (1786–1859) French actress and poet

Time is the great physician.

Benjamin Disraeli (1804–81) British statesman and novelist

There is no chance that does not return.

French proverb

Full many a gem of purest ray serene
The dark unfathom'd caves of ocean bear:
Full many a flower is born to blush unseen,
And waste its sweetness on the desert air.

Thomas Gray (1716–71) English poet *Elegy written in a Country Church-Yard*

God not only plays dice. He also sometimes throws them where they cannot be seen.
Stephen W. Hawking (1942–) British scientist

I wish you serendipity,
  A little magic in your life,
And gentle, calm serenity,
  To combat stress and strife.
I wish you sweet tranquillity,
  Along your future way,
And love to grow abundantly,
  To fill your world each day.
Iris Hesselden: quoted in *Francis Gay's Friendship Book* 1994

The critic is often an unsuccessful author, almost always an inferior one.
Leigh Hunt (1784–1859) English poet and writer

Know how sublime a thing it is to suffer and be strong.
Henry Wadsworth Longfellow (1807–82) American poet

Into each life some rain must fall.
Henry Wadsworth Longfellow *The Rainy Day*

Earth hath no sorrow that heaven cannot heal.
Thomas Moore (1779–1852) Irish poet

The nature of bad news infects the teller.
William Shakespeare (1564–1616) English playwright and poet *Antony and Cleopatra*

When sorrows come, they come
  not single spies,
But in battalions!
William Shakespeare *Hamlet*

I never wonder to see men wicked, but I often wonder to see them not ashamed.
Jonathan Swift (1667–1745) Anglo-Irish poet and satirist

❀ ❀ ❀ OPTIMISM ❀ ❀ ❀

The frailest hope is better than despair.
Maria Brooks (1795–1845) American poet

Hope, like the gleaming taper's
  light,
  Adorns and cheers our way;
And still, as darker grows the
  night,
  Emits a brighter ray.
Oliver Goldsmith (1728–74) Irish playwright, novelist and poet *The Captivity*

Every cloud has a silver lining.
Proverb

Things at the worst will cease, or else climb upward to what they were before.
William Shakespeare (1564–1616) English playwright and poet *Macbeth*

While there's life, there's hope.
Terence (195–159 BC) Roman dramatist *Heauton Timoroumenos*

'Tis easy enough to be pleasant,
When life flows along like a song;
But the man worth while is the one who will smile
When everything goes dead wrong.
Ella Wilcox (1855–1919) American journalist and poet

❋ SET–BACK ❋

To fall is neither dangerous nor disgraceful, but to remain prostrate is both.
Konrad Adenauer (1876–1967) German statesman

If at first you don't succeed you're running about average.
Margaret H. Alderson (1959–) journalist

There are always ten better things to do than to give up.
Anon

It is the little bits of things that fret and worry us;
we can dodge an elephant, but we can't dodge a fly.
Josh Billings (1818–85) American humorist

The maxim of the British people is 'Business as usual'.
Sir Winston Churchill (1874–1965) English statesman

Our greatest glory is not in never falling, but in rising every time we fall.
Confucius (551–479 BC) Chinese philosopher

A stumble may prevent a fall.
English proverb

If way to the Better there be, it exacts a full look at the worst.
Thomas Hardy (1840–1928) English novelist, poet and dramatist *De Profundis*

'Tis a lesson you should heed,
    Try, try again.
If at first you don't succeed,
    Try, try again.
William Edward Hickson (1803–70) Nonconformist preacher *Try and Try Again*

He knows not his own strength that hath not met adversity.
Ben Jonson (c.1572–1637) English dramatist

Half a calamity is better than a whole one.
T. E. Lawrence 'of Arabia' (1888–1935) Anglo-Irish soldier and Arabist

---

❈ DISAPPOINTMENTS ❈

It is not only fine feathers that make fine birds.

Aesop (c.550 BC) Greek fabulist

If you would know what the Lord God thinks of money, you only have to look at those to whom he gives it.

Maurice Baring (1874–1945) English journalist and author

I quickly laugh at everything, for fear of having to cry.

Pierre-Augustin de Beaumarchais (1732–99) French playwright *Le Barbier de Seville*

If it was raining soup, we'd be out with forks.

Brendan Behan (1923–64) Irish author

If of all words of tongue and pen,
The saddest are, 'It might have
  been',
More sad are these we daily see:
'It is, but hadn't ought to be'.

Francis Brett Harte (1836–1902) American author *Mrs Judge Jenkins*

Disappointments should be cremated, not embalmed.

Henry S. Haskins American writer *Meditations in Wall Street*

Little is the luck I've had,
  And Oh, 'tis comfort small

To think that many another lad
  Has had no luck at all.

A. E. Housman (1859–1936) English scholar and poet *Last Poems*

Were it not better to forget
Than but remember and regret?

Letitia Elizabeth Landon (1802–38) English poet and author *Despondency*

How disappointment tracks the steps of hope.

Letitia Elizabeth Landon

There's no point dwelling on what might or could have been. You just have to go forward.

Jack Nicholson (1937–) American film actor

These are the times that try men's souls.

Thomas Paine (1737–1809) American revolutionary philosopher and writer

Disappointment is often the salt of life.

Theodore Parker (1810–60) American Unitarian clergyman

Wisdom comes by disillusionment.

George Santayana (1863–1952) Spanish philosopher, poet and novelist *Reason in Common Sense*

For all sad words of tongue or pen,
The saddest are these: 'It might
  have been!'

John Greenleaf Whittier (1807–92) American Quaker and poet

❀ ❀ ERRORS AND ❀ ❀ MISTAKES

Forget your mistakes but not what caused them.
Anon

I would rather be first in a small village in Gaul than second-in-command in Rome.
Julius Caesar (c.100–44 BC) Roman general and statesman

There is something good in all weathers. If it doesn't happen to be good for my work today, it's good for some other man's today, and will come round for me tomorrow.
Charles Dickens (1812–70) English author

Some of the best lessons we ever learn we learn from our mistakes and failures. The error of the past is the wisdom and success of the future.
Tyron Edwards (1809–94) American theologian

No man ever became great or good except through many and great mistakes.
William Gladstone (1809–98) Liberal statesman

It is the true nature of mankind to learn from mistakes, not from example.
Fred Hoyle (1915–) English astronomer and mathematician

Only a mediocre person is always at his best.
William Somerset Maugham (1874–1965) British writer

It has taken thirty-three years and a bang on the head to get my values right.
Stirling Moss (1929–) British racing driver

The man who makes no mistakes does not usually make anything.
Edward John Phelps (1822–1900) American lawyer and diplomat

The best may slip, and the most cautious fall:
He's more than mortal that ne'er err'd at all.
John Pomfret (1667–1702) English poet *Love Triumphant Over Reason*

Oh Lord, give me an excuse.
Leo Rosten's Treasury of Jewish Quotations

O, call back yesterday, bid time return!
William Shakespeare (1564–1616) English playwright and poet *Richard II*

A life spent making mistakes is not only more honourable but more

useful than a life spent doing
nothing.
George Bernard Shaw (1856–
1950) Irish dramatist *The Doctor's
Dilemma*

We are none of us infallible –
not even the youngest of us.
William Hepworth Thompson
(1810–86)

Experience is one thing you can't
get for nothing.
Oscar Wilde (1854–1900) Irish
playwright, novelist and wit

❀ ❀ ❀ FAILURE ❀ ❀ ❀

'Tis better to have tried and failed
than never to have tried at all.
Anon

We are all of us failures – at least
the best of us are.
J. M. Barrie (1860–1937) Scottish
novelist and dramatist

There is much to be said for failure.
It is more interesting than success.
Max Beerbohm (1872–1956)
English writer and caricaturist
Mainly On The Air

In the lexicon of youth, which fate
  reserves
For a bright manhood, there is no
  such word

as – fail! . . . Never say 'Fail' again.
Edward Bulwer-Lytton (1803–73)
English novelist, playwright and
politician

The only people who never fail are
those who never try.
Ilka Chase

Say not that she did well or ill,
  Only 'She did her best'.
Dinah Maria Craik (1826–87)
English novelist *Poems*

Sometimes a noble failure serves
the world as faithfully as a
distinguished success.
Edward Dowden (1843–1913)
Irish critic

He's no failure. He's not dead yet.
Gwilym Lloyd George
(1894–1967) Welsh politician

There is nothing more
disappointing than failing to
accomplish a thing, unless it is to
see someone else accomplish it.
Henry S. Hasking American
writer

God will not look you over for
medals, degrees or diplomas, but
for scars.
Elbert Hubbard (1856–1915)
American author *Epigrams*

There is the greatest practical
benefit in making a few failures
early in life.
Thomas Henry Huxley (1825–95)
English biologist

It is better to die on your feet than to live on your knees.
Gomez Dolores Ibarruri (la Pasionaria) (1895–1989) Spanish writer and politician *Speech*, 1936

Not failure, but low aim, is crime.
James Russell Lowell (1819–91) American poet and essayist

Far better it is to dare mighty things, to win glorious triumphs, even though checkered by failure, than to take rank with those poor spirits who neither enjoy much nor suffer much, because they live in the grey twilight that knows not victory nor defeat.
Theodore Roosevelt (1858–1919) 26th American President

It is hard to fail, but it is worse never to have tried to succeed.
Theodore Roosevelt

Our business in life is not to succeed but to continue to fail in good spirits.
Robert Louis Stevenson (1850–94) Scottish novelist and poet

It's not true that nice people finish last. Nice people are winners before the game even starts.
Addison Walker, United Feature Syndicate quoted in *Reader's Digest*

He only is exempt from failures who makes no efforts.
Richard Whately (1787–1863) English scholar and prelate

Every failure is a step to success; every detection of what is false directs us toward what is true; every trial exhausts some tempting form of error.
William Whewell (1794–1866) English scholar

We women adore failures. They lean on us.
Oscar Wilde (1854–1900) Irish playwright, novelist and wit *A Woman of No Importance*

✱ HONOURABLE ✱
DEFEAT

You are never so near victory as when defeated in a good cause.
Henry Ward Beecher (1813–87) American Congregationalist clergyman

There's nothing worth the wear of winning
  But laughter and the love of friends.
Hilaire Belloc (1870–1953) British writer and poet *Dedicatory Ode*

'Tis not what a man does which exalts him, but what man would do!
Robert Browning (1812–89) English poet *Saul*

It is better to be defeated on principle than to win on lies.
Arthur Calwell (1896–1973) Australian politician

As always, victory finds a hundred fathers, but defeat is an orphan.
Count Galeazzo Ciano (1903–44) Italian politician *Diary entry* 9 September 1942

Whom the gods wish to destroy they first call promising.
Cyril Connolly (1903–74) English author and journalist

When there is no peril in the fight, there is no glory in the triumph.
Pierre Corneille (1606–84) French dramatist

I backed the right horse, and then the wrong horse went and won.
Henry Arthur Jones (1851–1929) English dramatist *The Silver King*

There was only one occasion in my life when I put myself on a strict diet . . . and it was the most miserable afternoon I've ever spent.
Denis Norden (1922–) English scriptwriter and broadcaster

Winning isn't everything, but wanting to win is.
Arnold Palmer (1929–) American golfer

What is defeat? Nothing but education, nothing but the first step to something better.
Wendell Phillips (1811–84) American abolitionist

Even if strength fail, boldness at least will deserve praise: in great endeavours even to have had the will is enough.
Sextus Propertius (c.48–c.15 BC) Roman poet

The test of courage is to bear defeat without losing heart.
Proverb

You may have to fight a battle more than once to win it.
Margaret Thatcher (1925–) English Conservative stateswoman

I would rather lose in a cause that I know some day will triumph, than triumph in a cause that I know some day will fail.
Wendell L. Wilkie (1892–1944) American politician

 MISHAPS ❖ ❖ ❖

An unwatched pot boils immediately.
H. F. Ellis (1907–) English writer and humorist

He is so unlucky that he runs into accidents which started out to happen to somebody else.
Donald Marquis (1878–1937) American novelist, playwright and poet

It's no use crying over spilt milk, because all the forces of the universe were bent on spilling it.
William Somerset Maugham (1874–1965) British writer *Of Human Bondage*

COLD
❋ ❋ COMFORT ❋ ❋

The gods help them that help themselves.
Aesop (c.550 BC) Greek fabulist *Hercules and the Waggoner*

Happiness is good health and a bad memory.
Ingrid Bergman (1915–82) Swedish film and stage actress

You may not realize it when it happens, but a kick in the teeth may be the best thing in the world for you.
Walt Disney (1901–66) American artist and film producer

Waste not fresh tears over old griefs.
Euripides (480 or 484–406 BC) Greek dramatist

If all the people in the world should agree to sympathize with a certain man at a certain hour, they could not cure his headache.
E. W. Howe (1853–1937) American author

Life is just one damned thing after another.
Elbert Hubbard (1856–1915) American author

Even the gods love their jokes.
Plato (c.427–c.347 BC) *Cratylus* Greek philosopher

There is ways to keep off some kinds of bad luck, but this wasn't one of them.
Mark Twain (1835–1910) American writer *Huckleberry Finn*

No man can lose what he never had.
Izaak Walton (1593–1683) English writer *The Compleat Angler*

Laugh, and the world laughs with you;
Weep, and you weep alone,
For the sad old earth must borrow its mirth,
But has trouble enough of its own.
Ella Wilcox (1850–1919) American journalist and poet *Solitude*

 **THE BIBLE**

The sun also ariseth and the sun goeth down, and hasteth to his place where he arose.
Ecclesiastes 1:5

Sorrow and sighing shall flee away.
Isaiah 35:10

These things I have spoken to you, that in Me you may have peace. In the world you may have tribulation; but be of good cheer, I have overcome the world.
John 16:33

Blessed are ye that hunger now: for ye shall be filled. Blessed are ye that weep now: for ye shall laugh.
Luke 6:21

Hope deferred makes the heart sick, but a longing fulfilled is a tree of life.
Proverbs 13:12

Many are the plans in a man's heart, but it is the Lord's purpose that prevails.
Proverbs 19:21

A righteous man may fall seven times and rise again.
Proverbs 24:16

Many are the afflictions of the righteous, but the Lord delivers him out of them all.
Psalm 34:19

Let us therefore cast off the works of darkness, and let us put on the armour of light.
Romans 13:12

CHAPTER EIGHTEEN

APOLOGY AND FORGIVENESS

❋ ❋ **COMING** ❋ ❋
CLEAN

The angry man always thinks he can do more than he can.
Albertano of Brescia (c.1190–c.1270) *Liber Consolationis*

Experience is the wisdom that enables us to recognize . . . the folly that we have already embraced.
Ambrose Bierce (1842–1914) American journalist

When a man forgets himself, he usually does something everybody else remembers,
James Coco quoted in *Reader's Digest*

Heaven has no rage like love to hatred turned,
Nor hell a fury, like a woman scorned.
William Congreve (1670–1729) English dramatist and poet *The Mourning Bride*

Confessions may be good for the soul but they are bad for the reputation.
Thomas, Lord Dewar (1864–1930) British distiller and writer

When I make a mistake it's a beaut!
Fiorello Henry la Guardia (1882–1947) American lawyer and politician *On an indefensible appointment.*

I've made an ass of myself so many times I often wonder if I am one.
Norman Mailer (1923–) American novelist and journalist

A man may be a fool and not know it, but not if he is married.
Henry L. Mencken (1880–1956) American journalist and linguist

It is not our wrong actions which it requires courage to confess, so much as those which are ridiculous and foolish.
Jean-Jacques Rousseau (1712–78) French political philosopher and novelist

O, my offence is rank, it smells to heaven.
William Shakespeare (1564–1616) English playwright and poet *Hamlet*

An angry man is again angry with himself when he returns to reason.
Publilius Syrus (First century BC)

Man is the only animal that blushes – or needs to.
Mark Twain (1835–1910) American writer *Following the Equator*

The great charm in argument is really finding one's own opinion, not other people's.
Evelyn Waugh (1903–66) English novelist and travel writer

My life is an open book. All too often open at the wrong page.
Mae West (1893–1980) American vaudeville and film actress

❀ ❀ DENIAL ❀ ❀

Beware of thinking yourself shrewd when you are only suspicious.
Anon

A truth that's told with bad intent
Beats all the Lies you can invent.
William Blake (1757–1827) English poet and artist *Auguries of Innocence*

Everyone threw the blame on me. I have noticed that they nearly always do. I suppose it is because they think I shall be able to bear it best.
Sir Winston Churchill (1874–1965) English statesman *My Early Life*

The average man is more interested in a woman who is interested in him than he is in a woman – any woman – with beautiful legs.
Marlene Dietrich (1904–92) German actress

How seldom a fact is accurately stated; how almost invariably when a story has passed through the mind of a third person it becomes little better than a falsehood.
Nathaniel Hawthorne (1804–64) American novelist *American Note-Books*

I claim not to have controlled events, but confess plainly that events have controlled me.
Abraham Lincoln (1809–65) 16th American President *Letter to A. G. Hodges*

I am a man
More sinned against than sinning.
William Shakespeare (1564–1616) English playwright and poet *King Lear*

I understand a fury in your words,
But not the words.
William Shakespeare *Othello*

Truth is never pure, and rarely simple.

Oscar Wilde (1854–1900) Irish playwright, novelist and wit

JUSTIFICATION,
❊ ❊ EXCUSES ❊ ❊
AND REASONS

Forgetfulness is a gift from God bestowed upon debtors in compensation for their destitution of conscience.

Ambrose Bierce (1842–1914) American journalist

Advice is like castor oil, easy enough to give but dreadful uneasy to take.

Josh Billings (1818–85) American humorist

Those who restrain Desire, do so because theirs is weak enough to be restrained.

William Blake (1757–1827) English poet and artist

There is, however, a limit at which forbearance ceases to be a virtue.

Edmund Burke (1729–97) Irish statesman and philosopher *Observations on a Publication, The Present State of the Nation.*

There is no Good, there is no Bad; these be the whims of mortal will:

What works me well that call I 'good',
 what harms and hurts I hold as 'ill'.

Richard Burton (1821–90) English orientalist and explorer *Kasidah*

An injury is much sooner forgotten than an insult.

Philip Stanhope, Earl of Chesterfield (1694–1773) English statesman, orator and wit *Letter to his Son*

No animal ever invented anything as bad as drunkenness – or as good as drink.

G. K. Chesterton (1874–1936) English critic and novelist

No explanation is necessary because none would be satisfactory.

Dwight D. Eisenhower (1890–1969) 34th American President

Don't view me with a critic's eye,
But pass my imperfections by.
Large streams from little fountains flow,
Tall oaks from little acorns grow.

David Everett (1770–1813) English author *Lines written for a school declamation*

Count not his broken pledges as a crime. He meant them, how he meant them – at the time.

Kensal Green *Premature Epitaphs*

How happy are astrologers, who are believed if they tell one truth to

a hundred lies, while other people lose all credit if they tell one lie to a hundred truths.
Francesco Guicciardini (1483–1540) Florentine historian and statesman

No man at one time can be wise and love.
Robert Herrick (1591–1674) English poet *Hesperides*

Anger is a brief madness
Horace (65–8 BC) Roman poet and satirist *Epistles*

Never explain – your friends do not need it and your enemies will not believe you anyway.
Elbert Hubbard (1856–1915) American author

Can a leopard change his spots?
Jeremiah 13:23

Apologies are seldom of any use.
Dr Samuel Johnson (1709–84) English writer and critic

Many things – such as loving, going to sleep or behaving unaffectedly – are done worst when we try hardest to do them.
C. S. Lewis (1898–1963) Irish-born academic and writer *Studies in Medieval and Renaissance Literature*

I am one of those unfortunates to whom death is less hideous than explanations.
Wyndham Lewis (1894–1969) English Catholic biographer

All childish errors are not made by children.
E. C. McKenzie American writer and compiler

No man is exempt from saying silly things. The misfortune is to say them seriously.
Michel Montaigne (1533–92) French essayist

No man can think clearly when his fists are clenched.
George Jean Nathan (1882–1958) American critic

Anger is not only inevitable; it is also necessary. Its absence means indifference, the most disastrous of human failings.
Arthur Ponsonby (1871–1946) English politician

There is nothing like desire for preventing the thing one says from bearing any resemblance to what one has in mind.
Marcel Proust (1871–1922) French novelist

The mind is always the dupe of the heart.
François, Duc de La Rochefoucauld (1613–80) French writer *Maxims*

Quarrels would not last long if the fault were only on one side.
François, Duc de la Rochefoucauld *Maxims*

A little inaccuracy sometimes saves tons of explanation.
  Saki (H. H. Munro) (1870–1916) British novelist

Oftentimes excusing of a fault
Doth make the fault worse by the excuse.
  William Shakespeare (1564–1616) English playwright and poet

To be wise and love
Exceeds man's might.
  William Shakespeare *Troilus and Cressida*

The more things a man is ashamed of, the more respectable he is.
  George Bernard Shaw (1856–1950) Irish dramatist *Man and Superman*

Never apologize and never explain – it's a sign of weakness.
  Laurence Stallings (1894–1968) American novelist and playwright *She Wore a Yellow Ribbon*

Two wrongs don't make a right, but they make a good excuse.
  Thomas Szasz (1920–) American psychiatrist *The Second Sin*

These times having the rare good fortune that you may think what you like and say what you think.
  Publius Tacitus (c.56–120) Roman historian

The point is that nobody likes having salt rubbed into their wounds, even if it is the salt of the earth.
  Rebecca West (1892–1983) Irish novelist and biographer

It is a folly to expect men to do all that they may reasonably be expected to do.
  Richard Whately (1787–1863) English scholar and prelate *Apophthegms*

❋ CAPITULATION AND ❋ APOLOGY

Dear pot,
   Sorry.
Love kettle.
  Anon

Life is a long lesson in humility.
  J. M. Barrie (1860–1937) Scottish novelist and dramatist *The Little Minister*

Apologize, *v*: To lay the foundations for a future offence.
  Ambrose Bierce (1842–1914) American journalist

Apologies only account for the evil which they cannot alter.
  Benjamin Disraeli (1804–81) British statesman and novelist

In real life it only takes one to make a quarrel.
  Ogden Nash (1902–71) American poet *The Ogden Nash Pocket Book*

The quickest way of ending a war is to lose it.

George Orwell (1903–50) English novelist *Shooting an Elephant*

Man does not live by words alone, despite the fact that sometimes he has to eat them.

Adlai Stevenson (1900–65) American Democrat politician

It's a good rule of life never to apologize. The right sort of people don't want apologies, and the wrong sort take a mean advantage of them.

P. G. Wodehouse (1881–1975) English novelist

❉ ❉ ❉ **REGRET** ❉ ❉ ❉

Time wounds all heels.

Jane Ace (1905–74) American radio performer

This is the curse of life! that not
A nobler, calmer train
Of wiser thoughts and feelings blot
Our passions from our brain!

Matthew Arnold (1822–88) English poet and critic *Absence*

There is another man within me that's angry with me.

Sir Thomas Brown (1915–)

Lord, deliver me from myself.

Thomas Browne (1605–82) English scholar and writer *Religio Medici*

Never love unless you can
Bear with all the faults of man:
Men will sometimes jealous be,
Though but little cause they see;
And hang the head, as discontent,
And speak what straight they will
    repent.

Thomas Campion (1567–1620) English physician and poet *Never Love*

True friendship is like sound health, the value of it is seldom known until it be lost.

Charles Caleb Colton (1780–1832) English clergyman and writer

Not sharp revenge, nor hell itself, can find a fiercer torment than a guilty mind.

John Dryden (1631–1700) English poet

This is the bitterest of all, to wear the yoke of our own wrong-doing.

George Eliot (1819–80) English novelist

To be left alone, and face to face with my own crime, has been just retribution.

Henry Wadsworth Longfellow (1807–82) American poet

There is no anguish like an error of which we feel ashamed.

Edward Lytton (1803–73) English novelist and playwright *Ernest Maltravers*

Anger begins in folly, and ends in repentance.
Pythagoras (Sixth century BC) Greek philosopher

It is not just when a villainous act has been committed that it torments us; it is when we think of it afterward, for the remembrance of it lasts forever.
Jean-Jacques Rousseau (1712–78) French political philosopher and novelist

I am afraid to think what I have
    done;
Look on't again I dare not.
William Shakespeare (1564–1616) English playwright and poet *Macbeth*

The loss of a friend is like that of a limb; time may heal the anguish of the wound, but the loss cannot be repaired.
Robert Southey (1774–1843) English poet and writer

He punishes himself who repents of his deeds.
Publilius Syrus (First century BC) *Moral Sayings*

Hindsight is always 20:20.
Billy Wilder (1906–) American film maker

BURYING
❋ ❋ ❋ THE ❋ ❋ ❋
HATCHET

Unusual irritability, which leads to quarrels, shortens life.
Alexander A. Bogomoletz (1881–1946) *The Prolongation of Life*

Little quarrels often prove to be new recruits of love.
Samuel Butler (1612–80) English satirist *Hudibras*

There's no substitute for moonlight and kissing.
Barbara Cartland (1901–) English romantic novelist

Next to the wound, what women make best is the bandage.
Jules Amédée Barbey D'Aurevilly (1808–89) French novelist, poet and critic

An olive-leaf he brings, pacific sign.
John Milton (1608–74) English poet *Paradise Lost, Book II*

A soft answer turneth away wrath.
Proverbs 15:1

A quarrel between friends, when made up, adds a new tie to friendship, as experience shows that the callosity formed round a broken bone makes it stronger than before.
St Francis de Sales (1567–1622) French theologian

No, I will be the pattern of all
   patience:
I will say nothing.
   William Shakespeare (1564–1616)
English playwright and poet *King Lear*

Making peace is harder than
making war.
   Adlai Stevenson (1900–65)
American politician *Address in 1946*

Many promising reconciliations
have broken down because, while
both parties come prepared to
forgive, neither party came
prepared to be forgiven.
   Charles Williams (1886–1945)
English novelist

❋ ❋ FORGIVENESS ❋ ❋

Young men soon give, and soon
forget affronts: Old age is slow in
both.
   Joseph Addison (1672–1719)
English essayist and politician *Cato*

Mutual Forgiveness of each vice,
Such are the Gates of Paradise.
   William Blake (1757–1827)
English poet and artist *The Gates of Paradise, Prologue*

Life that ever needs forgiveness
has for its first duty to forgive.
   Henry Bulwer (1801–72) English
diplomat and author

He that cannot forgive others
breaks the bridge over which he
must pass himself; for every man
has need to be forgiven.
   Thomas Fuller (1608–61) English
writer and clergyman

We never ask God to forgive
anybody except where we haven't.
   Elbert Hubbard (1856–1915)
American author

We read that we ought to forgive
our enemies; but we do not read
that we ought to forgive our
friends.
   Cosimo de Medici (1389–1464)
Florentine patron of art and
literature

To err is human, to forgive, divine.
   Alexander Pope (1688–1744)
English poet *An Essay on Criticism*

One forgives as much as one loves.
   **François, Duc de La
Rochefoucauld** (1613–80) French
writer *Maxims*

The truest joys the seldom prove
   Who free from quarrels live:
'Tis the most tender part of love
   Each other to forgive.
   John Sheffield (1648–1721)
English politician and writer *The Reconcilement*

Forgive these wild and wandering
   cries,
Confusions of a wasted youth:
Forgive the where they fail in
   truth,

And in thy wisdom make me wise.
Alfred, Lord Tennyson (1809–92)
English poet *In Memoriam*

❉ ❉ NEW RESOLVE ❉ ❉

If the hill will not come to
   Mahomet,
Mahomet will go to the hill.
Francis Bacon (1561–1626)
English philosopher and statesman
Essays of Love

We can work it out: Defiant phrase
used with respect to:
   1: Rocky relationships.
   2: Video recorder operation.
Mike Barfield (1962–) *Dictionary
For Our Time – 'The Oldie'*

Friendship, of itself a holy tie,
Is made more sacred by adversity.
Charles Caleb Colton (1780–1832)
English clergyman and writer

The falling out of faithful friends
renewing is of love.
Richard Edwards (c.1523–66) Poet
Amantium Irae

Right actions for the future are the
best apologies for the wrong ones
in the past.
Tyron Edwards (1809–94)
American theologian

A man, Sir should keep his
friendship in constant repair.
Dr Samuel Johnson (1709–84)
English writer and critic *Letter to
Lord Chesterfield*

I had rather be the cause of her
laughter, than her tears.
Caroline Lamb (1785–1828)
English novelist

But with the morning cool
repentance came.
Sir Walter Scott (1771–1832)
Scottish novelist and poet *Rob Roy*

❉ LOVE IN ADVERSITY ❉

Some people complain because
roses have thorns; rather be
thankful that thorns have roses.
Anon

Love he comes and love he tarries
Just as fate or fancy carries;
Longest stays, when sorest
   chidde;
Laughs and flies, when press'd
   and bidden.
J. Campbell *Freedom and Love*

The way to love anything is to
realize it might be lost.
G. K. Chesterton (1874–1936)
English critic and novelist

If yet I have not all thy love,
Dear, I shall never have it.
John Donne (1573–1631) English
poet *Lovers' Infiniteness*

Love's the noblest frailty of the mind.
  John Dryden (1631–1700) English poet *The Indian Emperor*

The only present love demands is love.
  John Gay (1685–1732) English poet *The Espousal*

Never a lip is curved with pain
That can't be kissed into smiles again.
  Francis Brett Harte (1836–1902) American author *The Last Galleon*

The greatest happiness of life is the conviction that we are loved, loved for ourselves, or rather loved in spite of ourselves.
  Victor Hugo (1802–85) French poet and author

A part of kindness consists in loving people more than they deserve.
  Joseph Joubert (1754–1824) French writer and moralist

The quarrels of lovers are like summer storms. Everything is more beautiful when they have passed.
  Madame Necker (1739–94) Swiss writer

What dire offence from am'rous causes springs,
What mighty contests rise from trivial things.
  Alexander Pope (1688–1774) English poet *The Rape of the Lock*

Of all affliction taught a lover yet,
'Tis sure the hardest science to forget!
How shall I lose the sin, yet keep the sense,
And love the offender, yet detest the offence?
  Alexander Pope *Translations and Imitations*

I hate the sin, but I love the sinner.
  Thomas Buchanan Read (1822–72) American poet *What a Word May Do*

Woman is like a teabag – you can't tell how strong she is until you put her in hot water.
  Nancy Reagan (1923–) American actress

Women and elephants never forget an injury.
  Saki (H. H. Munro) (1870–1916) British novelist

The course of true love never did run smooth.
  William Shakespeare (1564–1616) English playwright and poet *A Midsummer Night's Dream*

You are my true and honourable wife;
As dear to me as are the ruddy drops
That visit my sad heart.
  William Shakespeare *Julius Caesar*

But love is blind, and lovers cannot see

The petty follies that themselves
   commit.
   William Shakespeare *Merchant of
Venice*

Better a little chiding than a great
deal of heart-break.
   William Shakespeare *The Merry
Wives of Windsor*

As the sunlight clasps the earth,
And the moonbeams kiss the sea –
What are all these kissings worth,
If you do not kiss me?
   Percy Bysshe Shelley (1792–1822)
English poet *Love's Philosopher*

Trouble is a part of your life, and if
you don't share it, you don't give
the person who loves you a chance
to love you enough.
   Dinah Shore (1917–) American
singer

The feud between us was but of the
   house,
Not of the heart.
   Robert Southey (1774–1843)
English poet and writer *Roderick*

And blessings on the falling out
   That all the more endears,
When we fall out with those we
   love
   And kiss again with tears!
   Alfred, Lord Tennyson (1809–92)
English poet *The Princess*

Lovers' rows make love whole
again.
   Terence (195–159 BC) Roman
dramatist

The quarrels of lovers are the
renewal of love.
   Terence *Heauton Timoroumenos*

'Tis strange what a man may do,
and a woman yet think him an
angel.
   William Thackeray (1811–63)
English novelist *Henry Esmond*

Be she meeker, kinder, than
Turtle-dove or pelican
   If she be not so to me,
   What care I how kind she be?
   George Wither (1588–1667)
English poet *Shall I, Wasting in
Despair*

❉ ❉ MAKING LIGHT ❉ ❉

Blessed are they who can laugh at
themselves, for they shall always
be amused.
   Anon

I pick the loser every time. If ever
you see me in a queue at the
railway booking-office, join the
other one; because there'll be a
chap at the front of mine who's
trying to send a rhinoceros to
Tokyo.
   J. Basil Boothroyd (1910–)
English writer and broadcaster

I am not at all the sort of person
you and I took me for.
   Jane Carlyle (1801–66) Wife of
Thomas Carlyle, Scottish historian

One of love's April-fools.
  William Congreve (1670–1729)
English dramatist and poet *The Old Bachelor*

Lapp courtships are conducted pretty much in the same fashion as in other parts of the world. The aspirant, as soon as he discovers he has lost his heart, goes off in search of a friend and a bottle of brandy.
  Frederick Temple Hamilton, Lord Dufferin (1826–1902) British politician

I've never hated a man enough to give him his diamonds back.
  Zsa Zsa Gabor (1919–)
Hungarian film star

God will pardon me. It is his profession.
  Heinrich Heine (1797–1856)
German poet and essayist

The concept of two people living together for 25 years without having a cross word suggests a lack of spirit only to be admired in sheep.
  Alan P. Herbert (1890–1971)
English writer and politician *News Chronicle*, 1940

I make mistakes: I'll be the second to admit it.
  Jean Kerr (1923–) American playwright quoted in *Reader's Digest*

In every house of marriage there's room for an interpreter.
  Stanley Kunitz (1905–)
American poet *Route Six*

I wasn't kissing her I was whispering in her mouth.
  Chico Marx (1891–1961)
American comedian

Send two dozen roses to Room 424 and put 'Emily I love you' on the back of the bill.
  Groucho Marx (1895–1977)
American comedian

You think I'm an asshole now? You should've seen me when I was drunk.
  John Cougar Mellencamp (1951–)
American pop singer

It's a funny kind of month, October. For the really keen cricket fan it's when you discover that your wife left you in May.
  Denis Norden (1922–) English scriptwriter and broadcaster

Being wrong is a natural gift. You cannot learn it. Some of us have a particular genius in this direction and can be wrong for months at a time.
  Stephen Pile (1949–) English writer *The Book of Heroic Failures*

I manage my own affairs with as much care and steady attention and skill as – let us say – a drunken Irish tenor.
  J. B. Priestley (1894–1984) English novelist and playwright

Dontopedalogy is the science of opening your mouth and putting your foot in it, a science which I

have practised for a good many years.
Prince Philip (1921–) Duke of Edinburgh

Love means never having to say you're sorry.
Eric Segal (1937–) American screenplay writer from the film *Love Story*, 1970

When I say an ill-natured thing 'tis out of pure good-humour.
Richard Brinsley Sheridan (1751–1816) Irish dramatist

I presume you're mortal, and may err.
James Shirley (1596–1666) English dramatist *The Lady of Pleasure*

I couldn't help it. I can resist everything except temptation.
Oscar Wilde (1854–1900) Irish playwright, novelist and wit

I'm a modern, intelligent, independent-type woman. In other words, a girl who can't get a man.
Shelley Winters (1922–) American actress

He spoke with a certain what-is-it in his voice, and I could see that, if not actually disgruntled, he was far from being gruntled.
P. G. Wodehouse (1881–1975) English novelist *The Code of the Woosters*

A Christian is a man who feels repentance on a Sunday
For what he did on Saturday
And is going to do on Monday.
Thomas Russell Ybarra (1880–1971) American writer *The Christian*

CHAPTER NINETEEN

ABSENCE

❊ PUNCTUALITY AND ❊ ARRIVING ON TIME

Eighty per cent of success is showing up.
Woody Allen (1935–) American film director *Interview*

Never be punctual – people will think you have nothing better to do.
Anon

Punctuality: The art of wasting nobody's time but your own.
Anon

Punctuality is something that if you have it, nobody is ever around to appreciate it.
Hylda Baker (1909–82) English actress and humorist

I've arrived and, to prove it, I'm here.
Max Bygraves (1922–) English entertainer *Catchphrase*

I meant to be prompt, but it never occured to me that I had better try to be early.
Clarence Day (1874–1935) American author *Life With Father*

A man consumes the time you make him wait.
In thinking of your faults – so don't be late.
Arthur Guiterman *A Poet's Proverbs*

If you're there before it's over, you're on time.
James J. Walker (1881–1946) American lawyer and mayor of New York city

Punctuality is the virtue of the bored.
Evelyn Waugh (1903–66) English novelist and travel writer *Diaries, 'Irregular Notes', 26 March 1962*

Punctuality is the thief of time.
Oscar Wilde (1854–1900) Irish playwright, novelist and wit

❊ ❊ ❊ LATENESS ❊ ❊ ❊

Better late than never.
Anon

Better late than before anybody has invited you.
Ambrose Bierce (1842–1914) American journalist *The Devil's Dictionary*

It's far better to be 3 minutes late in this world than 60 years too early in the next.
Mabel Constanduros *speaking as her Grandma Buggins character*

Five minutes! Zounds! I have been five minutes too late all my lifetime!

Hannah Cowley (1743–1809) Dramatist *The Belle's Stratagem*

If you're one hour late, you might as well be two.

Kent Garbutt (1962–)

Better late than never.

John Heywood (1497–c.1580) English playwright and musician

The surest way to be late is to have plenty of time.

Leo Kennedy (1885–1965) British journalist

Some people are always late, like the late King George V.

Spike Milligan (1918–) British comedian *The Bald Twit Lion*

I've been on a calendar, but never on time,

Marilyn Monroe (1926–62) American film star

Better late than never, as Noah remarked to the Zebra, which had understood that passengers arrived in alphabetical order.

Bert Leston Taylor (1866–1921) American journalist *The So-called Human Race*

❀ ❀ UNWILLING ❀ ❀ ABSENCE

Life is always like this. Just as something nice and interesting occurred, destiny must intervene with some pressing engagement.

Conrad Aitken (1889–1973) American poet and novelist

Friends, though absent, are still present.

Marcus Cicero (106–43 BC) Roman statesman and orator

Absent in body, but present in spirit.

I Corinthians 5:3

'Presents', I often say, 'endear absents.'

Charles Lamb (1775–1834) English essayist *Essays*

Tell them I came, and no one answered,
That I kept my word.

Walter de la Mare (1873–1956) English poet and novelist *The Listeners*

❀ ❀ STRATEGIC ❀ ❀ ABSENCE

Woman's great strength lies in being late or absent.

Alain-Fournier (1868–1951) French philosopher and writer

I was court-martialled in my absence, and sentenced to death in my absence, so I said they could shoot me in my absence.
Brendan Behan (1923–64) Irish writer

Absentee, *n*: A person with an income who has had the forethought to remove himself from the sphere of exaction.
Ambrose Bierce (1842–1914) American journalist *Devil's Dictionary*

Of all the thirty-six alternatives, running away is best.
Chinese proverb

What is better than presence of mind in a railway accident? Absence of body.
Punch, 1849

Judicious absence is a weapon.
Charles Reade (1814–84) English novelist and playwright

The best defence against the atom bomb is not to be there when it goes off.
The British Army Journal, 1949

❁ ❁ ❁ EXCUSES ❁ ❁ ❁

Why is it that the later you are, the longer the length of the red light?
Paul Dickens *The Official Explanations* quoted in *Reader's Digest*

The absent are never without fault, nor the present without excuse.
Benjamin Franklin (1706–90) American statesman

I could keep out of bed all right if I once got out. It is the wrenching away of the head from the pillow that I find so hard.
Jerome K. Jerome (1859–1927) English humorous writer

The sun streamed into my room, and I said, it's a sin not to get up on a morning like this. And the more I said I ought to get up, the more delightful I found it to lie in bed.
William Somerset Maugham (1874–1965) British writer

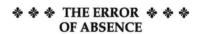

❁ ❁ ❁ THE ERROR OF ABSENCE

Absent, *adj*: Exposed to the attacks of friends and acquaintances; defamed; slandered.
Ambrose Bierce (1842–1914) American journalist *The Enlarged Devil's Dictionary*

Absent, *adj*: Peculiarly exposed to the tooth of detraction; vilified; hopelessly in the wrong; superseded in the consideration and affection of another.
Ambrose Bierce *The Enlarged Devil's Dictionary*

The absent are always in the wrong.
  Philippe Nericault (1680–1754) French playwright

✤ ✤ INVITATION ✤ ✤ DECLINED

Very sorry can't come. Lie follows by post.
  Charles, Lord Beresford (1846–1919) Irish-born naval commander *Telegram sent to the Prince Of Wales after being summoned to dine.*

You can include me out.
  Samuel Goldwyn (1882–1974) American film producer

One of the delights known to age, and beyond the grasp of youth, is that of not going . . . But don't I like to enjoy myself? By not going that is just what I am trying to do.
  J. B. Priestley (1894–1984) English novelist and playwright

The truly free man is the one who will turn down an invitation to dinner without giving an excuse.
  Jules Renard (Nineteenth century) French writer

CHAPTER TWENTY

PUBLIC SPEAKING

❉ ❉ OPENING LINES ❉ ❉

I am a man of few words who likes to come straight to the point, so I will not bore you with superfluous preamble . . . Never let it be said that I was a man who would use a sentence where a word would suffice.

Anon

Unaccustomed as I am to public speaking I feel this irresistible urge to prove it.

Anon

I want to thank everybody who made this day necessary.

Yogi Berra (1925–) American baseball player and coach

Many a man who couldn't direct you to the drugstore on the corner when he was thirty will get a respectful hearing when age has further impaired his mind.

Finley Peter Dunne (1867–1936) American humorist *Mr Dooley Remembers*

My wife . . . pleased me by laughing uproariously when reading the manuscript, only to inform me that it was my spelling that amused her.

Gerald Durrell (1925–) English writer and naturalist

You'd scarce expect one of my age
To speak in public on the stage;
And if I chance to fall below
Demosthenes or Cicero,
Don't view me with a critic's eye,
But pass my imperfections by.

David Everett (1770–1813) English author *Lines written for a School Declamation*

If there's anyone listening to whom I owe money. I'm prepared to forget it if you are.

Errol Flynn (1909–59) American actor *In a broadcast in Australia*

I intended to give you some advice but now I remember how much is left over from last year unused.

George Harris (1844–1922) American congressman

The dog, considered a sagacious beast,
Does not give tongue when he has had a feast.
Nor does the cow go mooing around the mead
To tell the world that she's enjoyed her feed . . .
But Modern Man, by some malignant fate,
When he has eaten, simply must orate.

Alan P. Herbert (1890–1971) English writer and politician

The human brain starts working the moment you are born and never stops until you stand up to speak in public.

George Jessel (1824–83) English judge

My dear friends – I will not call you ladies and gentlemen, since I know you too well.

William Petten *Among the Humorists*

It is my invariable custom to say something flattering to begin with so that I shall be excused if by any chance I put my foot in it later on.

Prince Philip (1921–) Duke of Edinburgh

Since brevity is the soul of wit,
And tediousness the limbs and
    outward flourishes,
I will be brief.

William Shakespeare (1564–1616) English playwright and poet *Hamlet*

There comes a time in every man's life and I've had many of them.

Casey Stengel (1889–1975) American baseball player and manager *Remark*

Churchill was always re-writing his speeches until he had to give them. But that's where my similarity to Churchill ends.

Adlai Stevenson (1900–65) American Democrat politician

Not that the story need be long, but it will take a long while to make it short.

Henry David Thoreau (1817–62) American essayist and poet *Letter to a Friend*

It usually takes me more than three weeks to prepare a good impromptu speech.

Mark Twain (1835–1910) American writer

It's hard to be funny when you have to be clean.

Mae West (1893–1980) American vaudeville and film actress

On an occasion of this kind it becomes more than a moral duty to speak one's mind – it becomes a pleasure.

Oscar Wilde (1856–1900) Irish playwright, novelist and wit

Sign in an executive's office: 'What I am about to say represents one four thousand-millionth of the world's opinion'

Jack Williams quoted in *Reader's Digest*

❖ ❖ MEETINGS AND ❖ ❖ DISCUSSIONS

We are growing serious, and, let me tell you, that's the very next step to being dull.

Joseph Addison (1672–1719) English essayist and politician *Cato*

He listens well who takes notes.
  Dante Alighieri (1265–1321)
Italian poet *The Divine Comedy*

It's better to debate a question
without settling it than to settle a
question without debating it.
  Joseph Joubert (1754–1824)
French writer and moralist

Let us never negotiate out of fear.
But let us never fear to negotiate.
  John F. Kennedy (1917–63) 35th
American President *Inaugural
Address* 20th Jan. 1961

When all think alike, no one is
thinking.
  Walter Lippmann (1899–1974)
American journalist

The Law of Triviality. Briefly
stated, it means that the time spent
on any item of the agenda will be
in inverse proportion to the sum
involved.
  Cyril Northcote Parkinson
(1909–) English political science
*High Finance or the Point of
Vanishing Interest*

A dinner lubricates business.
  William Scott Stowell (1745–
1836) English judge *Boswell's Life of
Johnson,* 1781

❋ ❋ ADVICE ON ❋ ❋ SPEECHES AND SPEAKING

As a general rule, any speech can
be improved by making it shorter.
  Anon

I take the view, and always have
done, that if you cannot say what
you have to say in twenty minutes,
you should go away and write a
book about it.
  Lord Brabazon of Tara (1884–
1964) English aviator and politician
Attributed

An after-dinner speech should be
like a lady's dress – long enough to
cover the subject and short enough
to be interesting.
  R. A. Butler (1902–82) English
Conservative politician

Have something to say; say it, and
stop when you've done.
  Tyron Edwards (1809–94)
American theologian

Blessed is the man, who having
nothing to say, abstains from
giving wordy evidence of the fact.
  George Eliot (1819–80) English
novelist

Speeches are like babies – easy to
conceive but hard to deliver.
  Pat O'Malley (1901–) English
actor

The most precious things in speeches are pauses.

Ralph Richardson (1902–83) English actor

My father gave me these hints on speech-making: 'Be sincere . . . be brief . . . be seated'.

James Roosevelt

The golden rule is that there are no golden rules.

George Bernard Shaw (1856–1950) Irish dramatist *Maxims for Revolutionists*

Preach not because you have to say something, but because you have something to say.

Richard Whately (1787–1863) English scholar and prelate *Apophthegms*

A little sincerity is a dangerous thing, and a great deal of it is absolutely fatal.

Oscar Wilde (1856–1900) Irish playwright, novelist and wit *The Critic as Artist*

❧ ❧ AUDIENCES ❧ ❧

The best audience is intelligent, well-educated, and a little drunk.

Alben W. Barkley (1877–1956) American politician

The people may be made to follow a course of action, but they may not be made to understand it.

Confucius (551–479 BC) Chinese philosopher *Analects*

Talk to a man about himself and he will listen for hours.

Benjamin Disraeli (1804–81) British statesman and novelist

Make 'em laugh; make 'em cry; make 'em wait.

Charles Reade (1814–84) English novelist and playwright *Attributed*

I know two kinds of audience only – one coughing and one not coughing.

Artur Schnabel (1882–1951) Austrian concert pianist *My Life and Music*

REPLIES
❧ ❧ ❧ AND ❧ ❧ ❧
RETORTS

It had been hard for him that spake it to have put more truth and untruth together in few words than in that speech.

Francis Bacon (1561–1626) English philosopher and statesman *Essays of Friendship*

There is less in this than meets the eye.

Tallulah Bankhead (1903–68) American actress

I have made mistakes but I have never made the mistake of claiming that I never made one.
 James Gordon Bennett (1795–1872) American journalist

If a thing goes without saying, let it.
 Jacob M. Braude *Treasury of Wit and Humour*

I don't mind lies, but I hate inaccuracy.
 Samuel Butler (1835–1902) English author, painter and musician

I can't think of an extemporaneous comment. As soon as I prepare one, I'll let you know.
 Mike DiSalle

A sophisticated rhetorician, inebriated with the exuberance of his own verbosity.
 Benjamin Disraeli (1804–81) British statesman and novelist *About W. E. Gladstone*

You shouldn't interrupt my interruptions:
That's really worse than interrupting.
 T. S. Eliot (1888–1965) British poet and critic *The Cocktail Party*

I know he is a truly great and good man, for he told me so himself.
 William S. Gilbert (1836–1911) English comic opera and verse writer

If you can't answer a man's arguments, all is not lost; you can still call him vile names.
 Elbert Hubbard (1856–1915) American author *Attributed*

One of the commonest ailments of the present day is premature forming of a opinion.
 Kin Hubbard (1868–1930) American humorist

Sir, you are like a pin, but without either it's head or it's point.
 Douglas Jerrold (1803–57) English author and dramatist *Attributed*

You ain't heard nothin' yet.
 Al Jolson (1886–1950) American singer and actor in *The Jazz Singer*

You look wise. Pray correct that error.
 Charles Lamb (1775–1834) English essayist *Essays of Elia*

When I want your opinion I'll give it to you.
 Laurence J. Peter (1918–) Canadian writer

I murdered my grandmother this morning.
 Franklin D. Roosevelt (1882–1945) 32nd American President *Said to get the attention of those to whom he was speaking.*

No matter how thin you slice it, it's still boloney.
 Alfred E. Smith (1873–1944) American Democrat politician

There are three kinds of lies: lies, damned lies, and statistics.
Mark Twain (1835–1910) American writer *Autobiography*

I disapprove of what you say, but I will defend to the death your right to say it.
Voltaire (1694–1778) French author *Attributed*

Ah! don't say you agree with me. When people agree with me I always feel that I must be wrong.
Oscar Wilde (1856–1900) Irish playwright, novelist and wit *The Critic as Artist*

🌼 DRAWING TO A CLOSE 🌼

I stand up when he nudges me. I sit down when they pull my coat.
Ernest Bevin (1881–1951) English Labour statesman

I do not object to people looking at their watches when I am speaking. But I strongly object when they start shaking them to make sure they are still going.
William, Lord Birkett (1883–1962) English lawyer and politician *from A. Andrews, Quotations for Speakers and Writers*

Don't clap too hard – it's a very old building.
John Osborne (1929–) English playwright and actor *The Entertainer*

Gentlemen, you have just been listening to that Chinese Sage On Too Long.
Will Rogers (1879–1935) American humorist-philosopher

🌼 TOASTS 🌼

Here's to the whole world, lest some stupid person take offence.
Anon

A man hath no better thing under the sun than to eat, and to drink, and to be merry.
Ecclesiastes 8:15

To better days – may the happiest days of your past be the saddest days of your future.
William Evans III and Andrew Frothingham: *Cheers! 101 Toasts for Every Occasion*

May the most you wish for be the least you get.
William Evans III and Andrew Frothingham: *Cheers! 101 Toasts for Every Occasion*

May we treat our friends with kindness and our enemies with generosity.
William Evans III and Andrew Frothingham: *Cheers! 101 Toasts for Every Occasion*

To perfect friends who were once perfect strangers.

William Evans III and Andrew Frothingham: *Cheers! 101 Toasts for Every Occasion*

To those who know me best and, for some reason, still love me.

William Evans III and Andrew Frothingham: *Cheers! 101 Toasts for Every Occasion*

Every day you look lovelier and lovelier – and today you look like tomorrow.

William Evans III and Andrew Frothingham: *Cheers! 101 Toasts for Every Occasion*

To our sweethearts and wives – may they never meet.

Lewis C. Henry (Editor) *Toasts for all Occasions*

May the roof above us never fall in, and may we friends gathered below never fall out.

Irish Distillers Group quoted in *Reader's Digest March* 1984

May you have warm words on a cold evening a full moon on a dark night and a smooth road all the way to your door.

Irish Distillers Group quoted in *Reader's Digest March* 1984

May your troubles in the coming New Year be as short-lived as your resolutions.

E. C. McKenzie American writer and compiler

IF ALL ELSE FAILS

CONGRATULATIONS AND
HAPPY BIRTHDAY ON YOUR
ANNIVERSARY THIS
VALENTINE'S DAY, BAR
MITZVAH BOY, HOPE YOU
FEEL BETTER SOON.
  Ed Brodsky

What shall I write about,
  What shall I say?
My butterfly thoughts
  Keep on flitting away.
My notepaper waiting,
  My stamps in a line,
The easiest part
  Is the name that I sign.
What shall I write about,
  What shall I do?
I'll just send a card
  Saying, 'Thinking of you!'
    Iris Hesselden quoted in *Francis
Gay's Friendship Book* 1994

INDEX

Abbott, Wenonah S.
Death and Bereavement (Of a Better Place) 130
Ace, Jane
Apology and Forgiveness (Regret) 181
Acheson, Dean
Good Luck (Humorous) 141
Adam, David
Moving/New Home (Bless This House) 80
Adams, Franklin P.
Birthday (Middle Age) 34
Christmas and Other Holidays (New Year) 45
Adams, Joey
Matrimony (Marriage: The Cynical View) 66
Home and Away (Other European Countries) 96,
   (America) 97
Addison, Joseph
Christmas and Other Holidays (Christmas) 42
Affairs of the Heart (Flattery) 51, *(The Essence of
   Love)* 57
Matrimony (Marriage: The Positive View) 65,
   (Marriage: The Cynical View) 66
Home and Away (Farewell and Bon Voyage) 84
Death and Bereavement (Consolation) 129, *(In
   the Line of Duty)* 136
Good Luck (Luck) 145
Apology and Forgiveness (Forgiveness) 183
Public Speaking (Meetings and Discussions)
   194
Ade, George
Matrimony (Marriage: The Cynical View) 66
Adenauer, Konrad
Misfortune (Set-Back) 168
Aeschylus
Words of Wisdom (Guidelines) 15, *(Support and
   Sympathy)* 27
Good Luck (Hope) 145
Aesop
Misfortune (Disappointments) 169, *(Cold
   Comfort)* 174
Agathon
Misfortune (Philosophical Thoughts) 163
Aitken, Conrad
Absence (Unwilling Absence) 190
Alain-Fournier
Absence (Strategic Absence) 190
Albertano of Brescia
Apology and Forgiveness (Coming Clean) 176
Alcott, Amos Bronson
Retirement (Life beyond Retirement) 122
Success and Happiness (Achievement) 153
Alderson, Margaret H.
Misfortune (Set-Back) 168
Aldrich, Henry
Birthday (Celebration and Drinking) 40
Aldrich, James
Death and Bereavement (Of a Better Place) 130

Ali, Muhammad
Retirement (Quitting While You're Ahead) 120
Alighieri, Dante
Mother's/Father's Day (Parents) 110
Death and Bereavement (Remembrance) 128
Good Luck (Major Challenge) 150
Misfortune (Sympathy) 166
Public Speaking (Meetings and Discussions) 195
Allen, Woody
Affairs of the Heart (Humorous) 47
Death and Bereavement (Black Humour) 139
Absence (Punctuality and Arriving) 189
Ambrose, St.
Home and Away (Italy) 95
Amiel, Henri Frédéric
Matrimony (The Bride) 70
Andersen, Hans Christian
Success and Happiness (The Good Life) 155
Anouilh, Jean
Affairs of the Heart (Advice for Lovers) 51
Anspacher, Louis K.
Matrimony (Marriage: The Positive View) 65
Antiphanes
Affairs of the Heart (Declarations of Love) 53
Arbiter, Petronius
Death and Bereavement (Of a Better Place) 130
Aristophanes
Birthday (Old Age) 38
Aristotle
Retirement (Well-Earned Rest) 120
Thanks and Fond Regards (Gratitude) 157
Arkell, Reginald
Togetherness (Anniversary) 113
Arlen, Michael
Home and Away (Parting and Leaving) 83
Armour, Richard
Birthday (Middle Age) 34, *(Age and the Signs of
   Aging)* 36
Retirement (Living with Leisure) 121
Armstrong, John
Good Luck (Advice) 142
Arnold, Matthew
Death and Bereavement (Consolation) 129,
   (Grief) 134
Apology and Forgiveness (Regret) 18
Arnold, Samuel J.
Good Luck (Major Challenge) 150
Ashford, Daisy
Affairs of the Heart (Love on the Rocks) 60
Asquith, Herbert, Lord
Birthday (Youth) 32
Astaire, Fred
Birthday (Old Age) 38
Astor, Nancy
Birthday (Old Age) 38
Success and Happiness (Humorous) 153

Auber, Daniel-François-Esprit
Birthday (Old Age) 38
Auden, Wystan Hugh
Affairs of the Heart (From the Heart) 55
Togetherness (Enduring Love) 114
Thanks and Fond Regards (Gratitude) 157
Austen, Jane
Matrimony (Marriage: The Cynical View) 66, 67
Home and Away (Climate and Weather) 86, 87
Togetherness (Happy Memories) 116
Austin, Mary
Christmas and Other Holidays (Christmas) 42
Ayckbourn, Alan
Affairs of the Heart (Humorous) 47
Aytoun, William Edmonstoune
Home and Away (Scotland, Wales, Ireland) 94
Babson, Roger W.
Misfortune (Encouragement) 164
Bacall, Lauren
Togetherness (Enduring Love) 114
Bacon, Francis
Words of Wisdom (Guidelines) 15, *(Worldly Observations)* 17
Birthday (Youth) 32, *(Age and the Signs of Aging)* 36
Affairs of the Heart (Flattery) 52
Moving/New Home (Of Houses and Home) 77
Home and Away (Travel) 81
Babies and Children (Children: The Negative View) 106
Ill Health (Medicine: Cures and Remedies) 124
Death and Bereavement (Of Death) 137, *(Life and Death)* 139
Good Luck (Opportunity) 143, *(Hope)* 145, *(Education and Study)* 150, *(Exams)* 151
Success and Happiness (Perseverance) 155
Thanks and Fond Regards (Gratitude) 157, *(Gratitude)* 157
Apology and Forgiveness (New Resolve) 184
Public Speaking (Replies and Retorts) 196
Bagehot, Walter
Matrimony (The Bride) 70
Bailey, Thomas
Thanks and Fond Regards (Hospitality) 159
Baker, Hylda
Absence (Punctuality and Arriving) 189
Balaam (Alias Thomas Pitt)
Words of Wisdom (Instructive Sayings) 25
Balchin, Nigel
Babies and Children (Children: The Negative View) 106
Balzac, Honoré de
Matrimony (Advice to the Newly Weds) 75
Babies and Children (Children: The Negative View) 106
Mother's/Father's Day (Mothers) 108
Good Luck (Advice) 142
Bankhead, Tallulah
Public Speaking (Replies and Retorts) 196
Barbauld, Anna Letitia
Home and Away (Parting and Leaving) 83

Barbellion, W. N. P.
Matrimony (Humorous) 62
Barfield, Mike
Birthday (Youth) 32, *(Old Age)* 38
Christmas and Other Holidays (Christmas) 42, *(Easter)* 46
Affairs of the Heart (Humorous) 47
Matrimony (Humorous) 62, *(Engagement)* 63, *(Marriage: The Cynical View)* 67
Babies and Children (Parenthood) 103
Togetherness (Anniversary) 113
Retirement (Early, Late or Not At All) 119
Good Luck (New Job) 148
Apology and Forgiveness (New Resolve) 184
Baring, Maurice
Misfortune (Disappointments) 169
Barkley, Alben W.
Public Speaking (Audiences) 196
Barnard, Mrs. C. A.
Togetherness (Happy Memories) 116
Barretto, Larry
Babies and Children (Babies) 102
Barrie, J. M.
Affairs of the Heart (Advice for Lovers) 51
Home and Away (Climate and Weather) 87
Togetherness (Happy Memories) 116, *(Of Wives)* 117
Death and Bereavement (Of Death) 137
Misfortune (Failure) 171
Apology and Forgiveness (Capitulation) 180
Barrymore, John
Home and Away (America) 97
Baruch, Bernard
Words of Wisdom (Support and Sympathy) 28
Baudelaire, Charles
Togetherness (Happy Memories) 116
Bax, Arnold
Good Luck (Taking the Plunge) 147
Bayle, Pierre
Quotes on Quotes 13
Bayly, Thomas H.
Home and Away (Absence) 87
Beattie, James
Retirement (Well-Earned Rest) 120
Death and Bereavement (Tributes) 132
Beaumarchais, Pierre de
Misfortune (Disappointments) 169
Beauvoir, Simone de
Matrimony (Advice to the Newly Weds) 75
Mother's/Father's Day (Mothers and Young Children) 109
Beckett, Samuel
Ill Health (Convalescence) 127
Beddoes, T. L.
Death and Bereavement (Final Rest) 135
Beecher, Henry Ward
Words of Wisdom (Instructive Sayings) 25
Affairs of the Heart (The Essence of Love) 57
Mother's/Father's Day (Mothers and Young Children) 109, *(Parents)* 111
Death and Bereavement (Of a Better Place) 130, *(Tributes)* 132

Good Luck (Advice) 142
Misfortune (Honourable Defeat) 172
Beerbohm, Max
Birthday (Insulting) 31
Misfortune (Failure) 171
Behan, Brendan
Matrimony (Marriage: The Positive View) 65
Home and Away (Canada) 97
Mother's/Father's Day (Parents) 111
Misfortune (Disappointments) 169
Absence (Strategic Absence) 191
Behn, Aphra
Affairs of the Heart (Advice for Lovers) 51
Bellay, Joachim du
Home and Away (Home and Homecoming) 91
Belloc, Hilaire
Misfortune (Honourable Defeat) 172
Belloy, P. L. B. du
Home and Away (Homesickness) 88
Belmondo, Jean-Paul
Birthday (Middle Age) 34
Benchley, Robert
Home and Away (Planes, Trains and Automobiles) 85
Ill Health (Accidents) 126
Bennett, Alan
Words of Wisdom (Wry Comment) 19
Togetherness (Anniversary) 113
Bennett, Arnold
Matrimony (Advice to the Newly Weds) 75
Ill Health (Sickness) 124
Bennett, James Gordon
Public Speaking (Replies and Retorts) 197
Bennett, W. C.
Thanks and Fond Regards (Gratitude) 157
Benny, Jack
Matrimony (The Bride) 70
Thanks and Fond Regards (Gratitude) 157
Benson, R. H.
Birthday (Youth) 32
Bentley, Nicolas
Retirement (Well-Earned Rest) 120
Berenson, Bernard
Words of Wisdom (Support and Sympathy) 28
Beresford, Charles, Lord
Absence (Invitation Declined) 192
Bergengren, Ralph
Christmas and Other Holidays (Christmas) 42
Bergman, Ingrid
Misfortune (Cold Comfort) 174
Berlin, Irving
Death and Bereavement (Remembrance) 128
Success and Happiness (Achievement) 153
Berra, Yogi
Public Speaking (Opening Lines) 193
Betjeman, John
Good Luck (New Job) 148
Bevin, Ernest
Public Speaking (Drawing to a Close) 198
Bibesco, Elizabeth
Words of Wisdom (Support and Sympathy) 28
Home and Away (Parting and Leaving) 83

Bible
Words of Wisdom (Worldly Observations) 18, *(Happiness and How to Achieve It)* 23, *(Instructive Sayings)* 27, *(Ten Inspired Quotes)* 29
Birthday (Celebration and Drinking) 41
Matrimony (Biblical) 74
Moving/New Home (Bless This House) 80
Home and Away (Absence) 88
Death and Bereavement (The Bible) 137
Good Luck (Advice) 143, *(Success and How to Achieve It)* 147, *(New Job)* 149
Success and Happiness (Good Fortune) 154, *(Congratulations)* 156
Thanks and Fond Regards (Friendship) 158
Misfortune (The Bible) 175
Apology and Forgiveness (Justification) 179, *(Burying the Hatchet)* 182
Absence (Unwilling Absence) 190
Public Speaking (Toasts) 198
Bieber, Margaret
Good Luck (Advice) 142
Bierce, Ambrose
Words of Wisdom (Wry Comment) 19, 20
Christmas and Other Holidays (Christmas) 42
Affairs of the Heart (Humorous) 47, *(Advice for Lovers)* 51, *(Love on the Rocks)* 60
Matrimony (Humorous) 62, *(The Groom)* 72, *(To the Happy Couple)* 73
Moving/New Home (Of Houses and Home) 77
Home and Away (Foreign Travel) 82, *(Absence)* 88, *(Homesickness)* 88, *(Holidays and Tourism)* 89, *(Home and Homecoming)* 91, *(Australia and New Zealand)* 98
Babies and Children (Babies) 102
Mother's/Father's Day (Fathers) 110
Ill Health (Doctors and Physicians) 126
Good Luck (Opportunity) 143
Thanks and Fond Regards (Compliments) 160
Misfortune (Humorous) 162
Apology and Forgiveness (Coming Clean) 176, *(Justification)* 178, *(Capitulation)* 180
Absence (Lateness) 189, *(Strategic Absence)* 191, *(The Error of Absence)* 191
Billings, Josh
Birthday (Old Age) 38
Home and Away (Holidays and Tourism) 89
Success and Happiness (Perseverance) 155
Misfortune (Set-Back) 168
Apology and Forgiveness (Justification) 178
Binyon, Laurence
Death and Bereavement (Remembrance) 128
Birdseye, George
Thanks and Fond Regards (Hospitality) 159
Birkett, William, Lord
Public Speaking (Drawing to a Close) 198
Bishop, Stephen
Affairs of the Heart (Humorous) 47
Blake, William
Affairs of the Heart (The Essence of Love) 58
Good Luck (Aiming High) 147
Apology and Forgiveness (Denial) 177,

(Justification) 178, *(Forgiveness)* 183
Bliss, Philip Paul
Home and Away (Home and Homecoming) 91
Bogomoletz, Alexander A.
Apology and Forgiveness (Burying the Hatchet)
182
Bohr, Niels
Good Luck (Luck) 145
Boileau, Nicolas
Retirement (Living with Leisure) 121
Boliska, Al
*Home and Away (Planes, Trains and
Automobiles)* 85
Bond, Simon
Birthday (Staying Young) 33
Matrimony (Advice to the Newly Weds) 75
Good Luck (New Job) 148
Boothroyd, J. Basil
Moving/New Home (Home Ownership) 79
*Home and Away (Planes, Trains and
Automobiles)* 85
Togetherness (Anniversary) 113
Ill Health (Medicine: Cures and Remedies)
124
Apology and Forgiveness (Making Light) 186
Borland, Hal
Christmas and Other Holidays (New Year) 45
Home and Away (Home and Homecoming) 91
Born, Bertrand le
*Christmas and Other Holidays (Traditional
Easter)* 46
Borrow, George Henry
Home and Away (England and the English) 93
Boucicault, Dion
Words of Wisdom (Worldly Observations) 18
Boulton, Harold E.
Home and Away (England and the English) 93
Bourdillon, William Francis
Affairs of the Heart (Love on the Rocks) 60
Bowen, Charles S. C.
Misfortune (Humorous) 162
Bowen, Edward Ernest
Birthday (Middle Age) 34
Brabazon of Tara, Lord
*Public Speaking (Advice on Speeches and
Speaking)* 195
Braham, John
Home and Away (Home and Homecoming) 91
Braude, Jacob M.
Public Speaking (Replies and Retorts) 197
Brenan, Gerald
Birthday (Old Age) 39
Briers, Richard
Birthday (Growing Older: The Drawbacks) 38
Brodsky, Ed
(If All Else Fails) 201
Brontë, Anne
Affairs of the Heart (Advice for Lovers) 51
Home and Away (Homesickness) 88
Brontë, Emily
Death and Bereavement (Tributes) 132
Thanks and Fond Regards (Gratitude) 157

Brooke, Rupert C.
Home and Away (Town and Country) 90, *(Home
and Homecoming)* 91, *(England and the
English)* 93
Death and Bereavement (In the Line of Duty) 136
Brooks, Maria
Misfortune (Optimism) 167
Broome, Rev. William
Good Luck (Major Challenge) 150
Brothers, Joyce
Matrimony (Marriage: The Cynical View) 67
Brougham, Henry Peter, Lord
Good Luck (Exams) 151
Brown, Gean
Misfortune (Humorous) 162
Brown, Heywood
Babies and Children (Birth) 99, *(Parenthood)* 104
Brown, Thomas
Apology and Forgiveness (Regret) 181
Browne, Charles Farrer
Words of Wisdom (Wry Comment) 20
Browne, Thomas
Death and Bereavement (An End to Suffering)
136
Apology and Forgiveness (Regret) 181
Browne, William
Matrimony (The Bride) 70
Browning, Elizabeth Barrett
Affairs of the Heart (From the Heart) 55
Matrimony (Engagement) 64
Togetherness (Enduring Love) 115
Browning, Robert
Birthday (Middle Age) 341
Affairs of the Heart (From the Heart) 55,
(Proposals) 59
Home and Away (England and the English) 93,
(Italy) 95
Babies and Children (Parenthood) 104
Mother's/Father's Day (Parents) 111
Togetherness (Happy Memories) 116
Misfortune (Honourable Defeat) 173
Bryan, William J.
Good Luck (Major Challenge) 150
Buchan, John
Words of Wisdom (Wry Comment) 20
Buck, Pearl S.
Mother's/Father's Day (Mothers) 108
Bulwer, Henry
Apology and Forgiveness (Forgiveness) 183
Bulwer-Lytton, Edward
Retirement (Living with Leisure) 121
Good Luck (Exams) 151
Thanks and Fond Regards (Compliments) 160
Misfortune (Failure) 171
Bunyan, John
Death and Bereavement (Of a Better Place) 131
Thanks and Fond Regards (Generosity) 160
Misfortune (Philosophical Thoughts) 163
Burchfield, Robert
Success and Happiness (Perseverance) 155
Burdette, Robert Jones
Good Luck (Worry and Fear) 145

Burgess, Anthony
Matrimony (Advice to the Newly Weds) 75
Death and Bereavement (Of Death) 137
Burke, Edmund
Words of Wisdom (Hard Truths) 23
Babies and Children (Babies) 102
Apology and Forgiveness (Justification) 178
Burke, Leo. J.
Babies and Children (Babies) 102
Burns, George
Birthday (Old Age) 39, *(Celebration and Drinking)* 40
Retirement (Early, Late or Not At All) 119
Burns, Robert
Affairs of the Heart (From the Heart) 55, *(Love on the Rocks)* 60
Matrimony (The Bride) 70
Death and Bereavement (Tributes) 132
Burns, Stan
Babies and Children (Birth) 99
Burton, Montague
Words of Wisdom (Guidelines) 15
Burton, Richard
Birthday (The Down Side) 31
Death and Bereavement (Grief) 134
Good Luck (Advice) 142
Apology and Forgiveness (Justification) 178
Burton, Robert
Matrimony (To the Happy Couple) 73
Togetherness (Of Wives) 117
Bush, Kate
Mother's/Father's Day (Mothers) 108
Bussy-Rabutin, Comte de
Home and Away (Absence) 88
Butler, Rab
Public Speaking (Advice on Speeches and Speaking) 195
Butler, Samuel (17th century)
Words of Wisdom (Worldly Observations) 18
Apology and Forgiveness (Burying the Hatchet) 182
Butler, Samuel (19th century)
Words of Wisdom (Worldly Observations) 18
Birthday (Old Age) 39
Matrimony (Marriage: The Cynical View) 67
Ill Health (Sickness) 124
Death and Bereavement (Remembrance) 128
Public Speaking (Replies and Retorts) 197
Bygraves, Max
Absence (Punctuality and Arriving) 189
Byrom, John
Christmas and Other Holidays (Traditional Christmas) 44
Byron, George Gordon, Lord
Birthday (The Down Side) 31, *(Youth)* 32, *(Middle Age)* 34, *(Celebration and Drinking)* 40
Affairs of the Heart (Advice for Lovers) 51, *(From the Heart)* 55
Matrimony (The Bride) 70
Home and Away (Parting and Leaving) 83, *(Farewell and Bon Voyage)* 84, *(Climate and Weather)* 87, *(Homesickness)* 88, *(Italy)* 96, *(Other European Countries)* 96
Death and Bereavement (Consolation) 129
Misfortune (Philosophical Thoughts) 163
Byron, H. J.
Birthday (Old Age) 39
Cabell, James Branch
Words of Wisdom (Worldly Observations) 18
Affairs of the Heart (Humorous) 47
Caesar, Julius
Misfortune (Errors and Mistakes) 170
Cagney, James
Success and Happiness (Achievement) 153
Calverley, Charles S.
Babies and Children (Children: The Positive View) 105
Togetherness (Happy Memories) 116
Calwell, Arthur
Misfortune (Honourable Defeat) 173
Campbell J.
Apology and Forgiveness (Love in Adversity) 184
Campbell, Mrs Patrick
Affairs of the Heart (Humorous) 47
Matrimony (Marriage: The Cynical View) 67
Campbell, Thomas
Home and Away (Homesickness) 88
Death and Bereavement (Remembrance) 128
Campion, Thomas
Apology and Forgiveness (Regret) 181
Canetti, Elias
Death and Bereavement (Of Death) 137
Capote, Truman
Home and Away (Italy) 96
Carlyle, Jane
Apology and Forgiveness (Making Light) 186
Carlyle, Thomas
Death and Bereavement (Tributes) 132
Carney, Julia
Thanks and Fond Regards (Gratitude) 157
Carryl, Charles E.
Home and Away (Planes, Trains and Automobiles) 85
Cartland, Barbara
Affairs of the Heart (Sex and Lust) 49
Apology and Forgiveness (Burying the Hatchet) 182
Cary, Joyce
Words of Wisdom (Hard Truths) 23
Catullus, Gaius
Affairs of the Heart (From the Heart) 55
Cervantes, Miguel de
Success and Happiness (Good Fortune) 154
Misfortune (Encouragement) 164, *(Advice)* 165
Chakiris, George
Affairs of the Heart (Humorous) 47
Chalmers, Allan K.
Words of Wisdom (Happiness and How to Achieve It) 22
Chalmers, Patrick Reginald
Misfortune (Encouragement) 164
Chandler, Raymond
Affairs of the Heart (Flattery) 52

Charles the Bold
Good Luck (Hope) 145
Charron, Pierre
Words of Wisdom (Guidelines) 15
Chase, Alexander
Death and Bereavement (An End to Suffering)
   136
Chase, Ilka
Matrimony (The Groom) 72
Misfortune (Failure) 171
Cher
Matrimony (Marriage: The Cynical View) 67
Earl Of Chesterfield, Philip Stanhope
Words of Wisdom (Worldly Observations) 18,
   (Happiness and How to Achieve It) 22
Matrimony (Advice to the Newly Weds) 75
Apology and Forgiveness (Justification) 178
Chesterton, G. K.
Words of Wisdom (Worldly Observations) 18,
   (Happiness and How to Achieve It) 22
Affairs of the Heart (Humorous) 47
Moving/New Home (Home Ownership) 79
Home and Away (Planes, Trains and
   Automobiles) 85, *(Holidays and Tourism)* 89,
   (Home and Homecoming) 91
Ill Health (Convalescence) 127
Good Luck (Opportunity) 143, *(Education and*
   Study) 151
Misfortune (Philosophical Thoughts) 163
Apology and Forgiveness (Justification) 178,
   (Love in Adversity) 184
Chevalier, Maurice
Birthday (Old Age) 39
Child, L. M.
Birthday (Old Age) 39
Choate, Joseph
Birthday (Old Age) 39
Christie, Agatha
Words of Wisdom (Guidelines) 15
Togetherness (Humorous) 113
Churchill, Charles
Home and Away (England and the English) 93
Churchill, Winston
Matrimony (Advice to the Newly Weds) 75
Home and Away (Other European Countries) 96,
   (India and the Far East) 98
Togetherness (Of Wives) 117
Death and Bereavement (Black Humour) 139
Good Luck (Worry and Fear) 145
Success and Happiness (Congratulations) 155
Misfortune (Set-Back) 168
Apology and Forgiveness (Denial) 177
Ciano, Count Galeazzo
Misfortune (Honourable Defeat) 173
Cibber, Colley
Matrimony (Marriage: The Cynical View) 67
Cicero, Marcus
Birthday (Old Age) 39
Death and Bereavement (Grief) 134
Absence (Unwilling Absence) 190
Clarke, James
Affairs of the Heart (From the Heart) 55

Clemenceau, Georges
Home and Away (America) 97
Cleveland, John
Home and Away (Home and Homecoming) 91
Clough, Arthur Hugh
Misfortune (Advice) 165
Cobb, Irvin S.
Birthday (Middle Age) 34
Coco, James
Apology and Forgiveness (Coming Clean) 176
Cocteau, Jean
Death and Bereavement (Black Humour) 140
Coke, Edward
Moving/New Home (Home Ownership) 79
Coleridge, Hartley
Affairs of the Heart (Flattery) 52, *(From the*
   Heart) 56
Coleridge, Samuel Taylor
Affairs of the Heart (The Essence of Love) 58
Mother's/Father's Day (Mothers) 108, *(Mothers*
   and Young Children) 109
Collier, Jeremy
Good Luck (Success and How to Achieve It) 146
Collins, William
Birthday (Insulting) 31
Death and Bereavement (In the Line of Duty) 136
Colton, Charles Caleb
Words of Wisdom (Guidelines) 15
Affairs of the Heart (Courting) 50
Home and Away (Foreigners and Foreign
   Countries) 82, *(Town and Country)* 90
Good Luck (Exams) 151
Thanks and Fond Regards (Gratitude) 157
Apology and Forgiveness (Regret) 181, *(New*
   Resolve) 184
Colum, Padraic
Moving/New Home (First Home) 78
Confucius
Words of Wisdom (Instructive Sayings) 25, 26
Misfortune (Set-Back) 168
Public Speaking (Audiences) 196
Congreve, William
Togetherness (Anniversary) 113
Apology and Forgiveness (Coming Clean) 176,
   (Making Light) 187
Connolly, Billy
Matrimony (Humorous) 62
Connolly, Cyril
Misfortune (Honourable Defeat) 173
Connor, T. W.
Matrimony (The Bride) 70
Constanduros, Mabel
Absence (Lateness) 189
Coolidge, Calvin
Words of Wisdom (Wry Comment) 20
Cooper, Jilly
Matrimony (The Groom) 72
Moving/New Home (House Buying) 78
Cope, Wendy
Affairs of the Heart (Advice for Lovers) 51,
   (Flattery) 52, *(Declarations of Love)* 53, *(The*
   Essence of Love) 58

Coren, Alan
Christmas and Other Holidays (Christmas) 42
Moving/New Home (House Buying) 78
Home and Away (France) 95, *(Other European Countries)* 96
Mother's/Father's Day (Fathers) 110
Corneille, Pierre
Misfortune (Honourable Defeat) 173
Courteline, Georges
Birthday (Youth) 32
Cousins, Norman
Good Luck (Exams) 151
Coute, Emile
Ill Health (Convalescence) 127
Coward, Noël
Home and Away (Travel) 81, *(Climate and Weather)* 87, *(Holidays and Tourism)* 89, *(England and the English)* 93
Cowley, Abraham
Death and Bereavement (Tributes) 132
Cowley, Hannah
Absence (Lateness) 190
Cowper, William
Home and Away (England and the English) 93
Retirement (Living with Leisure) 121
Death and Bereavement (Consolation) 129, *(Of a Better Place)* 131
Death and Bereavement (Grief) 134
Success and Happiness (Congratulations) 155
Craik, Dinah Maria
Misfortune (Failure) 171
Crane, Nathalia
Good Luck (Major Challenge) 150
Crashaw, Richard
Affairs of the Heart (Flattery) 52
Death and Bereavement (Grief) 134
Crisp, Quentin
Moving/New Home (Home Ownership) 79
Home and Away (England and the English) 93
Crockett, David
Good Luck (Taking the Plunge) 147
Cromwell, Oliver
Good Luck (Faith and Trust) 144
Crowell, Grace
Thanks and Fond Regards (Gratitude) 157
Cuppy, William
Birthday (Humorous) 30
Curie, Marie
Words of Wisdom (Guidelines) 15
Curtis, George William
Birthday (Staying Young) 33
D'Aurevilly, Barbey
Apology and Forgiveness (Burying the Hatchet) 182
D'Urfrey, Thomas
Affairs of the Heart (Flattery) 52
Dale, Daphne
Affairs of the Heart (Declarations of Love) 53
Dali, Salvador
Words of Wisdom (Wry Comment) 20
Davies, Hunter
Home and Away (Town and Country) 90

Davies, William H.
Christmas and Other Holidays (Christmas) 42
Affairs of the Heart (From the Heart) 56
Home and Away (Home and Homecoming) 91
Retirement (Living with Leisure) 121
Thanks and Fond Regards (Gratitude) 157
Davis, Thomas Osborne
Home and Away (Home and Homecoming) 92
Day, Clarence
Absence (Punctuality and Arriving) 189
Day, Doris
Birthday (Middle Age) 34
Deffand, Marquise du
Good Luck (Taking the Plunge) 147
Defoe, Daniel
Death and Bereavement (Tributes) 133
Misfortune (Advice) 165
Degas, Edgar
Birthday (Youth) 32
Deighton, Len
Home and Away (England and the English) 93
Delafield, E. M.
Home and Away (Holidays and Tourism) 89
Delaney, Shelagh
Affairs of the Heart (Humorous) 48
Desbordes-Valmore, Marceline
Death and Bereavement (Of Death) 138
Misfortune (Sympathy) 166
Descartes, René
Words of Wisdom (Ten Inspired Quotes) 29
Dewar, Thomas, Lord
Togetherness (Of Husbands) 118
Apology and Forgiveness (Coming Clean) 176
Dewey, John
Retirement (Life beyond Retirement) 122
Dewing, Thomas W.
Home and Away (America) 97
Dickens, Charles
Words of Wisdom (Hard Truths) 24
Christmas and Other Holidays (Christmas) 42
Matrimony (Engagement) 64
Babies and Children (Babies) 102
Good Luck (New Job) 148
Misfortune (Errors and Mistakes) 170
Dickens, Monica
Moving/New Home (Home Ownership) 79
Dickens, Paul
Absence (Excuses) 191
Dickinson, Emily
Death and Bereavement (Of a Better Place) 131, *(Of Death)* 138
Dietrich, Marlene
Apology and Forgiveness (Denial) 177
Diller, Phyllis
Matrimony (Advice to the Newly Weds) 75
Babies and Children (Children: The Negative View) 106
Dirksen, Everett
Misfortune (Advice) 165
Disalle, Mike
Public Speaking (Replies and Retorts) 197

Disney, Walt
Misfortune (Cold Comfort) 174
Disraeli, Benjamin
Quotes on Quotes 13
Birthday (The Down Side) 315
Babies and Children (Children: The Positive View) 105
Togetherness (Enduring Love) 115
Retirement (Early, Late or Not At All) 119
Good Luck (Success and How to Achieve It) 146
Success and Happiness (Achievement) 153, *(Congratulations)* 156
Thanks and Fond Regards (Hospitality) 159
Misfortune (Sympathy) 166
Apology and Forgiveness (Capitulation) 180
Public Speaking (Audiences) 196, *(Replies and Retorts)* 197
Dixon, Margaret
Misfortune (Encouragement) 164
Dobson, Henry A.
Birthday (The Down Side) 31
Death and Bereavement (The Inevitability of Death) 138
Dodd, Ken
Home and Away (America) 97
Dodsley, Robert
Home and Away (Parting and Leaving) 83
Donleavy, James Patrick
Words of Wisdom (Wry Comment) 20
Ill Health (Sickness) 125
Donne, John
Affairs of the Heart (From the Heart) 56, *(The Essence of Love)* 58, *(Proposals)* 59
Matrimony (Engagement) 64
Togetherness (Enduring Love) 115
Death and Bereavement (Of a Better Place) 131
Apology and Forgiveness (Love in Adversity) 184
Dorr, Julia C.
Birthday (Humorous) 30
Douglas, Norman
Moving/New Home (First Home) 78
Home and Away (Foreigners and Foreign Countries) 82
Dow, Dorothy
Affairs of the Heart (Flattery) 52
Dowden, Edward
Misfortune (Failure) 171
Doyle, Arthur Conan
Words of Wisdom (Guidelines) 151, *(Instructive Sayings)* 260
Success and Happiness (Achievement) 153
Droste-Hülshoff, Annette Elizabeth von
Death and Bereavement (Grief) 134
Drucker, Peter
Success and Happiness (Good Fortune) 154
Drummond, Thomas
Moving/New Home (Home Ownership) 79
Dryden, John
Home and Away (Absence) 88
Retirement (Life beyond Retirement) 122

Death and Bereavement (Of a Better Place) 131
Good Luck (Faith and Trust) 144
Thanks and Fond Regards (Hospitality) 159
Apology and Forgiveness (Regret) 181, *(Love in Adversity)* 185
Dublin, Al
Affairs of the Heart (Humorous) 48
Dudley, Henry
Success and Happiness (Congratulations) 156
Dumas, Alexandre (Dumas père)
Words of Wisdom (Guidelines) 15
Dumas, Alexandre (Dumas fils)
Babies and Children (Children: The Negative View) 107
Duncan, Isadora
Matrimony (Marriage: The Cynical View) 67
Dunne, Finley P.
Babies and Children (Babies) 102
Public Speaking (Opening Lines) 193
Durrell, Gerald
Public Speaking (Opening Lines) 193
Dylan, Bob
Words of Wisdom (Guidelines) 15
Edgeworth, Maria
Moving/New Home (Of Houses and Home) 77
Good Luck (New Job) 148
Edison, Thomas Alva
Good Luck (Worry and Fear) 145, *(Education and Study)* 151
Edward VIII
Mother's/Father's Day (Parents) 111
Togetherness (Anniversary) 113
Edwards, Bob
Words of Wisdom (Hard Truths) 24
Edwards, Oliver
Words of Wisdom (Happiness and How to Achieve It) 22
Edwards, Richard
Apology and Forgiveness (New Resolve) 184
Edwards, Tyron
Birthday (Old Age) 39
Death and Bereavement (Of a Better Place) 131
Misfortune (Errors and Mistakes) 170
Apology and Forgiveness (New Resolve) 184
Public Speaking (Advice on Speeches and Speaking) 195
Eikerenkoetter, Frederick J.
Retirement (Life beyond Retirement) 122
Einstein, Albert
Good Luck (Advice) 142
Eisenhower, Dwight D.
Apology and Forgiveness (Justification) 178
Eliot, T. S.
Birthday (Middle Age) 352
Public Speaking (Replies and Retorts) 197
Eliot, George
Words of Wisdom (Happiness and How to Achieve It) 22
Home and Away (Foreign Travel) 82
Apology and Forgiveness (Regret) 181
Public Speaking (Advice on Speeches and Speaking) 195

Elliott, Ebenezer
Death and Bereavement (The Inevitability of Death) 138
Ellis, H. F.
Misfortune (Humorous) 162, *(Accidents)* 173
Ellison, Phyllis
Retirement (Life beyond Retirement) 122
Emerson, Ralph Waldo
Quotes on Quotes 13
Moving/New Home (Of Houses and Home) 77, *(House Buying)* 78
Good Luck (Advice) 142, *(Success and How to Achieve It)* 146
Success and Happiness (Achievement) 153
Thanks and Fond Regards (Gratitude) 157, *(Hospitality)* 159
Misfortune (Philosophical Thoughts) 163
Engel, Sigmund Z.
Birthday (Growing Older: The Benefits) 37
Enright, D. J.
Death and Bereavement (Grief) 135
Epicurus
Thanks and Fond Regards (Gratitude) 157
Erasmus, Desiderius
Words of Wisdom (Worldly Observations) 18, *(Hard Truths)* 24
Estienne, Henri
Birthday (Growing Older: The Drawbacks) 38
Euripides
Misfortune (Cold Comfort) 174
Evans III, William
Public Speaking (Toasts) 198, 199
Everett, David
Good Luck (Aiming High) 148
Apology and Forgiveness (Justification) 178
Public Speaking (Opening Lines) 193
Everett, Edward
Words of Wisdom (Guidelines) 16
Fabiano, Victoria
Birthday (Humorous) 30
Farrar, Frederic
Good Luck (Faith and Trust) 144
Faulkner, William
Death and Bereavement (Grief) 135
Fawkes, Guy
Good Luck (Major Challenge) 150
Feather, William
Words of Wisdom (Worldly Observations) 18
Retirement (Well-Earned Rest) 120
Fenton, James
Affairs of the Heart (From the Heart) 56
Fiebig, Jim
Babies and Children (Parenthood) 104
Field, Eugene
Babies and Children (Babies) 102
Fielding, Henry
Affairs of the Heart (The Essence of Love) 58
Matrimony (Marriage: The Cynical View) 67
Death and Bereavement (Of Death) 138
Fields, W. C.
Birthday (Celebration and Drinking) 41
Babies and Children (Birth) 99

Ill Health (Hospitals) 126
Good Luck (Humorous) 141
Misfortune (Humorous) 162, *(Advice)* 165
Fishback, Margaret
Birthday (Humorous) 30
Babies and Children (Babies) 102
Fisher, Dorothy Canfield
Birthday (Growing Older: The Benefits) 37
Fitzgerald, F. Scott
Words of Wisdom (Guidelines) 16
Affairs of the Heart (Humorous) 48
Fitzgerald, Zelda
Affairs of the Heart (From the Heart) 56
Florio, John
Ill Health (Medicine: Cures and Remedies) 124
Flynn, Errol
Public Speaking (Opening Lines) 193
Foch, Marshal Ferdinand
Misfortune (Encouragement) 164
Forbes, B. C.
Words of Wisdom (Happiness and How to Achieve It) 22
Misfortune (Philosophical Thoughts) 163
Ford, Henry
Words of Wisdom (Guidelines) 16
France, Anatole
Quotes on Quotes 13
Retirement (Life beyond Retirement) 122
Good Luck (Faith and Trust) 144
Franklin, Benjamin
Words of Wisdom (Wry Comment) 20, *(Happiness and How to Achieve It)* 22, *(Ten Inspired Quotes)* 29
Christmas and Other Holidays (Traditional Christmas) 44
Matrimony (Advice to the Newly Weds) 75
Retirement (Living with Leisure) 121
Ill Health (Medicine: Cures and Remedies) 124
Good Luck (New Job) 149, *(Education and Study)* 151
Thanks and Fond Regards (Generosity) 160
Absence (Excuses) 191
Freeman, Thomas
Home and Away (England and the English) 94
Freud, Clement
Christmas and Other Holidays (New Year) 45
Frey, Glenn
Birthday (Middle Age) 35
Frost, D.
Good Luck (Success and How to Achieve It) 146
Frost, Robert
Birthday (Humorous) 30
Home and Away (Home and Homecoming) 92
Death and Bereavement (Life and Death) 139
Frothingham, Andrew
Public Speaking (Toasts) 198, 199
Fuller, John
Affairs of the Heart (Flattery) 52
Fuller, Thomas
Words of Wisdom (Guidelines) 16
Matrimony (The Bride) 70
Apology and Forgiveness (Forgiveness) 183

Gabor, Zsa Zsa
Matrimony (Humorous) 62, (Marriage: The Cynical View) 67
Apology and Forgiveness (Making Light) 187
Gage, Francis
Home and Away (Home and Homecoming) 92
Gandhi, Mohandas K.
Words of Wisdom (Ten Inspired Quotes) 29
Garbutt, Kent
Absence (Lateness) 190
Garland, Judy
Affairs of the Heart (Declarations of Love) 53
Garner, James
Matrimony (Second Marriage) 69
Gay, John
Affairs of the Heart (The Essence of Love) 582
Apology and Forgiveness (Love In Adversity) 185
George, David Lloyd
Home and Away (England and the English) 94
Good Luck (Aiming High) 148
George, Gwilym Lloyd
Misfortune (Failure) 171
Getty, John Paul
Good Luck (Humorous) 141, (Success and How to Achieve It) 146
Gibbs, Philip
Thanks and Fond Regards (Generosity) 160
Gibran, Kahlil
Matrimony (Marriage: The Positive View) 65, (To the Happy Couple) 73
Babies and Children (Parenthood) 104
Death and Bereavement (Of a Better Place) 131
Good Luck (Exams) 152
Gilbert, William S.
Birthday (Humorous) 30, (Insulting) 31
Ill Health (Sickness) 125, (Accidents) 126
Good Luck (Advice) 142
Public Speaking (Replies and Retorts) 197
Giles, Herbert
Matrimony (Marriage: The Positive View) 65
Gillilan, Strickland
Mother's/Father's Day (Mothers and Young Children) 109
Gilmour, William
Birthday (Celebration and Drinking) 41
Giraudoux, Jean
Home and Away (Home and Homecoming) 92
Gladstone, William
Misfortune (Errors and Mistakes) 170
Glasow, Arnold H.
Words of Wisdom (Hard Truths) 24
Godfrey, Mr P.
Home and Away (Home and Homecoming) 92
Goethe, Johann Wolfgang von
Moving/New Home (Home Ownership) 79
Good Luck (Advice) 142
Goldsmith, Oliver
Birthday (Old Age) 39
Home and Away (Homesickness) 88
Mother's/Father's Day (Mothers) 108
Togetherness (Of Wives) 117

Misfortune (Optimism) 167
Goldwyn, Samuel
Babies and Children (Babies) 103
Good Luck (Humorous) 141
Absence (Invitation Declined) 192
Goodrich, Samuel G.
Babies and Children (Parenthood) 104
Gordon, Richard
Home and Away (Planes, Trains and Automobiles) 85
Ill Health (Hospitals) 126
Gourmont, Remy de
Ill Health (Hospitals) 126
Gracian, Baltasar
Words of Wisdom (Guidelines) 16
Grahame, Kenneth
Home and Away (Planes, Trains and Automobiles) 86
Graves, Robert
Affairs of the Heart (Proposals) 59
Gray, Thomas
Words of Wisdom (Hard Truths) 24
Misfortune (Sympathy) 166
Greeley, Horace
Home and Away (Farewell and Bon Voyage) 84
Green, Kensal
Apology and Forgiveness (Justification) 178
Green, Michael
Christmas and Other Holidays (Christmas) 43
Moving/New Home (House Buying) 78
Gregg, Hubert
Christmas and Other Holidays (Christmas) 43
Grenfell, Joyce
Home and Away (Parting and Leaving) 83
Babies and Children (Parenthood) 104
Death and Bereavement (Life and Death) 139
Gresley, Nigel
Home and Away (Travel) 81
Gropius, Walter
Words of Wisdom (Guidelines) 16
Guardia, Fiorello Henry la
Apology and Forgiveness (Coming Clean) 176
Guicciardini, Francesco
Apology and Forgiveness (Justification) 179
Guiterman, Arthur
Words of Wisdom (Instructive Sayings) 26
Home and Away (Climate and Weather) 87
Absence (Punctuality and Arriving) 189
Guizot, François
Good Luck (Advice) 142
Gunter, John
Words of Wisdom (Happiness and How) 22
Hagen, Walter C.
Good Luck (Worry and Fear) 145
Hale, Matthew
Matrimony (Marriage: The Positive View) 66
Hall, Jerry
Matrimony (Humorous) 62
Hall, Peter
Togetherness (Enduring Love) 115
Hall, William
Matrimony (Marriage: The Positive View) 65

Halleck, Fitz-Greene
Death and Bereavement (Tributes) 133
Halm, Friedrich
Affairs of the Heart (The Essence of Love) 58
Hamilton, Lord Dufferin, Frederick Temple
Apology and Forgiveness (Making Light) 187
Haraucourt, Edmond
Home and Away (Parting and Leaving) 83
Hardy, Thomas
Christmas and Other Holidays (Christmas) 43
Misfortune (Set-Back) 168
Harington, John
Home and Away (Farewell and Bon Voyage) 85
Harris, George
Good Luck (Humorous) 141
Public Speaking (Opening Lines) 193
Harris, Jean
Thanks and Fond Regards (Gratitude) 157
Harris, Sydney J.
Words of Wisdom (Wry Comment) 20
Matrimony (The Bride) 70
Misfortune (Humorous) 162
Harrison, Benjamin
Death and Bereavement (Tributes) 133
Harte, Francis Brett
Misfortune (Disappointments) 169
Apology and Forgiveness (Love in Adversity)
187
Hartley, Leslie P.
Words of Wisdom (Worldly Observations) 18
Haskins, Henry S.
Misfortune (Disappointments) 169, (Failure)
171
Hawes, Judy
Good Luck (Aiming High) 148
Hawking, Stephen W.
Misfortune (Sympathy) 167
Hawthorne, Alice
Mother's/Father's Day (Mothers) 108
Hawthorne, Nathaniel
Words of Wisdom (Ten Inspired Quotes) 29
Death and Bereavement (Consolation) 129
Apology and Forgiveness (Denial) 177
Hays, Brooks
Success and Happiness (Humorous) 153
Hazlitt, William
Home and Away (Foreign Travel) 82, (Town and
Country)* 90
Healey, Dennis
Misfortune (Advice) 165
Heath, Robert
Affairs of the Heart (Flattery) 52
Heimel, Cynthia
Words of Wisdom (Wry Comment) 20
Affairs of the Heart (Declarations of Love) 53
*Home and Away (Planes, Trains and
Automobiles)* 86
Heine, Heinrich
Matrimony (To the Happy Couple) 73
Apology and Forgiveness (Making Light) 187
Hellelden, Iris
Birthday (Old Age) 39

If all Else Fails 201
Heller, Joseph
Death and Bereavement (Black Humour) 140
Helps, Arthur
Thanks and Fond Regards (Gratitude) 157
Hemans, Felicia D.
Home and Away (England and the English) 94
Mother's/Father's Day (Mothers) 108
Death and Bereavement (Remembrance) 128
Hemingway, Ernest
Affairs of the Heart (Sex and Lust) 49
Babies and Children (Parenthood) 104
Henley, William Ernest
Good Luck (Faith and Trust) 144
Misfortune (Encouragement) 164
Henry, Lewis C.
Public Speaking (Toasts) 199
Henry, Matthew
Success and Happiness (The Good Life) 155
O. Henry
Matrimony (The Bride) 70
Good Luck (New Job) 149
Herbert, Alan P.
Birthday (Celebration and Drinking) 41
Matrimony (Advice to the Newly Weds) 75
Apology and Forgiveness (Making Light) 187
Public Speaking (Opening Lines) 193
Herbert, George
Moving/New Home (First Home) 78
Herold, Don
Retirement (Living with Leisure) 121
Herrick, Robert
Affairs of the Heart (Advice for Lovers) 51,
(Flattery)* 52, (Proposals)* 59
Matrimony (Second Marriage) 69, (The Bride)
70, (The Groom)* 72
Herrick, Robert
Togetherness (Enduring Love) 115
Death and Bereavement (Grief) 135
Apology and Forgiveness (Justification) 179
Hesburgh, Theodore M.
Babies and Children (Parenthood) 104
Hesselden, Iris
Misfortune (Sympathy) 167
Heywood, John
Words of Wisdom (Instructive Sayings) 26
Affairs of the Heart (Flattery) 521
Success and Happiness (Good Fortune) 154
Absence (Lateness) 190
Hicks, Edward Seymour
Birthday (Youth) 33
Hickson, William Edward
Misfortune (Set-Back) 168
Hippo, St. Augustine of
Affairs of the Heart (Advice for Lovers) 51
Hippocrates
Words of Wisdom (Hard Truths) 24
Hitchcock, Alfred
Togetherness (Humorous) 113
Good Luck (Worry and Fear) 146
Hoffenstein, Samuel
Babies and Children (Babies) 103

Holland, Henry Scott
Death and Bereavement (Consolation) 129
Holland, Norah M.
Death and Bereavement (Life and Death) 139
Holmes, Oliver Wendell
Words of Wisdom (Worldly Observations) 18
Birthday (Staying Young) 33, *(Growing Older: The Drawbacks)* 38, *(Old Age)* 40
Matrimony (Engagement) 64, *(The Bride)* 70
Togetherness (Enduring Love) 115, *(Happy Memories)* 117
Retirement (Well-Earned Rest) 120
Homer
Matrimony (The Bride) 70
Death and Bereavement (Tributes) 133
Hood, Thomas
Affairs of the Heart (From the Heart) 56
Home and Away (France) 95
Death and Bereavement (Tributes) 133
Hope, Bob
Birthday (Humorous) 30, *(Middle Age)* 35
Horace
Words of Wisdom (Guidelines) 16, *(Happiness and How to Achieve It)* 22
Affairs of the Heart (Proposals) 59
Death and Bereavement (Remembrance) 128, *(In the Line of Duty)* 136, *(Of Death)* 138
Good Luck (Advice) 143
Misfortune (Advice) 166
Apology and Forgiveness (Justification) 179
Housman, Alfred E.
Good Luck (New Job) 149
Misfortune (Disappointments) 169
Howe, E. W.
Words of Wisdom (Support and Sympathy) 28
Misfortune (Cold Comfort) 174
Howells, William D.
Words of Wisdom (Instructive Sayings) 26
Death and Bereavement (Grief) 135
Hoyle, Fred
Misfortune (Errors and Mistakes) 170
Hubbard, Elbert
Retirement (Well-Earned Rest) 120
Good Luck (Success and How to Achieve It) 146
Misfortune (Failure) 171, *(Cold Comfort)* 174
Apology and Forgiveness (Justification) 179, *(Forgiveness)* 183
Public Speaking (Replies and Retorts) 197
Hubbard, Kin
Words of Wisdom (Wry Comment) 20
Birthday (Middle Age) 35
Birthday (Growing Older: The Drawbacks) 38
Matrimony (The Groom) 72
Togetherness (Of Wives) 117
Good Luck (Success and How to Achieve It) 147
Public Speaking (Replies and Retorts) 197
Hugo, Victor
Words of Wisdom (Instructive Sayings) 26
Birthday (Middle Age) 35
Apology and Forgiveness (Love In Adversity) 185
Humphrey, Hubert
Matrimony (The Groom) 72

Misfortune (Humorous) 162
Hunt, Helen Friske
Death and Bereavement (An End to Suffering) 136
Hunt, Leigh
Christmas and Other Holidays (Christmas) 43
Home and Away (Town and Country) 91
Misfortune (Sympathy) 167
Hurst, Gerald
Words of Wisdom (Hard Truths) 24
Huxley, Aldous
Words of Wisdom (Worldly Observations) 18, *(Hard Truths)* 24
Good Luck (Advice) 143
Huxley, Thomas Henry
Misfortune (Failure) 171
Ibarruri, Gomez Delores
Misfortune (Failure) 172
Ibsen, Henrik
Babies and Children (Babies) 103
Inchbald, Elizabeth
Affairs of the Heart (Courting) 50
Inge, William R.
Good Luck (Worry and Fear) 146
Ingersoll, Robert Green
Good Luck (Faith and Trust) 144
Irving, Washington
Birthday (Age and the Signs of Aging) 36
Thanks and Fond Regards (Hospitality) 159
Jackson, Holbrook
Birthday (Growing Older: The Benefits) 37
James, William
Words of Wisdom (Happiness and How to Achieve It) 22
Jarrell, Randall
Home and Away (America) 97
Jefferson, Thomas
Good Luck (Luck) 145
Jerome, Jerome K.
Words of Wisdom (Wry Comment) 20, *(Happiness and How to Achieve It)* 22
Affairs of the Heart (Humorous) 48
Babies and Children (Babies) 103
Retirement (Living with Leisure) 121
Success and Happiness (Humorous) 153
Absence (Excuses) 191
Jerrold, Douglas
Birthday (Old Age) 40
Matrimony (Engagement) 64, *(Second Marriage)* 69
Moving/New Home (Of Houses and Home) 77
Public Speaking (Replies and Retorts) 197
Jessel, George
Public Speaking (Opening Lines) 194
Jewett, Sarah
Birthday (The Down Side) 31
Johnson, Dr Samuel
Words of Wisdom (Instructive Sayings) 26, *(Ten Inspired Quotes)* 29
Birthday (Youth) 33
Matrimony (Marriage: The Positive View) 65, *(Second Marriage)* 69

Home and Away (Foreigners and Foreign Countries) 82, *(France)* 95, *(Italy)* 96
Retirement (Early, Late or Not At All) 119
Death and Bereavement (Consolation) 130
Good Luck (Humorous) 141, *(Faith and Trust)* 144, *(Major Challenge)* 150
Thanks and Fond Regards (Friendship) 159
Misfortune (Encouragement) 164
Apology and Forgiveness (Justification) 179, *(New Resolve)* 184
Johnson, Gerald W.
Words of Wisdom (Hard Truths) 24
Johnson, Lyndon B.
Matrimony (The Bride) 71
Johnson, Philander
Misfortune (Humorous) 162
Jolson, Al
Public Speaking (Replies and Retorts) 197
Jones, Franklin P.
Babies and Children (Parenthood) 104
Togetherness (Enduring Love) 115
Jones, Henry Arthur
Misfortune (Honourable Defeat) 173
Jong, Erica
Words of Wisdom (Worldly Observations) 18
Jonson, Ben
Affairs of the Heart (Courting) 50
Death and Bereavement (Tributes) 133
Misfortune (Set-Back) 168
Joubert, Joseph
Birthday (Old Age) 40
Matrimony (The Bride) 71
Apology and Forgiveness (Love in Adversity) 185
Public Speaking (Meetings and Discussions) 195
Joyce, John Alexander
Togetherness (Enduring Love) 115
Kafka, Franz
Misfortune (Encouragement) 164
Kauffman, Max
Matrimony (Humorous) 62
Keats, John
Home and Away (Travel) 81, *(Town and Country)* 91
Babies and Children (Children: The Positive View) 105
Keble, John
Home and Away (Homesickness) 89
Keeler, Christine
Words of Wisdom (Worldly Observations) 18
Keller, Helen
Affairs of the Heart (The Essence of Love) 58
Misfortune (Philosophical Thoughts) 163, *(Encouragement)* 165
Kennedy, John F.
Good Luck (Worry and Fear) 146
Public Speaking (Meetings and Discussions) 195
Kennedy, Leo
Absence (Lateness) 190
Kennedy, Robert F.
Words of Wisdom (Instructive Sayings) 26
Kenyon, John
Babies and Children (Parenthood) 104

Kernahan, Coulson
Ill Health (Accidents) 126
Kerr, Jean
Words of Wisdom (Wry Comment) 20
Matrimony (Marriage: The Cynical View) 68
Home and Away (Planes, Trains and Automobiles) 86
Misfortune (Humorous) 163
Apology and Forgiveness (Making Light) 187
Key, Ellen
Matrimony (Marriage: The Positive View) 65
Kierkegaard, Soren
Words of Wisdom (Hard Truths) 24
King Jr., Martin Luther
Matrimony (Marriage: The Positive View) 65
Kinnay, Coates
Mother's/Father's Day (Mothers and Young Children) 109
Kipling, Rudyard
Words of Wisdom (Guidelines) 16
Home and Away (Travel) 81, *(India and the Far East)* 98
Babies and Children (Children: The Positive View) 105
Mother's/Father's Day (Mothers) 108, *(Parents)* 111
Kissinger, Henry Alfred
Misfortune (Humorous) 163
Knowles, F. M.
Christmas and Other Holidays (New Year) 45
Home and Away (Home and Homecoming) 92
Knox, Ronald
Babies and Children (Babies) 103
Kraus, Karl
Retirement (Early, Late or Not At All) 119
Kreer, Anne
Success and Happiness (Good Fortune) 154
Kunitz, Stanley
Apology and Forgiveness (Making Light) 187
Lamb, Caroline
Apology and Forgiveness (New Resolve) 184
Lamb, Charles
Christmas and Other Holidays (New Year) 45, 46
Matrimony (Humorous) 62
Absence (Unwilling Absence) 190
Public Speaking (Replies and Retorts) 197
Lance, Bert
Words of Wisdom (Instructive Sayings) 26
Landon, Letitia Elizabeth
Home and Away (Parting and Leaving) 83
Misfortune (Disappointments) 169
Lang, Andrew
Affairs of the Heart (From the Heart) 56
Home and Away (Parting and Leaving) 84
Lao-tze
Good Luck (Taking the Plunge) 147
Lardner, Ring
Babies and Children (Birth) 99
Larkin, Philip
Death and Bereavement (Remembrance) 128
Larson, Doug
Home and Away (Holidays and Tourism) 89

Lattista, O. A.
Matrimony (Marriage: The Cynical View) 68
Lawrence, Bill
Matrimony (Humorous) 63
Lawrence, Commander James
Misfortune (Encouragement) 165
Lawrence 'of Arabia', T. E.
Misfortune (Set-Back) 168
Leacock, Stephen
Words of Wisdom (Support and Sympathy) 28
Matrimony (Marriage: The Cynical View) 68
Lebowitz, Fran
Birthday (Youth) 33
Affairs of the Heart (Humorous) 48
Babies and Children (Parenthood) 104, *(Children: The Negative View)* 107
Lehman, Earnest
Success and Happiness (The Good Life) 155
Leibniz, Gottfried Wilhelm von
Matrimony (Marriage: The Positive View) 65
Lennon, John
Affairs of the Heart (Humorous) 48
Lessing, Gotthold E.
Affairs of the Heart (Love on the Rocks) 60
Lewis, C. S.
Words of Wisdom (Hard Truths) 24
Apology and Forgiveness (Justification) 179
Lewis, Cecil Day
Birthday (A Special Day) 32
Lewis, Wyndham
Apology and Forgiveness (Justification) 179
Liberace
Success and Happiness (The Good Life) 155
Lincoln, Abraham
Words of Wisdom (Instructive Sayings) 26
Birthday (Growing Older: The Benefits) 37
Matrimony (Marriage: The Cynical View) 68
Mother's/Father's Day (Mothers) 108
Apology and Forgiveness (Denial) 177
Lippmann, Walter
Moving/New Home (First Home) 78
Public Speaking (Meetings and Discussions) 195
Little, Mary Wilson
Retirement (Living with Leisure) 121
Loader, Philip
Words of Wisdom (Hard Truths) 24
Matrimony (Advice to the Newly Weds) 75
Logan, John
Home and Away (Parting and Leaving) 84
Lombardi, Vince
Good Luck (Advice) 143, *(Success and How to Achieve It)* 147
Longfellow, Henry Wadsworth
Christmas and Other Holidays (Traditional Christmas) 44, *(Traditional Easter)* 46
Affairs of the Heart (Declarations of Love) 54
Home and Away (Home and Homecoming) 92
Death and Bereavement (Tributes) 133
Good Luck (Aiming High) 148
Misfortune (Sympathy) 167
Apology and Forgiveness (Regret) 181

Loos, Anita
Retirement (Quitting While You're Ahead) 120
Lowell, James Russell
Words of Wisdom (Ten Inspired Quotes) 29
Birthday (Youth) 33
Misfortune (Failure) 172
Lownes, Victor
Affairs of the Heart (Humorous) 48
Lucan
Death and Bereavement (Consolation) 130
Lucretius
Death and Bereavement (Consolation) 130, *(Life and Death)* 139
Luther, Martin
Matrimony (Marriage: The Positive View) 65
Togetherness (Anniversary) 113
Thanks and Fond Regards (Gratitude) 157
Lynd, Robert
Christmas and Other Holidays (Christmas) 43
Lytton, Edward
Apology and Forgiveness (Regret) 181
Lytton, Edward, Lord
Thanks and Fond Regards (Hospitality) 160
MacArthur, Douglas
Good Luck (Opportunity) 143
Macaulay, Thomas B.
Words of Wisdom (Support and Sympathy) 28
Macaulay, Rose
Home and Away (Foreign Travel) 82
Machiavelli, Niccolò
Retirement (Quitting While You're Ahead) 120
Good Luck (Luck) 145
Mackintosh, James
Words of Wisdom (Happiness and How to Achieve It) 22
Maclaine, Shirley
Affairs of the Heart (Humorous) 48
Home and Away (Parting and Leaving) 84
Madan, Geoffrey
Retirement (Life beyond Retirement) 122
Mahaffy, John Pentland
Home and Away (Scotland, Wales, Ireland) 94
Mailer, Norman
Apology and Forgiveness (Coming Clean) 176
Mancroft, Samuel, Lord
Home and Away (Planes, Trains and Automobiles) 86
Manley, Mary
Affairs of the Heart (Proposals) 59
Mann, Thomas
Home and Away (Holidays and Tourism) 90
Mansfield, Katherine
Misfortune (Advice) 166
Marceau, Marcel
Affairs of the Heart (Declarations of Love) 54
Marcy, William
Success and Happiness (Congratulations) 156
Marden, O. S.
Ill Health (Medicine: Cures and Remedies) 124
Mare, Walter de la
Absence (Unwilling Absence) 190

Marlowe, Christopher
Affairs of the Heart (Flattery) 53, *(Proposals)* 59
Marmion, Shackerley
Birthday (Old Age) 40
Marquis, Donald
Misfortune (Accidents) 174
Martial, Marcus
Birthday (A Special Day) 32
Togetherness (Happy Memories) 117
Ill Health (Sickness) 125
Martin, Dean
Birthday (Celebration and Drinking) 41
Marvell, Andrew
Affairs of the Heart (From the Heart) 56
Babies and Children (Birth) 99
Marx, Chico
Apology and Forgiveness (Making Light) 187
Marx, Groucho
Birthday (Humorous) 30, *(Old Age)* 40
Affairs of the Heart (Humorous) 48, *(Proposals)* 60
Thanks and Fond Regards (Hospitality) 160
Apology and Forgiveness (Making Light) 187
Masefield, John
Home and Away (Town and Country) 91
Thanks and Fond Regards (Generosity) 161
Mason, Monica
Babies and Children (Babies) 103
Massinger, Philip
Good Luck (Advice) 143
Apology and Forgiveness (New Resolve) 184
Maugham, William Somerset
Words of Wisdom (Wry Comment) 20
Christmas and Other Holidays (New Year) 46
Home and Away (England and the English) 94
Good Luck (Education and Study) 151
Misfortune (Errors and Mistakes) 170, *(Accidents)* 174
Absence (Excuses) 191
Maurier, George L. du
Ill Health (Doctors and Physicians) 127
Maxwell, Elsa
Death and Bereavement (The Inevitability of Death) 138
McCreery, John L.
Death and Bereavement (Of a Better Place) 131
McEvoy, J. P.
Matrimony (Humorous) 63
Misfortune (Advice) 166
McFee, William
Babies and Children (Birth) 99
McKenzie, E. C.
Words of Wisdom (Happiness and How to Achieve It) 22, *(Instructive Sayings)* 26
Birthday (Insulting) 31, *(Staying Young)* 34
Christmas and Other Holidays (Traditional Christmas) 44
Affairs of the Heart (Humorous) 48, *(Courting)* 50
Matrimony (Engagement) 64, *(The Bride)* 71
Home and Away (Holidays and Tourism) 90
Mother's/Father's Day (Fathers) 110

Togetherness (Anniversary) 114, *(Of Husbands)* 118
Ill Health (Sickness) 125, *(Accidents)* 126, *(Doctors and Physicians)* 127
Good Luck (Worry and Fear) 146
Success and Happiness (Perseverance) 155, *(The Good Life)* 155
Thanks and Fond Regards (Friendship) 159
Apology and Forgiveness (Coming Clean) 176, *(Justification)* 179
Public Speaking (Toasts) 199
Medici, Cosimo de
Apology and Forgiveness (Forgiveness) 183
Mellencamp, John Cougar
Apology and Forgiveness (Making Light) 187
Melville, Herman
Retirement (Well-Earned Rest) 120
Menander
Death and Bereavement (Tributes) 133
Misfortune (Encouragement) 165
Mencken, Henry L.
Words of Wisdom (Wry Comment) 21, *(Hard Truths)* 24
Matrimony (Marriage: The Cynical View) 68
Togetherness (Of Husbands) 118
Ill Health (Medicine: Cures and Remedies) 124
Death and Bereavement (Black Humour) 140
Apology and Forgiveness (Coming Clean) 176
Menotti, Gian Carlo
Togetherness (Enduring Love) 115
Meredith, George
Affairs of the Heart (Proposals) 60
Matrimony (Humorous) 63
Togetherness (Enduring Love) 115
Michelangelo
Death and Bereavement (Tributes) 133
Middleton, Thomas
Home and Away (Home and Homecoming) 92
Mill, John Stuart
Words of Wisdom (Happiness and How to Achieve It) 22
Matrimony (Marriage: The Cynical View) 68
Millay, Edna St. Vincent
Home and Away (Planes, Trains and Automobiles) 86
Milligan, Spike
Babies and Children (Parenthood) 104
Ill Health (Sickness) 125
Success and Happiness (Good Fortune) 154
Absence (Lateness) 190
Milton, John
Words of Wisdom (Ten Inspired Quotes) 29
Birthday (Youth) 33
Christmas and Other Holidays (Traditional Christmas) 44
Matrimony (To the Happy Couple) 73
Moving/New Home (First Home) 79
Togetherness (Of Wives) 117
Apology and Forgiveness (Burying the Hatchet) 182
Mitchell, Margaret
Misfortune (Encouragement) 165

Mitchum, Robert
Affairs of the Heart (Humorous) 48
Mitford, Nancy
Home and Away (Foreigners and Foreign Countries) 82
Babies and Children (Children: The Negative View) 107
Mizner, Wilson
Birthday (Old Age) 40
Good Luck (New Job) 149
Monkhouse, (William) Cosmo
Babies and Children (Birth) 99
Monroe, Marilyn
Absence (Lateness) 190
Montaigne, Michel
Quotes on Quotes 13
Words of Wisdom (Hard Truths) 25
Apology and Forgiveness (Justification) 179
Montesquieu, Baron de
Words of Wisdom (Guidelines) 16
Montgomery, James
Home and Away (Holidays and Tourism) 90
Death and Bereavement (Life and Death) 139
Montgomery, Robert
Home and Away (Home and Homecoming) 92
Moore, George
Home and Away (Home and Homecoming) 92, *(Scotland, Wales, Ireland)* 94
Moore, Professor Clement C.
Christmas and Other Holidays (Traditional Christmas) 44
Moore, Thomas
Affairs of the Heart (Declarations of Love) 54, *(The Essence of Love)* 58
Togetherness (Anniversary) 114
Misfortune (Sympathy) 167
Morell, Dr Thomas
Success and Happiness (Achievement) 154
Morgan, Julia
Good Luck (New Job) 149
Morley, Christopher
Words of Wisdom (Guidelines) 16
Matrimony (Humorous) 63, *(Second Marriage)* 69
Morley, Robert
Home and Away (France) 95
Morpurgo, J. E.
Home and Away (Other European Countries) 96
Morrow, Dwight W.
Good Luck (Advice) 143
Moss, Stirling
Misfortune (Errors and Mistakes) 170
Muggeridge, Malcolm
Affairs of the Heart (Humorous) 48
Retirement (Quitting While You're Ahead) 121
Muir, Frank
Home and Away (Scotland, Wales, Ireland) 94
Nabokov, Vladimir
Affairs of the Heart (Sex and Lust) 50
Nash, Ogden
Birthday (Celebration and Drinking) 41

Matrimony (Humorous) 63, *(Marriage: The Positive View)* 66, *(Advice to the Newly Weds)* 76
Babies and Children (Children: The Negative View) 107
Apology and Forgiveness (Capitulation) 180
Nashe, Thomas
Ill Health (Sickness) 125
Nathan, George Jean
Apology and Forgiveness (Justification) 179
Necker, Madame
Apology and Forgiveness (Love in Adversity) 185
Nericault, Philippe
Absence (The Error of Absence) 192
Nesbit, Wilber D.
Togetherness (Happy Memories) 117
Nevill, Dorothy, Lady
Words of Wisdom (Guidelines) 17
Nichols, Robert
Affairs of the Heart (From the Heart) 56
Nicolson, Harold
Words of Wisdom (Hard Truths) 25
Matrimony (Advice to the Newly Weds) 76
Nicholson, Jack
Misfortune (Disappointments) 169
Nietzsche, Friedrich
Affairs of the Heart (Sex and Lust) 50
Misfortune (Encouragement) 165
Nightingale, Florence
Ill Health (Hospitals) 126
Norden, Denis
Birthday (Middle Age) 35
Misfortune (Honourable Defeat) 173
Apology and Forgiveness (Making Light) 187
Norman, Greg
Mother's/Father's Day (Parents) 111
Norris, Kathleen
Birthday (Age and the Signs of Aging) 36
Northcote, James
Good Luck (Success and How to Achieve It) 147
Norton, Caroline
Affairs of the Heart (Declarations of Love) 54
Death and Bereavement (Of a Better Place) 131
O'Brien, Edna
Affairs of the Heart (Humorous) 49
O'Malley, Austin
Mother's/Father's Day (Fathers) 110
O'Malley, Pat
Public Speaking (Advice on Speeches and Speaking) 195
O'Rourke, P. J.
Words of Wisdom (Wry Comment) 21
Christmas and Other Holidays (Christmas) 43
Affairs of the Heart (Humorous) 49
Home and Away (Travel) 81, *(Foreigners and Foreign Countries)* 83
Orwell, George
Words of Wisdom (Hard Truths) 25
Birthday (Middle Age) 35
Apology and Forgiveness (Capitulation) 181
Osborne, John
Public Speaking (Drawing to a Close) 198

Osler, William
Words of Wisdom (Happiness and How to Achieve It) 23
Osmond, Marie
Misfortune (Philosophical Thoughts) 163
Ouida
Home and Away (Parting and Leaving) 84
Ovid
Ill Health (Convalescence) 127
Owen, John
Togetherness (Anniversary) 114
Ill Health (Doctors and Physicians) 127
Paine, Thomas
Misfortune (Disappointments) 169
Palin, Michael
Home and Away (Travel) 81
Palmer, Arnold
Misfortune (Honourable Defeat) 173
Palmer, Janet
Retirement (Living with Leisure) 121
Palmerston, Henry, Lord
Ill Health (Doctors and Physicians) 127
Panchatantra
Words of Wisdom (Instructive Sayings) 26
Papprill, Ross F.
Words of Wisdom (Wry Comment) 21
Parker, Dorothy
Affairs of the Heart (Humorous) 49, *(Advice for Lovers)* 51
Babies and Children (Birth) 99
Parker, Dr Edward H.
Death and Bereavement (Final Rest) 135
Parker, Theodore
Matrimony (Humorous) 63
Misfortune (Disappointments) 169
Parkinson, Cyril Northcote
Good Luck (New Job) 149
Public Speaking (Meetings and Discussions) 195
Pascal, Blaise
Words of Wisdom (Wry Comment) 21, *(Instructive Sayings)* 26
Affairs of the Heart (From the Heart) 56
Matrimony (Engagement) 64
Patton Jr., George S.
Death and Bereavement (Tributes) 133
Paul, Elliot
Home and Away (France) 95
Payne, John Howard
Home and Away (Home and Homecoming) 92
Peacock, Thomas Love
Birthday (Celebration and Drinking) 41
Matrimony (Humorous) 63
Penn, William
Babies and Children (Children: The Negative View) 107
Pepys, Samuel
Matrimony (The Bride) 71, *(To the Happy Couple)* 73
Peter, Laurence J.
Home and Away (America) 97
Thanks and Fond Regards (Gratitude) 157

Public Speaking (Replies and Retorts) 19
Petten, William
Public Speaking (Opening Lines) 194
Phelps, Edward John
Misfortune (Errors and Mistakes) 170
Phillips, Stephen
Birthday (Old Age) 40
Phillips, Wendell
Misfortune (Honourable Defeat) 173
Picasso, Pablo
Birthday (Old Age) 40
Pile, Stephen
Apology and Forgiveness (Making Light) 187
Pitkin, Walter B.
Birthday (Middle Age) 35
Plato
Misfortune (Cold Comfort) 174
Plautus, Titus Maccius
Words of Wisdom (Instructive Sayings) 26
Good Luck (Advice) 143
Thanks and Fond Regards (Friendship) 159
Pliny the Elder
Home and Away (Home and Homecoming) 92
Good Luck (Education and Study) 151
Plunkitt, George Washington
Success and Happiness (Good Fortune) 154
Plutarch
Retirement (Well-Earned Rest) 120
Poe, Edgar Allan
Mother's/Father's Day (Mothers) 108
Death and Bereavement (Final Rest) 135
Pomfret, John
Misfortune (Errors and Mistakes) 170
Ponsonby, Arthur
Apology and Forgiveness (Justification) 179
Pope, Alexander
Words of Wisdom (Hard Truths) 25, *(Instructive Sayings)* 26, *(Support and Sympathy)* 28
Affairs of the Heart (The Essence of Love) 58
Babies and Children (Birth) 99
Retirement (Life beyond Retirement) 123
Apology and Forgiveness (Forgiveness) 183, *(Love in Adversity)* 185
Porchia, Antonio
Words of Wisdom (Instructive Sayings) 27
Porter, Cole
Mother's/Father's Day (Fathers) 110
Pound, Ezra
Birthday (Growing Older: The Benefits) 37
Powell, Anthony
Birthday (Age and the Signs of Aging) 36
Praed, Winthrop M.
Affairs of the Heart (The Essence of Love) 58
Prentiss, Elizabeth
Babies and Children (Babies) 103
Priestley, J. B.
Apology and Forgiveness (Making Light) 187
Absence (Invitation Declined) 192
Prince Philip
Retirement (Living with Leisure) 122
Apology and Forgiveness (Making Light) 188
Public Speaking (Opening Lines) 194

Princess Anne
Matrimony (The Groom) 72
Princess Margaret
Death and Bereavement (Of a Better Place) 131
Prior, Matthew
Matrimony (The Bride) 71
Pritchett, Oliver
Christmas and Other Holidays (Christmas) 43
Affairs of the Heart (Humorous) 49
Ill Health (Sickness) 125
Prochnow, Herbert V.
Matrimony (The Groom) 72
Propertius, Sextus
Good Luck (Aiming High) 148
Misfortune (Honourable Defeat) 173
Proust, Marcel
Apology and Forgiveness (Justification) 179
Pyke, Magnus
Misfortune (Philosophical Thoughts) 164
Pythagoras
Apology and Forgiveness (Regret) 182
Raban, Jonathan
Home and Away (Foreigners and Foreign Countries) 83
Rabelais, François
Babies and Children (Children: The Positive View) 106
Ramsay, William
Good Luck (Education and Study) 151
Randall, Stanley J.
Good Luck (New Job) 149
Ransome, Arthur
Good Luck (Opportunity) 144
Raphael, Frederic
Birthday (Middle Age) 35
Read, Thomas Buchanan
Apology and Forgiveness (Love in Adversity) 185
Reade, Charles
Togetherness (Of Wives) 117
Absence (Strategic Absence) 191
Public Speaking (Audiences) 196
Reagan, Nancy
Birthday (A Special Day) 32
Apology and Forgiveness (Love in Adversity) 185
Reagan, Ronald
Affairs of the Heart (Sex and Lust) 50
Reed, Rev. David
Moving/New Home (Home Ownership) 80
Renard, Jules
Absence (Invitation Declined) 192
Rhodes, Cecil
Home and Away (England and the English) 94
Ribblesdale, Lord
Quotes on Quotes 13
Richardson, Ralph
Public Speaking (Advice on Speeches and Speaking) 196
Richter, Jean Paul
Babies and Children (Children: The Positive View) 106

Death and Bereavement (Remembrance) 128, *(Of a Better Place)* 131
Rickenbacker, Eddie
Good Luck (Worry and Fear) 146
Riley, Janet
Babies and Children (Children: The Positive View) 106
Rittenhouse, Jessie
Togetherness (Enduring Love) 115
Robinson, Therese
Affairs of the Heart (Love on the Rocks) 60
Rochefoucauld, François, Duc de la
Words of Wisdom (Guidelines) 17, *(Worldly Observations)* 19
Birthday (Old Age) 40
Affairs of the Heart (Love on the Rocks) 60
Matrimony (To the Happy Couple) 74
Home and Away (Absence) 88, *(Homesickness)* 89
Success and Happiness (Good Fortune) 154
Apology and Forgiveness (Justification) 179, *(Forgiveness)* 183
Rockefeller, John D.
Words of Wisdom (Instructive Sayings) 27
Rogers, Samuel
Affairs of the Heart (Humorous) 49
Rogers, Will
Words of Wisdom (Happiness and How to Achieve It) 23, *(Instructive Sayings)* 27
Success and Happiness (Congratulations) 156
Misfortune (Humorous) 163
Public Speaking (Drawing to a Close) 198
Roosevelt, Eleanor
Words of Wisdom (Support and Sympathy) 28
Roosevelt, Franklin D.
Words of Wisdom (Support and Sympathy) 28
Public Speaking (Replies and Retorts) 197
Roosevelt, James
Public Speaking (Advice on Speeches and Speaking) 196
Roosevelt, Theodore
Words of Wisdom (Ten Inspired Quotes) 29
Misfortune (Failure) 172
Rosen, Marc
Matrimony (To the Happy Couple) 74
Rosewarne, Pilot Officer V. A.
Death and Bereavement (Tributes) 133
Rossetti, Christina
Christmas and Other (Traditional Easter) 46
Home and Away (Town and Country) 91
Death and Bereavement (Remembrance) 128
Misfortune (Advice) 166
Rostand, Jean
Matrimony (To the Happy Couple) 74
Rousseau, Jean-Jacques
Words of Wisdom (Worldly Observations) 19
Apology and Forgiveness (Coming Clean) 176, *(Regret)* 182
Rowland, Helen
Matrimony (Marriage: The Cynical View) 68, *(The Bride)* 71, *(The Groom)* 72

Rowley, William
Babies and Children (Babies) 103
Rubinstein, Helena
Birthday (Age and the Signs of Aging) 37
Ruffini, Giovanni
Mother's/Father's Day (Mothers and Young Children) 109
Runbeck, Margaret Lee
Words of Wisdom (Happiness and How to Achieve It) 23
Ruskin, John
Home and Away (France) 95
Russell, Bertrand
Affairs of the Heart (Declarations of Love) 54
Matrimony (Engagement) 64
Home and Away (Holidays and Tourism) 90
Russell, Mark
Home and Away (Planes, Trains and Automobiles) 86
Saint-Exupery, Antoine de
Affairs of the Heart (The Essence of Love) 59
Home and Away (Travel) 81
Saki (H. H. Munro)
Birthday (Age and the Signs of Aging) 37
Babies and Children (Children: The Negative View) 107
Success and Happiness (Humorous) 153
Apology and Forgiveness (Justification) 180, *(Love in Adversity)* 185
Sales, St. Francis de
Apology and Forgiveness (Burying the Hatchet) 182
Sand, George
Affairs of the Heart (The Essence of Love) 58
Matrimony (Advice to the Newly Weds) 76
Sanders, George
Retirement (Early, Late or Not At All) 119
Santayana, George
Words of Wisdom (Wry Comment) 21
Home and Away (Foreign Travel) 82
Babies and Children (Parenthood) 104
Togetherness (Enduring Love) 115
Misfortune (Disappointments) 169
Sassoon, Vidal
Good Luck (Success and How to Achieve It) 147
Schachtel, Hyman Judha
Words of Wisdom (Happiness and How to Achieve It) 23
Togetherness (Enduring Love) 115
Schiller, Friedrich von
Birthday (Youth) 33
Schnabel, Arthur
Public Speaking (Audiences) 196
Schopenhauer, Arthur
Matrimony (Marriage: The Cynical View) 68
Schubert, Franz
Words of Wisdom (Hard Truths) 25
Schumann, Robert
Matrimony (Humorous) 63
Schurz, Carl
Words of Wisdom (Happiness and How to Achieve It) 23

Schwarzenegger, Arnold
Misfortune (Encouragement) 165
Schweitzer, Albert
Words of Wisdom (Happiness and How to Achieve It) 23
Thanks and Fond Regards (Compliments) 160
Scott, Walter
Birthday (Middle Age) 35
Christmas and Other (Traditional Christmas) 45
Babies and Children (Babies) 103
Success and Happiness (Achievement) 154
Apology and Forgiveness (New Resolve) 184
Scott-Maxwell, Florida
Mother's/Father's Day (Mothers) 109
Seeger, Alan
Death and Bereavement (In the Line of Duty) 136
Segall, Eric
Apology and Forgiveness (Making Light) 188
Segall, Lee
Misfortune (Philosophical Thoughts) 164
Seldon, John
Birthday (Celebration and Drinking) 41
Sellar, W. C.
Good Luck (Exams) 152
Seneca, Lucius Annaeus
Words of Wisdom (Instructive Sayings) 27
Home and Away (Travel) 81
Ill Health (Medicine: Cures and Remedies) 124
Death and Bereavement (The Inevitability of Death) 138
Misfortune (Philosophical Thoughts) 164
Sexton, Ann
Birthday (Old Age) 40
Shakespeare, William
Words of Wisdom (Guidelines) 172, *(Worldly Observations)* 19, *(Hard Truths)* 25, *(Instructive Sayings)* 27, *(Support and Sympathy)* 28
Birthday (Insulting) 31
Affairs of the Heart (Courting) 50, *(Advice for Lovers)* 51, *(Flattery)* 53, *(Declarations of Love)* 54, *(From the Heart)* 56, *(The Essence of Love)* 59
Matrimony (Humorous) 63, *(The Bride)* 71, *(To the Happy Couple)* 74
Moving/New Home (Of Houses and Home) 77
Home and Away (Parting and Leaving) 84, *(Farewell and Bon Voyage)* 85, *(Homesickness)* 89, *(Holidays and Tourism)* 90
Mother's/Father's Day (Mothers) 109, *(Fathers)* 110
Togetherness (Anniversary) 114, *(Enduring Love)* 116
Ill Health (Sickness) 125
Death and Bereavement (Of a Better Place) 132, *(Tributes)* 133, *(Final Rest)* 135, *(An End to Suffering)* 136, *(In the Line of Duty)* 137
Good Luck (Worry and Fear) 146
Success and Happiness (Good Fortune) 154
Thanks and Fond Regards (Gratitude) 157, 158, *(Friendship)* 159, *(Hospitality)* 160

Misfortune (Encouragement) 165, *(Advice)* 166,
(Sympathy) 167, *(Optimism)* 167, *(Errors and
Mistakes)* 170
Apology and Forgiveness (Coming Clean) 176,
(Denial) 177, *(Justification)* 180, *(Regret)* 182,
(Burying the Hatchet) 183, *(Love in Adversity)*
185, 186
Public Speaking (Opening Lines) 194
Sharpe, Gareth
Matrimony (To the Happy Couple) 74
Sharpe, R. L.
Togetherness (Anniversary) 114
Shaw, George Bernard
Words of Wisdom (Worldly Observations) 19,
(Instructive Sayings) 27
Birthday (Middle Age) 35, *(Celebration and
Drinking)* 41
Affairs of the Heart (Flattery) 53
Matrimony (Marriage: The Positive View) 66,
(Marriage: The Cynical View) 68, *(The Bride)*
71
Moving/New Home (Of Houses and Home) 77
*Home and Away (Foreigners and Foreign
Countries)* 83
Babies and Children (Parenthood) 105
Mother's/Father's Day (Parents) 111
Togetherness (Enduring Love) 116, *(Happy
Memories)* 117
Retirement (Well-Earned Rest) 120, *(Living with
Leisure)* 122
Ill Health (Convalescence) 127
Death and Bereavement (Consolation) 130,
(Tributes) 134
Good Luck (Education and Study) 151
Misfortune (Errors and Mistakes) 171
Apology and Forgiveness (Justification) 180
*Public Speaking (Advice on Speeches and
Speaking)* 196
Sheffield, John
Apology and Forgiveness (Forgiveness) 183
Shelley, Percy Bysshe
Affairs of the Heart (From the Heart) 57
Death and Bereavement (Remembrance) 129, *(Of
a Better Place)* 132, *(An End to Suffering)* 136,
(Of Death) 138, *(Life and Death)* 139
Misfortune (Encouragement) 165
Apology and Forgiveness (Love in Adversity)
186
Shenstone, William
Home and Away (Homesickness) 89
Sheridan, Richard Brinsley
Togetherness (Humorous) 113
Apology and Forgiveness (Making Light) 188
Sherriff, R. C.
Retirement (Living with Leisure) 122
Death and Bereavement (Final Rest) 135
Shirley, James
Apology and Forgiveness (Making Light) 188
Shore, Dinah
Apology and Forgiveness (Love in Adversity) 186
Sibelius, Jean
Good Luck (Advice) 143

Sidney, Philip
Matrimony (The Groom) 72
Good Luck (Major Challenge) 150
Sinclair, Upton
Christmas and Other Holidays (Christmas) 44
Skinner, Burrhus F.
Words of Wisdom (Instructive Sayings) 27
Smiles, Samuel
Good Luck (Advice) 143
Smith, Alexander
Birthday (Middle Age) 35
Smith, Alfred E.
Public Speaking (Replies and Retorts) 197
Smith, Frederick E.
Good Luck (Faith and Trust) 144
Smith, Logan Pearsall
*Words of Wisdom (Happiness and How to
Achieve It)* 23
Home and Away (Climate and Weather) 87
Death and Bereavement (Black Humour) 140
Smith, Rev. Sydney
Moving/New Home (Home Ownership) 80
Home and Away (Scotland, Wales, Ireland) 94
Smith, Sydney
Matrimony (Marriage: The Positive View) 66
Babies and Children (Birth) 99
Smith, Wolfman Jack
Quotes on Quotes 13
Togetherness (Anniversary) 114
Socrates
Matrimony (Marriage: The Cynical View) 69
Sophocles
*Babies and Children (Children: The Negative
View)* 107
South, Robert
Thanks and Fond Regards (Generosity) 161
Southey, Robert
Birthday (Youth) 33
*Babies and Children (Children: The Positive
View)* 106
Death and Bereavement (Remembrance) 128, *(Of
a Better Place)* 132
Apology and Forgiveness (Regret) 182, *(Love in
Adversity)* 186
Spellman, Cardinal Francis
Birthday (Humorous) 30
Spencer, Herbert
Birthday (Age and the Signs of Aging) 37
Spenser, Edmund
Affairs of the Heart (Flattery) 53, *(From the
Heart)* 57
Matrimony (To the Happy Couple) 74
Babies and Children (Birth) 100
Spock, Dr. Benjamin
Babies and Children (Parenthood) 105
Staël, Madame de
Affairs of the Heart (Love on the Rocks) 60
Death and Bereavement (Consolation) 130
Stallings, Laurence
Apology and Forgiveness (Justification) 180
Stanton, Elizabeth Cady
Moving/New Home (First Home) 79

Steele, Richard
Words of Wisdom (Instructive Sayings) 27
Togetherness (Anniversary) 114
Stein, Gertrude
Home and Away (America) 97
Stengel, Casey
Public Speaking (Opening Lines) 194
Sterne, Laurence
Affairs of the Heart (Courting) 50
Home and Away (Foreign Travel) 82
Retirement (Quitting While You're Ahead) 121
Stevenson, Adlai
Apology and Forgiveness (Capitulation) 181,
 (Burying the Hatchet) 183
Public Speaking (Opening Lines) 194
Stevenson, Edward
Words of Wisdom (Wry Comment) 21
Stevenson, Robert Louis
Birthday (Youth) 33
Matrimony (Marriage: The Cynical View) 69
Moving/New Home (First Home) 79
*Home and Away (Planes, Trains and
 Automobiles)* 86
Togetherness (Of Wives) 117
Misfortune (Failure) 172
Stoppard, Tom
Birthday (Growing Older: The Drawbacks) 38
Death and Bereavement (Tributes) 134
Stowe, Harriet
Death and Bereavement (Grief) 135
Stowell, William Scott
Public Speaking (Meetings and Discussions) 195
Strange, William
Death and Bereavement (Epitaphs) 140
Strong, Leonard A. G.
Matrimony (Marriage: The Cynical View) 69
Su Tung-P'O
Babies and Children (Birth) 100
Sutton, Dudley
Home and Away (Climate and Weather) 87
Sweeney, Paul
Home and Away (Climate and Weather) 87
Swift, Jonathan
Birthday (Age and the Signs of Aging) 37,
 (Growing Older: The Benefits) 37
Affairs of the Heart (Humorous) 49
Matrimony (Marriage: The Cynical View) 69
Home and Away (Home and Homecoming) 93
Ill Health (Sickness) 12
Death and Bereavement (An End to Suffering)
 136, *(Epitaphs)* 140
Good Luck (Advice) 143, *(New Job)* 149
Misfortune (Sympathy) 167
Swinburne, Algernon Charles
Affairs of the Heart (From the Heart) 57, *(Love on
 the Rocks)* 60
Swope, Herbert Bayard
Good Luck (Success and How to Achieve It) 147
Syrus, Publilius
Words of Wisdom (Instructive Sayings) 27
Apology and Forgiveness (Coming Clean) 177,
 (Regret) 182

Szasz, Thomas
Apology and Forgiveness (Justification) 180
Tacitus, Publius
Apology and Forgiveness (Justification) 180
Tarkington, Booth
Matrimony (Advice to the Newly Weds) 76
Tawney, Richard Henry
Retirement (Life beyond Retirement) 123
Taylor, Ann
*Mother's/Father's Day (Mothers and Young
 Children)* 109
Taylor, Bert Leston
Absence (Lateness) 190
Tennyson, Alfred, Lord
Words of Wisdom (Worldly Observations) 193
Christmas and Other Holidays (New Year) 46
Affairs of the Heart (From the Heart) 57, *(The
 Essence of Love)* 59, *(Love on the Rocks)* 61
Matrimony (Engagement) 64, *(The Bride)* 71
Death and Bereavement (Remembrance) 129,
 (Tributes) 134, *(An End to Suffering)* 136, *(The
 Inevitability of Death)* 138
Misfortune (Encouragement) 165
Apology and Forgiveness (Forgiveness) 184,
 (Love in Adversity) 186
Terence
Misfortune (Encouragement) 165, *(Optimism)*
 168
Apology and Forgiveness (Love in Adversity) 186
Thackeray, William M.
Affairs of the Heart (Flattery) 53
Apology and Forgiveness (Love in Adversity)
 186
Thatcher, Margaret
Babies and Children (Birth) 100
Misfortune (Honourable Defeat) 173
Theroux, Paul
Home and Away (Travel) 81, *(Climate and
 Weather)* 87
Thirkell, Angela
Good Luck (Humorous) 141
Thomas, Dylan
Death and Bereavement (Remembrance) 129,
 (Consolation) 130
Thomas, Gwyn
Home and Away (Scotland, Wales, Ireland) 95
Thomas, Jack
Matrimony (The Groom) 73
Thompson, Harold
Matrimony (Engagement) 64
Thompson, Hunter S.
Birthday (Celebration and Drinking) 41
Thompson, William Hepworth
Misfortune (Errors and Mistakes) 171
Thomson, James
Death and Bereavement (Grief) 135
Thoreau, Henry D.
Birthday (Middle Age) 35
Good Luck (Opportunity) 144
Public Speaking (Opening Lines) 194
Tibullus, Albius
Togetherness (Enduring Love) 116

Tickell, Thomas
Home and Away (Parting and Leaving) 84
Titcomb, Charles
Matrimony (Marriage: The Positive View) 66
Trevino, Lee
Birthday (Age and the Signs of Aging) 37
Trollope, Anthony
Misfortune (Advice) 166
Trotsky, Leon
Birthday (Old Age) 40
Trowbridge, J. T.
Good Luck (Major Challenge) 150
Trublet, Nicolas Charles
Quotes on Quotes 13
Trueblood, D. Elton
Words of Wisdom (Instructive Sayings) 27
Tupper, Martin Farquhar
Babies and Children (Children: The Positive View) 106
Turgenev, Ivan
Death and Bereavement (In the Line of Duty) 137
Turnball, Margaret
Mother's/Father's Day (Fathers) 110
Tusser, Thomas
Christmas and Other Holidays (Traditional Christmas) 45
Home and Away (Home and Homecoming) 93
Twain, Mark
Words of Wisdom (Guidelines) 17
Birthday (The Down Side) 31, *(Growing Older: The Drawbacks)* 38
Moving/New Home (Of Houses and Home) 77
Home and Away (Italy) 96, *(India and the Far East)* 98
Mother's/Father's Day (Fathers) 110
Good Luck (Humorous) 141, *(Success and How to Achieve It)* 147
Misfortune (Humorous) 163, *(Cold Comfort)* 174
Apology and Forgiveness (Coming Clean) 177
Public Speaking (Opening Lines) 194, *(Replies and Retorts)* 198
Universo, El
Birthday (Middle Age) 36
Ustinov, Peter
Mother's/Father's Day (Parents) 111
Vaughan, Bill
Home and Away (Holidays and Tourism) 90
Retirement (Early, Late or Not At All) 119
Vaughan, Henry
Matrimony (The Bride) 71
Vauvenargues, Marquis de
Words of Wisdom (Guidelines) 17
Vidal, Gore
Success and Happiness (Congratulations) 156
Vinci, Leonardo da
Retirement (Life beyond Retirement) 123
Virgil
Words of Wisdom (Support and Sympathy) 28, *(Ten Inspired Quotes)* 29
Affairs of the Heart (Declarations of Love) 54
Togetherness (Enduring Love) 116

Good Luck (Faith and Trust) 144
Misfortune (Philosophical Thoughts) 164
Voltaire
Ill Health (Medicine: Cures and Remedies) 124
Misfortune (Philosophical Thoughts) 164
Public Speaking (Replies and Retorts) 198
Vries, Peter de
Matrimony (Marriage: The Positive View) 66
Babies and Children (Parenthood) 105
Walker, Addison
Misfortune (Failure) 172
Walker, James J.
Absence (Punctuality and Arriving) 189
Walpole, Horace
Words of Wisdom (Support and Sympathy) 28
Walton, Izaak
Thanks and Fond Regards (Compliments) 160
Misfortune (Cold Comfort) 174
Ward, Artemus
Matrimony (The Groom) 73
Ward, Christopher
Christmas and Other Holidays (Christmas) 44
Warhol, Andy
Good Luck (New Job) 149
Warner, Charles Dudley
Home and Away (Climate and Weather) 87
Washburn, Henry S.
Death and Bereavement (Remembrance) 129
Washington, Booker T.
Success and Happiness (Perseverance) 155
Waugh, Evelyn
Matrimony (The Groom) 73
Apology and Forgiveness (Coming Clean) 177
Absence (Punctuality and Arriving) 189
Webb, Sidney
Matrimony (Marriage: The Cynical View) 69
Webster, John
Death and Bereavement (The Inevitability of Death) 138, 139
Welles, Orson
Home and Away (Other European Countries) 97
Wesley, Charles
Christmas and Other Holidays (Traditional Easter) 46
West, Mae
Affairs of the Heart (Sex and Lust) 50
Home and Away (Foreigners and Foreign Countries) 83
Apology and Forgiveness (Coming Clean) 177
Public Speaking (Opening Lines) 194
West, Rebecca
Apology and Forgiveness (Justification) 180
Whately, Richard
Misfortune (Failure) 172
Apology and Forgiveness (Justification) 180
Public Speaking (Advice on Speeches and Speaking) 196
Whewell, William
Misfortune (Failure) 172
Whistler, James
Babies and Children (Babies) 103

White, Elwyn B.
Christmas and Other Holidays (Traditional Christmas) 45
Whitehorn, Katharine
Birthday (A Special Day) 32
Good Luck (New Job) 149
Whittier, John Greenleaf
Misfortune (Disappointments) 169
Whitton, Charlotte
Good Luck (New Job) 150
Wilcox, Ella
Misfortune (Optimism) 168, *(Cold Comfort)* 174
Wilde, Oscar
Words of Wisdom (Worldly Observations) 19, *(Hard Truths)* 25
Birthday (Middle Age) 36, *(Age and the Signs of Aging)* 37
Affairs of the Heart (Sex and Lust) 50, *(Proposals)* 60
Matrimony (Engagement) 64, *(Marriage: The Cynical View)* 69
Babies and Children (Children: The Negative View) 107
Mother's/Father's Day (Mothers) 109
Ill Health (Sickness) 125
Death and Bereavement (Grief) 135
Success and Happiness (Achievement) 154
Misfortune (Errors and Mistakes) 171, *(Failure)* 172
Apology and Forgiveness (Denial) 178, *(Making Light)* 188
Absence (Punctuality and Arriving) 189
Public Speaking (Opening Lines) 194, *(Advice on Speeches and Speaking)* 196, *(Replies and Retorts)* 198
Wilder, Billy
Home and Away (France) 95
Apology and Forgiveness (Regret) 182
Wilder, Thornton Niven
Matrimony (Humorous) 63
Wilkie, Wendell L.
Misfortune (Honourable Defeat) 173
Wilkinson, Marguerite
Mother's/Father's Day (Parents) 111
Williams, Charles
Apology and Forgiveness (Burying the Hatchet) 183
Williams, Hugo
Home and Away (Planes, Trains and Automobiles) 86
Williams, Jack
Public Speaking (Opening Lines) 194
Wilmot, Earl of Rochester, John
Affairs of the Heart (Love on the Rocks) 61
Togetherness (Enduring Love) 116
Wilson, Earl
Birthday (Humorous) 30, *(Middle Age)* 36, *(Growing Older: The Drawbacks)* 38

Moving/New Home (Of Houses and Home) 77
Home and Away (Foreign Travel) 82
Wilson, Harold
Good Luck (Faith and Trust) 144
Winters, Shelley
Apology and Forgiveness (Making Light) 188
Wither, George
Christmas and Other Holidays (Traditional Christmas) 45
Apology and Forgiveness (Love in Adversity) 186
Wodehouse, P. G.
Words of Wisdom (Guidelines) 17, *(Wry Comment)* 21
Christmas and Other Holidays (Christmas) 44
Matrimony (The Groom) 73
Babies and Children (Children: The Negative View) 107
Success and Happiness (Humorous) 153
Apology and Forgiveness (Capitulation) 181, *(Making Light)* 188
Wood, Ellen
Affairs of the Heart (Advice for Lovers) 51
Woolcott, Alexander
Home and Away (Climate and Weather) 87
Wordsworth, William
Affairs of the Heart (From the Heart) 57
Home and Away (Home and Homecoming) 93, *(England and the English)* 94, *(Scotland, Wales, Ireland)* 95
Togetherness (Of Wives) 118
Death and Bereavement (Remembrance) 129
Wright, Frank Lloyd
Birthday (Staying Young) 34
Yates, Douglas
Matrimony (The Bride) 71
Ybarra, Thomas Russell
Apology and Forgiveness (Making Light) 188
Yeatman, R. J.
Good Luck (Exams) 152
Yeats, William Butler
Affairs of the Heart (Declarations of Love) 54, *(From the Heart)* 57
Death and Bereavement (Epitaphs) 140
Young, Brigham
Moving/New Home (House Buying) 78
Young, Edward
Words of Wisdom (Instructive Sayings) 27
Birthday (Middle Age) 36
Death and Bereavement (Life and Death) 139
Good Luck (Aiming High) 148
Yutang, Lin
Babies and Children (Parenthood) 105
Zadora, Pia
Matrimony (The Groom) 73